ATTACHMENT AND
DYNAMIC PRACTICE

Attachment and Dynamic Practice

An Integrative Guide for Social Workers and Other Clinicians

Jerrold R. Brandell and
Shoshana Ringel

COLUMBIA UNIVERSITY PRESS   New York

Columbia University Press
Publishers Since 1893

New York   Chichester, West Sussex
Copyright © 2007 Columbia University Press
All rights reserved

Library of Congress Cataloging-in-Publication Data
Brandell, Jerrold R.
Attachment and dynamic practice : an integrative guide for social
workers and other clinicians / Jerrold R. Brandell and Shoshana Ringel.
p.   cm.
Includes bibliographical references and index.
ISBN 978-0-231-13390-6 (cloth : alk. paper)
ISBN 978-0-231-13391-3 (pbk. : alk. paper)
ISBN 978-0-231-50855-1 (e-book)
1. Attachment behavior in children. 2. Attachment behavior in children—
Cross-cultural studies. I. Ringel, Shoshana. II. Title.
BF723.A75B73 2007
155.4'18—dc22

2006027644

∞

Columbia University Press books are printed on permanent
and durable acid-free paper.
This book is printed on paper with recycled content.

Printed in the United States of America

c 10 9 8 7 6 5 4 3 2 1
p 10 9 8 7 6 5 4 3 2

In memory of my mother, Edna Bernice Honoroff Brandell,
my first safe haven
—Jerrold Brandell

To Yehudah and Gvanit, with all my love
—Shoshana Ringel

Contents

Acknowledgments

A number of individuals provided much-appreciated assistance and support during the preparation of this book. We are grateful to the late John Michel, who until his untimely death in 2005 was senior executive editor at Columbia University Press. John was not only our editor but a good friend, as he was to so many others. We also wish to thank Lauren Dockett, executive editor, for her efficiency and professionalism during the short time we have worked with her, as well as our copyeditor, Jan McInroy, for her meticulous attention to detail and consummate professionalism. We thank our respective deans, Phyllis I. Vroom of the Wayne State University School of Social Work and Jesse Harris of the University of Maryland School of Social Work, for their willingness to support our research. Last, but most assuredly not least, we express gratitude to our psychotherapy patients, who have so enriched our understanding of attachment within a clinical context, and to our graduate students, whose penetrating questions about the nature of attachment have challenged us to write this book.

Two chapters in this book contain clinical case material drawn from previously published works. Several of the brief clinical vignettes used in chapter 5 are based on cases that originally appeared in Jerrold Brandell's book *Of Mice and Metaphors: Therapeutic Storytelling with Children*, published in

2000 by Basic Books. The lengthier case illustration used in chapter 5 is an adaptation of "Psychotherapy of a Traumatized Ten-Year-Old Boy: Theoretical Issues and Clinical Considerations," originally published in 1992 by Jerrold Brandell in *Smith College Studies in Social Work, 62*, 123–138. Two of the case illustrations appearing in chapter 7 are based on papers previously published by Shoshana Ringel. The first (Howie) is adapted from "The Man Without Words: Attachment Style as an Evolving Dynamic Process," *Psychoanalytic Social Work, 11*(2), 71–82 (Summer/Fall 2004). The other (Nicole) is adapted from "Play and Impersonation: Finding the Right Intersubjective Rhythm," *Clinical Social Work Journal, 31*(4), 371–381 (Fall 2003).

Introduction

Attachment theory is rooted in observational studies that seek to examine the relational bonds between young children and their caregivers, typically mothers. Over time, researchers have established that children's affectional bonds with their caregivers are rooted in psychological, as well as biological, motives. Attachment studies across cultures have found that children seek a primary attachment with one caregiver and that most children are securely attached. Moreover, with the advance of attachment research, it has been discovered that childhood attachment patterns affect later adult personality styles and that children frequently develop an attachment style similar to that of their parents.

Attachment theory traces its origins to several scientific and social fields, most notably psychoanalysis, social work, behaviorism, ethology, evolution, and biology. The "father" of modern attachment theory, John Bowlby, motivated by his own frustration with then-prevailing psychoanalytic ideas regarding clinical practice and human development, believed that answers to the most perplexing questions surrounding human attachment were not available from any single discipline. In direct consequence of this approach, scientific findings that have accrued from research on human attachment ever since continue to be broadly applicable to the social and behavioral sciences, rather than concentrated in a single disciplinary domain.

Attachment theory and research are also very closely aligned with the traditional interests of the social work profession. Both have emphasized infant and child welfare, the importance of relationships with primary caregivers, and the contributions of the extramural environment in shaping human functioning and pathology. The human attachment field has also gained global currency as a result of international research investigations conducted in Asian and African cultures. Indeed, after more than half a century of research on human attachment, the universality of the need for "affectional bonds," the term Bowlby used to characterize children's primordial need for their parents' love and protection, is now taken for granted. Bowlby's and Mary Ainsworth's research helped to clarify the notion of intergenerational transmission of trauma and the development of mental disorders. More recently, an even stronger link has been forged between this body of research and social work practice as the findings of attachment research have been applied to clinical methods of prevention and treatment in such diverse areas as child welfare, trauma and eating disorders, and personality disorders.

Research findings from the attachment field have also helped us understand the impact of attachment disruptions on children's personality development and on their evolving relationships. These findings have, moreover, dramatically altered the content and structure of parent education programs, as well as the training of mental health providers throughout the United States and other parts of the world.

The relationship between attachment theory and research and clinical practice has evolved only gradually. For many years, attachment researchers focused on investigating the influence of attachment disruptions on children's and adults' behaviors. Unfortunately, Bowlby's ideas were not especially well received by the psychoanalytic community, nor were they judged to be truly consonant with existing clinical frameworks. Attachment theory, however, has proven to be a far more natural "fit" with relational and intersubjective theories, ideas that are considered by many to be at the forefront of contemporary psychodynamic practice. Such theories, no longer wedded to earlier psychoanalytic conceptions of the biological primacy of the instinctual drives, had already accorded far greater emphasis to human relationships, or what some psychoanalytic researchers have termed the "preexisting tie to the human environment" (Greenberg & Mitchell, 1983). Furthermore, psychodynamic practice had long been in search of a more robust empirical framework to which certain assumptions regarding human development, psychopathology, and psychoanalytic conceptions of treatment might be anchored. Attachment theory and research have furnished a sound empirical basis for psychodynamic practice principles, particularly those associated with self psychology and relational theory. Moreover, while attachment theory does not provide an integrated clinical approach, we will show how attachment concepts can inform the treatment process.

Both of us are experienced clinicians who became interested in how attachment theory might be meaningfully applied to psychodynamic practice. We soon realized that little had been published on this topic in the social work literature, and in discussions with the late John Michel, who was at that time senior executive editor at Columbia University Press, we recognized the importance of writing this book. We are both also deeply involved in the academic world, and it has been our impression that many social work graduate students receive little, if any, exposure to attachment theory. To the extent that they do become acquainted with attachment theory, it is chiefly through two routes—the developmental psychology research literature and condensed summative reviews in graduate-level textbooks—neither of which addresses clinical applications. Furthermore, most of these publications do not provide much emphasis on the sequelae of attachment patterns for later development. We therefore decided to collaborate on an introductory text that could be used by students in graduate practice classes across three distinct curricular areas: human development, psychopathology, and clinical practice. We hope that this book will offer a clear and accessible introduction to attachment theory and research, that it will prove useful to students in their efforts to understand the relationship between early attachment patterns and later personality development, and, finally, that students will be able to extrapolate from the findings of attachment research and apply this knowledge to the broad range of clinical situations involving children, adolescents, and adults. To this end, we have included a number of illustrative clinical cases in the last three chapters of the book, each of which is thoroughly discussed and analyzed.

Our decision to coauthor this book followed a number of previous collaborations on various writing projects, and it underscores our mutual interest in developing and promoting psychodynamic theories and practice principles for clinical social work. As we became immersed in this project, we also found Jerry's rich clinical experience with children and adolescents and Shoshana's interest in cross-cultural practice to be especially complementary.

In the first part of the book, we focus on theoretical precursors of attachment theory in both social work and psychoanalysis, the history of attachment theory and research, the application of ideas regarding attachment to interpersonal and relational theories, and important research developments in the field of attachment over the last few decades. We have included the foremost figures in attachment research, starting with John Bowlby and Mary Ainsworth and moving on to Mary Main, Allan Sroufe, and Peter Fonagy, among others. In the last three chapters, we show how attachment concepts can inform diagnostic concerns and the treatment process with children, adolescents, and adults.

We hope that we have provided a succinct yet sufficiently detailed introduction to the field of attachment, its history, and its most important research findings and that students will be able to identify with the illustrative vignettes we have used. Bearing in mind that Bowlby's ideas regarding attachment could not help but be shaped by the panoply of psychoanalytic theories that arose from the rich theoretical climate of the mid-twentieth century, we have closely examined the relationship between other psychoanalytic developmental models and attachment theory. In keeping with current thinking in our field, we have also emphasized human diversity as it applies both to attachment research and to clinical practice. In this regard, we have selected cases that might be considered exemplars for clinical practice with diverse and special populations, including an urban African American adolescent, a Caribbean American woman, and a young adult with a neurological disability. Finally, we have highlighted the important relationship between attachment and pathology, especially insofar as the influence of trauma is concerned.

ATTACHMENT AND
DYNAMIC PRACTICE

Beginnings | ONE

Early Conceptions of the
Mother-Infant Relationship

Even before the formalization of John Bowlby's attachment theory in the late 1950s and 1960s, others had attributed importance to this concept and had begun to explore its characteristics. Konrad Lorenz, a fundamental figure in the field of ethology (the scientific study of animal behavior), whose work will be summarized in chapter 2, was one such theorist. A number of psychoanalysts, among them Freudian disciple Sandor Ferenczi and pioneering child psychoanalyst Melanie Klein, were also interested in the nature of the relations between parents and infants, a theoretical precursor to the idea of attachment. Klein's theories, controversial as they were, may in fact be seen as providing a significant link in the chain extending from Freud to the object relational ideas of the next generation of analytic developmentalists. Perhaps most influential within the psychoanalytic field, however, were those analysts associated with the "middle" or independent tradition of British object relations theory. These psychoanalytic theorists, who in addition to John Bowlby included such figures as D. W. Winnicott, W. R. D. Fairbairn, and Michael Balint (and perhaps more arguably the developmentalists Ian Suttie and Imre Hermann), were specifically disenchanted with classical conceptions of early development and are credited with being the architects of what is now termed the "relational/structure" model in contemporary psychoanalysis (Greenberg

& Mitchell, 1983). This chapter provides a concise summary of the work and influence of these early theorists, as well as a discussion of how their thinking may have shaped modern ideas of attachment.

The Beginning: Freudian Theory

In 1905, with the publication of *Three Essays on the Theory of Sexuality*, Freud offered a developmental schema to account for an elemental force, sexual energy, and its transformations from earliest infancy to puberty. This model, termed *libido theory*, made several important assertions about the nature of the infant's relationship to the external world. Freud believed that the libido progresses through various stages; each involves sensual pleasures and is experienced in association with sensitive parts of the body, such as the skin, the mouth, the anus, and the genitals. Freud believed that these bodily organs, which he termed the *erogenous zones*, are *cathected*, or charged with libidinal or sexual-drive energy according to a specific developmental sequence.

The earliest stage of libidinal development, which Freud termed the *oral stage*, begins at birth and continues through the middle of the second year of development. Some psychoanalysts believed that two subphases exist within the oral stage, the first of which involves sucking and the second, oral sadism (biting and devouring), but there was general recognition of the preeminence of oral needs, perceptions, and an oral mode of expression focused on the mouth, lips, tongue, and oral mucosa during this earliest developmental epoch. The next stage, termed the *anal stage* (from approximately one to three years), commences with the neuromuscular maturation of the anal sphincter. Such maturation was regarded as significant inasmuch as it furnishes the infant with appreciably greater voluntary control over the expulsion or retention of fecal products. Freud believed that there is a pleasure associated with the exercise of anal functions, which he termed *anal erotism*. Subsequent elaborations of this stage suggested the existence of two subphases, the *anal-sadistic* (destructive-expulsive) and *anal-erotic* (mastering-retaining) phases. The anal stage, according to the theory, is superseded by the *phallic stage* of development (from approximately three to five or six years), at which time erotic pleasure becomes firmly linked for the first time to stimulation of the penis or vagina. Central to the phallic stage is Freud's theory of the *Oedipus complex*, a conflict-laden configuration of psychological forces characterized by the concentration of sexual wishes directed at one parent, usually of the opposite sex, and the concurrent emergence of hostile feelings toward the remaining parent, the child's rival in love.[1] The phallic stage is followed by a period of libidinal quiescence, referred to as *latency* (from approximately five to eleven years), during which there is relative inactivity of the libidinal drive, a situation that permits a fuller resolution of oedipal or triangular conflicts.

Although Freud later became more interested in the nature of the infant's actual relations with human objects, his 1905 theory of the libido makes several critical assumptions, among which is that there is no preexisting tie to (libidinal) objects, to the human environment. Indeed, Freud believed that infantile emotional life begins in a state of *primary narcissism*, in which self is not differentiated from object and investment in libidinal objects does not occur (Meissner, 2000). As the infant begins to mature, a different distribution of libido, termed *autoerotism*, becomes possible. Autoerotism, unlike the state of primary narcissism, is not objectless; by definition, it consists of those actions through which the infant uses her or his own body or body parts to achieve sexual satisfaction, a classic illustration of which is thumb-sucking. Such gratifications, however, are most usefully thought of as substitutes for the love object (mother) or the part object (maternal breast), which are not always attainable and hence are unreliable. Mature object relations, in which libido becomes available for deployment in the interpersonal realm, is in Freud's view achieved only through autoerotism and in consequence of the progression of the libido to the oedipal phase of development.

The "object" in this model of development, it is emphasized, is originally "created by the individual," a result of experiences of satisfaction and frustration of the expression of libidinal desire (Greenberg & Mitchell, 1983, p. 44). In Freud's libido theory, it is the object's *suitability* to the impulse that is paramount. A related assumption is that of the individual as a discrete entity, a "closed" system whose psychosexual development proceeds largely irrespective of any interpersonal context. Such a model seems to suggest that parents exercise relatively little influence over what is fundamentally an endogenously arising and sequentially unfolding developmental process. And, to the degree that they might exist, actual parental deficiencies receive comparatively little attention. Within such a framework, the concept of attachment as an organizing principle for infant development would be radical indeed.

Freud had at various times also grappled with phenomena associated with separation, loss, and the mourning process, in essays such as "Mourning and Melancholia" (Freud, 1915/1917) and "Inhibitions, Symptoms, and Anxiety" (Freud, 1926). Of particular interest to Bowlby was Freud's understanding of the nature of separation anxiety, which he ultimately explains as "a reaction to the felt loss of the object" (Freud, 1926, p. 137). However, because Freud theorizes that infants' attachment to their mothers does not constitute a primary drive—since in the Freudian schema there is no preexisting tie to the object—he explains the longing experienced by an infant when the mother is unavailable primarily by invoking the economic hypothesis. In other words, physical separation leads to an accumulation of tension in the infant as a consequence of the possibility of nonsatisfaction of its needs. The real danger, according to Freud, is not the separation of the infant from her mother but the "economic disturbance" caused by the growing tensions, which the infant must somehow rid itself of (Freud, 1926). Freud, however, seems less than certain of this explanation. Indeed, in a later passage in the same work, he speculates that the infantile fear of loss of the object might conceivably be in the hardwiring, that it "might perhaps be accounted for as vestigial traces of the congenital preparedness to meet real dangers" found in other primates (Freud, 1926, p. 168). Bowlby, however, was far more confident than Freud had been. He became convinced that not only attachment behavior but also the child's behavioral response to separations from the caregiver—the now famous sequence of protest, despair, and detachment initially identified by Bowlby and James and Joyce Robertson—possesses an instinctual basis. Yet another important difference between traditional psychoanalytic ideas about development and those advanced by Bowlby was the latter's contention that children, even infants, are capable of mourning. Mourning, according to traditional psychoanalytic theory, is intimately linked to the attainment of a more or less fully functioning ego, a developmental accomplishment that is not theoretically possible until late childhood.[2]

In fact, a careful examination of Freud's conception of object relations, the Oedipus complex, the function of anxiety, the phenomenology of mourning, and the stages of the libido reveals basic assumptions regarding the primacy of intrapsychic processes and the relative insignificance of the interpersonal environment in shaping human growth and behavior—ideas that appear to be at considerable variance with those of attachment theory, as we shall discover. Attachment theory tends to give far greater importance to the environmental surround of developing infants and, more specifically, to the nature of the affectional bond between infants and mothers. For

Bowlby—who, like Fairbairn and other object relations theorists, became convinced of the critical role played by *real* experiences—the Freudian vision of erogenous impulses in search of an object to facilitate discharge simply did not correspond to systematic observations of infants and mothers. Moreover, when infants were deprived of such vital interpersonal contact, traumatic sequelae and other forms of psychopathology were judged far more likely to occur.[3]

Bowlby was also critical of the evidentiary basis advanced in support of the claims that classical psychoanalysis made about human development and psychopathology, which were almost exclusively retrospective in nature. He wrote:

> Most of the concepts that psychoanalysts have about early childhood have been arrived at by a process of historical reconstruction based on data derived from older subjects. This remains true even of ideas that stem from child analysis: the events and processes inferred belong to a phase of life that is already passed.... In creating this body of theory not only Freud but virtually all subsequent analysts have worked from an end-product backwards. Primary data are derived from studying, in the analytic setting, a personality more or less developed and already functioning more or less well; from those data the attempt is made to reconstruct the phases of personality that have preceded what is now seen.
>
> (Bowlby, 1969, pp. 3–4)

In his approach, Bowlby proceeded in exactly the opposite direction. Employing observational data of very young children and their behavior in specific situations, he endeavored to describe the earliest stages of personality functioning and development, data from which he would then attempt to "extrapolate forwards." Bowlby did not view his method, which embodied four components—prospective study, a focus on pathogenic influences and their sequelae, direct infant/child observation, and the use of animal data— as fundamentally incompatible with Freud's views and methods, although he characterized them as largely unfamiliar to most psychoanalysts.[4]

An Early Challenge: The Work of Sandor Ferenczi

Sandor Ferenczi was an early adherent of classical psychoanalysis who made a number of important theoretical and clinical contributions, among which were ideas about the salience of pre-oedipal experience and somewhat more controversial ideas about incest trauma (Rachman, 2000), the significance of actual maternal deprivation (Greenberg & Mitchell, 1983), and a technical innovation (the "active technique") designed to shorten the overall length of psychoanalyses (Tosone, 1997). Arguably more controversial was Ferenczi's position on "mutual analysis," a radical modification of psychoanalytic technique in which the patient and the analyst become full-fledged analytic partners in the interest of "eliminating the patient's feelings of inferiority to, and distance from the analyst" (Gay, 1988, p. 580). Interestingly, Ferenczi's most systematic foray into the realm of psychoanalytic developmental theory, "Versuch einer Genitaltheorie" (Ferenczi, 1924), was not notably controversial. In this paper, he emphasizes the subjugation of each libidinal stage—with particular attention to that of genitality—to the primal effort to reestablish an original state of pleasure associated with intrauterine existence.

Ferenczi's relationship with Freud, which had been strained on more than one occasion, finally became damaged beyond repair over the issue of childhood sexual abuse. In the late 1890s, Freud renounced what has come to be known as the seduction hypothesis. Although at one time he had believed his patients' reports of sexual trauma to represent veridical accounts, he gradually understood such reports to be deeply rooted oedipal fantasies,[5] a discovery that permitted a fuller elaboration of the Oedipus complex. Also referred to in the literature as the "nuclear complex" of the neuroses, the Oedipus complex gradually attained a position of superordinate importance in classical psychoanalytic theory and practice over the next thirty-five years. Ferenczi, however, on the basis of his own clinical work in the late 1920s and early 1930s, "rediscovered" the seduction hypothesis that Freud had abandoned more than three decades earlier. Although he accepted the existence of infantile sexuality, Ferenczi became convinced that *actual* occurrences of parental sexual abuse were a relatively ubiquitous phenomenon—in any event, hardly the exception suggested by Freud's theory. Indeed, Ferenczi was convinced that his patients had supplied him "with evidence of infantile seduction and rape, not fantasized, but real" (Gay, 1988, p. 583). What is especially noteworthy about Ferenczi's position is its assumption of veridicality in such matters, as well as the presumption that ongoing, reality-based relationships between infants and significant objects in their environmental surround possess a pivotal significance in the development of later psychopathology.

Although these ideas are referenced in Ferenczi's *Clinical Diary* (Dupont, 1988) and elsewhere, his last published paper, "Confusion of Tongues Between Adult and Child" (1949), appears to offer the clearest exposition of his high valuation of *real*-object experiences in the manufacture of neurotic disorders:

> I obtained above all new corroborative evidence for my supposition that the trauma, especially the sexual trauma, as the pathogenic factor cannot be valued highly enough. Even children of very respectable, sincerely puritanical families, fall victim to real violence or rape much more often than one had dared to suppose.
>
> (p. 227)

Ferenczi's contributions to clinical theory, according to Bacciagaluppi (1993), can be seen to encompass several themes, among them the importance of a loving approach to the patient; the possibility that the analyst can make therapeutic mistakes and the crucial importance of acknowledging such errors; and, finally, the notion of reciprocity in the relationship between analyst and patient. Bowlby was most certainly influenced by Ferenczi, in particular by the importance the latter attached to real events and relationships, as well as his early recognition of the pivotally significant role played by maternal deprivation in the formation of later psychopathology. Furthermore, Bowlby's ideas about trauma, which he linked closely to external events and real-object experiences, appear far closer to the model formulated by Ferenczi than to Freud's conception, which remains arguably reliant on the economic hypothesis of tension accumulation and discharge. It may in fact be argued that Ferenczi's influence is at the heart of Bowlby's theory of attachment, where one finds "two innate and complementary sets of behavior: attachment and parental caregiving—fundamentally, a reciprocal loving relationship" (Bacciagaluppi, 1993, p. 193).

Since Ferenczi died prematurely in the same year in which the English translation of the "Confusion of Tongues" paper was published (1933), he was never able to explore more systematically the potential of his ideas regarding pathological influences on infantile object relations for the study of *normal* infant development, a task left in part to such theorists as Winnicott, Fairbairn, Balint, Suttie, and Hermann. All of these independent-tradition theorists, however, were also influenced by Melanie Klein—in certain cases perhaps more in reaction against the radical ideas she proposed than in concert with them.

Infants and Mothers in the Kleinian Framework

Melanie Klein's controversial ideas, even today a subject of debate among psychoanalytic scholars and practitioners, have pervaded virtually every aspect of psychoanalytic theory and practice, although her perspective on infant development and on the infant's relationship with the outside world will be of greatest concern to us here.

Klein's influence on the course of contemporary psychoanalysis, which some have suggested may be second only to that of Freud (Mitchell & Black, 1995), was first felt keenly in the protracted and at times bitter debate that emerged during the 1930s and 1940s within the British psychoanalytic establishment. Largely in consequence of Klein's positions, which were felt to be at fundamental variance with those of Anna Freud, three separate schools of psychoanalytic thought gradually emerged in Britain (classical/ego psychological, English, and independent). Klein was also the first psychoanalyst to treat children with the psychoanalytic method, although her developmental premises as well as her clinical approach to child analysis, which called for little modification of the analytic method used in work with adult patients, were met with skepticism, criticism, and outright disdain.[6]

Klein was a productive scholar, publishing a series of theoretical and clinical papers and several books over a forty-year period. She steadfastly maintained her allegiance to Freud, asserting that all of her observations, her clinical work with children, and so on were intended only to confirm or amplify Freud's own theoretical innovations. There is certainly a modicum of support for Klein's professed allegiance to classical theory and developmental principles: her emphasis on the oral component in the infant's relatedness to its mother, on the salience of Freudian dual instinct theory, and the primacy of the Oedipus complex, are among the more prominent illustrations of this claim. Nevertheless, upon closer examination, Klein's ideas seem very unlike those of Freud; her portrayal of the mind as "a continually shifting, kaleidoscopic stream of primitive, phantasmagoric images, fantasies, and terrors" (Mitchell & Black, 1995, p. 87) suggests a mental life, in terms of both structure and content, that differs vastly from what Freud proposed.

In Freud's theory of object relations, infants proceed from a primary narcissistic state to object love, but only through the detour of autoerotism; moreover, "true" object love, in Freud's theoretical formulation, is possible only after the libido has been redistributed in the phallic-genital stage, which of course coincides with the Oedipus complex; whatever object relations might occur before this time—i.e., the pregenital stages—are to be considered regressive elaborations of the Oedipus complex (Fenichel, 1945; Grotstein, 1996).

It is here that Kleinian theory seems most transparently dyssynchronous with the classical framework. In the first place, Klein's theory is entirely psychological in nature, notable for its effort to "account for the contents and processes of mental dynamics" without recourse to biological explanations (Weininger & Whyte-Earnshaw, 1998, p. 198). Even Bowlby notes that in "contrast with Anna Freud, Melanie Klein is an advocate of the view that there is more in the infant's relation to his mother than the satisfaction of physiological needs" (1969, p. 367). The Kleinian baby, in stark contrast with the classical vision, is both psychologically separate and object seeking—rather than pleasure seeking—from the moment of birth (Grotstein, 1996; Klein, 1964). As noted, Klein's understanding of the infant's impulse life differs significantly from classical characterizations. For Freud, as we have mentioned, the object is in a sense a mental creation whose sole purpose resides in its suitability with/for the impulse. This, however, is in marked contrast to Klein's essential belief that

> objects are built into the experience of the impulse itself... [so that] the object of desire was implicit in the experience of desire itself. The libidinal impulse to love and protect contained, embedded within it, an image of a lovable and loving object; the aggressive impulse to hate and destroy contained, embedded within it, an image of a hateful and hating object.
>
> (Mitchell & Black, 1995, p. 91)

Such ideas also throw into much sharper relief one of attachment theory's most strenuous objections to the Kleinian conception of object relations—namely, Klein's contention that object relations are to be understood as completely *internal* phenomena. As perhaps the best known of Melanie Klein's many clinical supervisees during her years in London, Bowlby had gradually developed the "view that real-life events—the way parents treat a child—[are] of key importance in determining development," a perspective of which Melanie Klein was completely dismissive. Indeed, Klein forbade him to have contact with the families of his child patients, largely owing to her view that the child-mother relationship was of far less import than how it had become internalized (Karen, 1998). "The notion that internal relationships reflect external relationships," Bowlby later complained, "was totally missing from her thinking."[7]

Bowlby had been similarly critical of the Kleinian emphasis on orality, food, and the significance of the breast, thematic elements that served to secure the link Klein had gone to such effort to establish between her ideas and those of Freud. In spite of Klein's preoccupation with preserving this continuity between classical ideas and her clinical descriptions and theoretical formulations, Bowlby notes with a certain satisfaction, Klein's own observations sometimes called for a very different conclusion. In a publication from the early fifties, Klein wrote:

> Some children who, although good feeders, are not markedly greedy, show unmistakable signs of love and of a developing interest in the mother at a very early age—an attitude which contains some of the essential elements of an object-relation. I have seen babies as young as three weeks interrupt their sucking for a short time to play with mother's breast or to look towards her face. I have also observed that young infants—even as early as in the second month—would in wakeful periods after feeding lie on the mother's lap, look up at her, listen to her voice and respond to it by their facial expression; it was like a loving conversation between mother and baby. Such behavior implies that gratification is as much related to the object which gives the food as the food itself.
>
> (Klein, 1952, p. 239)

Such ideas, as we have shown in our review of classical psychoanalytic theory, represented a significant departure from then-prevailing conceptions about infancy and instinctual life. Klein, however, did not stop here. She also theorized a psychological existence for infants that, in spite of her claims to the contrary, seemed much less an extension of classical theory than an alternative to it.

Klein proposed that three-week-old infants experience a primitive anxiety state, which she terms *persecutory anxiety*, which is in turn hypothetically linked to schizoid mechanisms (e.g., splitting, projective identification, idealization, and magical, omnipotent denial). She asserts that such intrapsychic experiences form the basis for the *paranoid-schizoid position*, the first developmental organizer of infancy (Klein, 1964). Klein prefers the term *position* to Freud's term, *stage*, to highlight the "to and fro" movement of infant development, a process that she believed to be gradual and flexible and characterized by an almost unending series of progressive and regressive steps (Weininger & Whyte-Earnshaw, 1998). In the paranoid-schizoid position, the infant's *paranoia* is referable to "anxiety over threatened, fantasied annihilation by persecutory internal objects" (Moore & Fine, 1990, p. 110), while *schizoid* is used to designate the defensive configuration (as per above). Both ego and object are split into "good" and "bad," which, in the Kleinian view, gradually enables the infant to attain order and coherence out of primordial chaos—what can only be described as a bifurcated and fragmented experience of objects and of self. In this way, the dangers of *bad* objects, whether internal or external, are kept separate and isolated from the self and *good* objects (Greenberg & Mitchell, 1983). In Klein's framework, the object relations of the paranoid-schizoid position are defined as being either all good or all bad, though never constituted as an admixture of the two. Whole-object relations do eventually become possible with the gradual integration of experiences of good and bad, but only following a critical developmental shift that Klein hypothesized to occur beginning at four to six months, termed the *depressive position*.

The depressive position is the second developmental organizer of infancy, the successor to the paranoid-schizoid position. At this developmental juncture, the infant strives to integrate "love and hate for objects, their 'good' and 'bad' aspects, other partial representations of them ... and external reality with intrapsychic reality or fantasy" (Moore & Fine, 1990, p. 107). The central theme of the depressive position is concern for the object's welfare, which, of course, had until now been the recipient of hateful fantasies of vengeance and annihilation (emblematic of the earlier paranoid-schizoid position). The newly emerging capacity for whole-object relations means that the infant is now capable of experiencing ambivalence—that is, good (loving) and bad (hateful) feelings toward the *same* object. While this represents a critical developmental achievement for the infant, it also gives rise to new dangers: recognition that the maternal object may be destroyed or lost as a consequence of aggressive impulses within the infant's self, as well as oedipal conflict.[8] The affects of sadness, regret, sorrow, and guilt become internally available to the infant at this time and fuel efforts to make "reparations" for the earlier damage the infant believes itself responsible for. These fantasies are intended to repair the damage and transform the annihilated object into a whole object once again.

Although our interest has primarily been with the influence that Klein's theories have had on object relations theories and more particularly on the development of Bowlby's ideas regarding attachment, it may be useful to note that other writers have been critical of Klein on several grounds. For example, some have argued that in those fields (e.g., the neurosciences and cognitive psychology) where evidence might be offered in support of a fundamental Kleinian premise—that infants are capable of a complex fantasy life at birth— little if any exists (Tyson & Tyson, 1990). Others have been critical of Klein's lack of theoretical clarity regarding the relationship between fantasy and the establishment of character or psychic structure (Fairbairn, 1952; Kernberg, 1980; Mishne, 1993), and still others have faulted her for becoming the "adoptive parent" of Freud's much maligned and "largely ignored" death instinct (Karen, 1998).

The Independent, or Middle, Tradition: Winnicott, Fairbairn, and Balint

The independent, or middle, group consisted of a number of important thinkers, most of whom were associated with the British Psychoanalytical Society of the 1940s and 1950s. This group included D. W. Winnicott, W. R. D. Fairbairn, Michael Balint, and, somewhat less notably, Ian Suttie and Imre Hermann. Each of these theorists developed a view of object relations in accord with an important basic postulate: that an infant is from the moment of birth object seeking. Although this basic theoretical premise is attributable to the pioneering work of Melanie Klein, the middle traditionalists rejected a critical theoretical premise of Kleinian theory—that of constitutional aggression—and proposed as an alternative "an infant wired for harmonious interaction and nontraumatic development but thwarted by inadequate parenting" (Mitchell & Black, 1995, p. 114).

D. W. Winnicott

Usually considered the best-known representative of the independent group, Winnicott began his professional career as a pediatrician and only later sought training as a psychoanalyst. His oft-quoted axiom "There is no such thing as an infant; there is only the infant and its mother" (Winnicott, 1960b, p. 39) reinforces the pivotal significance that he attributes to the earliest object relations between infant and caregiver. For Winnicott, the relationship between mothers and babies—and more particularly the quality of mothering—is central. Disruptions to this vital mother-infant bond, whether in consequence of environmental vicissitudes or poor mothering, might have far-reaching, if not disastrous, consequences. Such ideas seem to have led Winnicott and Bowlby down fundamentally similar pathways. In fact, Bowlby was well aware of these similarities and observed on numerous occasions that Winnicott expressed many of the same ideas in poetic language that he, Bowlby, endeavored to present in scientific terms (Karen, 1998). For example, Bowlby noted with satisfaction that Winnicott's view of infantile anxiety seemed to favor a perspective that, like his own, focused on the relation of primitive anxiety to attachment failures (Bowlby, 1973).[9]

Winnicott's opinion of Bowlby and his contributions reflected greater ambivalence, however. Though he cited Bowlby in his own papers—going so far as to suggest that "psychoanalysis needs Bowlby's emphasis on deprivation" if it is ever to arrive at a fuller understanding of antisocial character pathology (Winnicott, 1958b, p. 310n)—he was at other times quite critical of Bowlby. It was in fact Winnicott, then president of the British Psychoanalytical Society, who reacted so negatively to a paper linking ethological studies to attachment formation, privately confiding in a note to Bowlby's former training analyst, Joan Riviere, that acceptance of Bowlby's ideas would signify rejection of many of the ideas Freud had struggled to advance (Karen, 1998).

Their common interests notwithstanding, there were also important differences between the two theorists. Bowlby was chiefly concerned with the environment and with elucidating a scientific basis for the infant's interpersonal relationships, while Winnicott focused his attention on the subjective dimension of infantile experience (Karen, 1998). In formulating ideas such as primary maternal preoccupation, good-enough mothering, the holding environment, true and false self, and the concept of the transitional object, Winnicott offered a vision of infancy that seemed quite dissimilar from much that had preceded it.

Winnicott believed that the emergence of a health-promoting psychological milieu for each human infant is determined by her or his mother's capacity for what he terms *primary maternal preoccupation*. In the state of primary maternal preoccupation, mothers engage in a sort of adaptive withdrawal from the external world, focusing increasingly on the baby developing inside themselves. Although such withdrawal might under other circumstances be considered pathological, the mother's concentrated focus on her unborn child is critically necessary for the infant's transition from prenatal experience to that of the world outside the womb (Moore & Fine,

1990). Indeed, mothers find their own "personal interests... rhythms and concerns... fading into the background" (Mitchell & Black, 1995, p. 125). Using the language of classical psychoanalysis, Meissner describes this unique form of empathic attunement between mother and unborn child as the result of a maternal "narcissistic cathexis" that has the effect of permitting "mother to identify with the child" and, more specifically, with the child's "inner needs" as though the latter "were... an extension of her own self" (Meissner, 2000, p. 199).

Good-enough mothering denotes the mother's ability to offer her wholly dependent baby an *optimal* degree of comfort and environmental constancy (Moore & Fine, 1990). Commencing with the mother's primary maternal preoccupation, this at first requires that she meet the symbiotic needs of her newborn infant, whose dependence upon caregiving is regarded as total or absolute and therefore is much like the symbiotic-phase infant of developmentalist Margaret Mahler[10] (Meissner, 2000). Such needs initially involve the regulation of basic physiological processes, though they gradually grow in variety and complexity, so that complete satisfaction of the infant's needs, if such a thing were ever possible, becomes increasingly unlikely as the infant matures. Indeed, in Winnciott's view, the mother's *shortcomings* are as essential to good mothering as her *successes*, a viewpoint that parallels the self psychological notion of optimal frustration/optimal gratification as a necessary basis for the child's transmuting internalizations.[11] Occurring in tandem with the child's psychological development and enhanced locomotor abilities, which lead to increasingly frequent physical separations between the child and the mother, there is the painful recognition that neither mother nor infant is omnipotent (Moore & Fine, 1990). However, the infant's exuberant forays into the object world outside the infant-mother matrix offer a compensatory pleasure that offsets the loss of the infantile fantasy of omnipotence (Winnnicott, 1958a, 1965).

Although the attunement between mothers and infants can never be perfect, Winnicott stresses the idea that whatever is offered to the infant is offered at the "right time" for the infant rather than being timed to meet the mother's own needs. The mother's capacity to provide empathically attuned support or *holding* thereby equips her baby in situations that evoke frustration, aggression, or loss. Such holding, which possesses equally important physical and emotional dimensions, also gradually furnishes the infant with a "first sense of a world that can be trusted sufficiently for the process of separation to occur" (Frogget, 2002, p. 42). Maternal holding in effect provides

for containment of the infant's anxiety and thus permits creative exploration not only of the world outside mother's body and physical reach but also
of the inner world—the world of thought, fantasy, and introspection. Such
ideas appear to translate readily into the developmental framework and ty-
pology ultimately devised by Bowlby and his followers that highlighted *secure* versus *insecure* forms of attachment.

Winnicott also emphasizes that such exploration of the child's inner and
outer environments occurs within a *potential space* between mother and infant, a "hypothetical area of mutual creativity" (Moore & Fine, 1990, p. 206).
In a caregiving environment that is good enough, this potential space may
ultimately become internalized by the child, who is then equipped to repro-
duce or re-create it in other circumstances and with other objects.

Winnicott also believed that all human beings begin life with a *true
self*, an "inherited potential" that may be understood to represent the infant's core self or essence. In an attuned and growth-promoting, facilitative
human environment, the true self, which has been described as a spontaneous expression of the id, is progressively elaborated and gradually becomes
firmly established. However, when the mother, owing to environmental
limitations, personal pathology, or perhaps a combination of the two, is
unable to respond to the "sensorimotor, gestural, 'id' self of the infant" but
offers instead a distorted reflection of what she observes, somewhat akin
to that of the fun-house mirror, a *false self* forms alongside or in place of
the true self. Put somewhat differently, the false self may be thought of
as a facade erected by the infant child so as to comply with the mother's
inadequate adaptations, whether such failures take the form of deprivations or impingements on the child's growth (Goldstein, 1995). Meissner
has observed that

> infants who develop in the direction of a false self mode have not experienced
> the security and mutual satisfaction of [an attuned mother-infant] ... relation-
> ship. Such mothers are out of contact with the child and react largely on the
> basis of their own inner fantasies, narcissistic needs, or neurotic conflicts. The
> child's survival depends on the capacity to adapt to this pattern of the mother's
> response, which is so grossly out of phase with the child's needs. This estab-
> lishes a pattern of gradual training *in compliance with whatever the mother is
> capable of offering, rather than the seeking out and finding of what is needed and
> wanted* [emphasis added].

(2000, pp. 202–203)

Infants who are locked into such patterns of forced compliance and negation of their own needs are able to survive, but, in Winnicott's view, only at the cost of "living falsely" (Winnicott, 1960a, 1965). Winnicott believed the bifurcation of self-experience into "true" and "false" structures is invariably present—even in normal infants—though only in the most disturbed children, adolescents, and adults does the false self organization elide its counterpart so completely.[12]

Winnicott treated many patients who suffered from various pathologies of the self, such as schizoid, borderline, or narcissistic personality disorders, individuals whose suffering seemed linked to a profound inner alienation. Such patients, Winnicott noted, may act and function normally, but they experience a fundamental disorder of their personhood. In effect, a critical dimension of subjectivity becomes subverted in such cases, so that the individual's true self, if not completely supplanted by a false self organization, is well hidden. "Winnicott's most profound and most productive insight," Mitchell and Black have noted, was the connection he made between false self disorders occurring in later life and "the subtle variations he observed in mother-infant interactions from the very beginning of life" (1995, p. 125). These observations seemed strongly to suggest significant if not striking continuities between infants' experiences with their mothers and "the quality and nuances of adult subjectivity," thereby offering important new opportunities for understanding not just the process of development but that of therapy as well (1995, p. 125).

Perhaps the most widely known of Winnicott's theoretical ideas is his concept of the *transitional object*. Winnicott believed that transitional objects, typically consisting of children's blankets, stuffed animals, pillows, toys, and other inanimate but nonetheless cherished possessions, serve to promote the developing child's gradually increasing independence. Such objects are endowed with soothing and calming qualities that become especially evident at times of heightened anxiety, for example, during stressful separations from caregivers or at bedtime (Winnicott, 1951), although the use of transitional objects is not by any means limited to such times. The transitional object has particular characteristics, including texture and odor, that are believed to remind the infant of the mother; indeed, efforts to "sanitize" such objects when they become dirty or foul-smelling may evoke strong protests in the child, who reacts to such a measure as a break in the continuity of her experience—a disruption that "may destroy the meaning and value" of the object (Winnicott, 1951, p. 232). The transitional object is transitional not only because it enables the infant to sustain the illusion of a calming, comforting mother in the mother's absence, but also because it "helps to bridge the gap between *me* and *not-me*... the space between the self and external reality." It is in this space, Winnicott notes, where "symbolization occurs, meaningful, affective, sharing-yet-separate companionship and love grow, [and]...play and illusion are maintained in the spontaneous, creative activities of healthy people" (Fonagy & Target, 2003, pp. 139–140).[13]

Winnicott's conception of transitional objects and of transitional experience was initially formulated within a developmental context, although he ultimately extended this framework to include various aspects of adult experience. Conceiving of the transitional experience as occurring within an intermediate domain or realm of illusion that "embraces both inner and external reality," Winnicott believed that its essential characteristics might be preserved in "areas of adult functioning having to do with... imaginative capacities [such] as creativity, religious experience, and art" (Meissner, 2000, pp. 200–201). Whereas the transitional experience for the infant or young child is intimately linked to a capacity for play, for the adult, transitional experience would be more likely to involve "playing with" new ideas and fantasies and the cultivation of one's own creative impulses.

W. R. D. Fairbairn

Fairbairn's *object relations theory* of development, like the framework developed by Winnicott, also represented a radical departure from classical psychoanalytic conceptions of libidinal drive and Freudian conceptions of the nature of the earliest relations between mothers and infants. First and foremost, Fairbairn's concept of ego is that of a structure "present from birth rather than developed from the id" in consequence of its commerce with reality (Moore & Fine, 1990, p. 71). Fairbairn's infantile ego, furthermore, possesses an energy all its own, thus obviating the need for the classical formulation of the id as the source of all psychic energy. In effect, the distribution of libidinal energy in the Fairbairnian model has become an *ego function*, and the id as an independent agency has therefore ceased to exist. Equally important is Fairbairn's conception of the *nature* of libidinal energy. Like Winnicott and other middle-tradition theorists, Fairbairn was more or less convinced that libido was object seeking rather than pleasure seeking. In effect, he believed the object to be "built into" the impulse from the very beginning. In such a scheme, pleasure is no longer conceived as the ultimate goal of the impulse but rather as a vehicle through which a relational tie can be established (Greenberg & Mitchell, 1983). Fairbairn was undoubtedly influenced in the formulation of these ideas by his extensive experience in working with abused children. As Mitchell and Black observe,

> He was struck by the intensity of their attachment and loyalty to [their] abusive parents; the lack of pleasure and gratification did not at all weaken the bonds. Rather, these children came to seek pain as a form of connection, the preferred connection, to others. Children, and later adults, seek from others the kinds of contact they experienced early on in their development. Just as ducklings become imprinted onto and follow around whatever caretaking object shows up at the right time ... so, in Fairbairn's view, do children become powerfully attached to and build their subsequent emotional lives around the kinds of interactions they had with their early caregivers.
>
> (1995, pp. 116–117)

Fairbairn's theory also represents a significant challenge to classical ideas about the origins of psychopathology. In Freud's articulation of the structural model—essentially, that conflict inheres in all mental activity and that there are specific conflict-mediating structures—a basic theoretical premise is the existence of instinctual aims of a hedonistic nature that strive for satisfaction or "discharge." When such aims are interfered with, whether the result of internal superego prohibitions, external constraints, or a combination of the two, various adaptations are possible; some of these may be adaptive and relatively conflict-free resolutions, while others may be conflict-laden, fundamentally neurotic defensive accommodations. Even psychotic disturbances, which might be said to reflect a failure of defense, are understood within the classical framework to represent the "outcome of a ... disturbance in the relations between the ego and the external world" that, like the neuroses, "originate[s] in the ego's conflicts with its various ruling agencies" (Freud, 1924, pp. 149, 152). In contrast, Fairbairn views psychopathology as the sequela of insurmountable obstacles to the infant's efforts to develop and maintain relationships with significant others or, in his language, "natural objects." Interferences with the infant's or young child's efforts to establish such relational ties lead to the formation of internalized objects, which are "compensatory substitutes for unsatisfactory relations with real, external objects" (Mitchell, 1994, p. 82).

Fairbairn's characterization of internalized object relations appears in certain respects to parallel Bowlby's ideas, particularly in relation to Bowlby's later elaboration of representational or internal working models, which is described in detail in chapter 2. Bowlby's concept of the internal working model is not necessarily a negatively valenced one, however, inasmuch as he assumes that *all* infants develop such representational models on the basis of their attachment experiences; for some, the model is an open, flexible one, revealing the subject's capacity to assimilate new information and anchored in a fundamentally secure attachment experience, whereas for others the model might reflect a kind of attachment rigidity, a foreshortening or derailment of development, perhaps linked to insecure or anxious attachment experiences. Although Fairbairn views all internalized objects as compensatory, the notion that such internal phenomena might distort or otherwise influence external object relationships is also clearly present in Bowlby's idea of representational models.

Not surprisingly, Fairbairn's understanding of human emotional development differs markedly from the libidinal phase model of classical theory. Unlike Freud, Karl Abraham, and other architects of libido theory, Fairbairn develops a conception of developmental stages that is not tied to a maturational sequence that shifts from one erotogenic zone to another. Rather, he theorizes a developmental process rooted in the individual's evolving capacity for relatedness to others. "What changes is not the body part, serving as a focus of instinctual tension, but the quality and complexity of relatedness to others" (Greenberg & Mitchell, 1983, p. 160). As individuals mature, they gradually exchange infantile dependency for mutuality and interdependence. Postpartum life, in Fairbairn's estimation, is the continuation of the intrauterine mental state, one characterized by a near-absolute merger with mother/mother's body. Fairbairn also refers to this infantile relationship to the mother as one of "primary identification," which in his view represents "the cathexis [libidinal investment] of an object which has not yet been differentiated from the cathecting subject" (Fairbairn, 1941, p. 34n).[14]

Fairbairn's theory of development, like the Freud/Abraham theory of libidinal development, also consists of three phases. Fairbairn's framework, however, is a model for the development of object relationships with the changing quality of the child's dependence on mother serving as the central organizing theme, a model that along with the progressive differentiation of infantile self from maternal object also emphasizes "a process of relinquishing narcissistic or self-centered attitudes in favor of loving and caring ones, and a process of more or less successful actualization of one's ideals in a relationship" (Robbins, 1994, p. 306). The three developmental stages that

Fairbairn identifies in this maturational schema are *infantile dependence,* *quasi independence,* and *mature dependence.*

Stage I: Infantile dependence

In this stage the infant's dependence on the mother is absolute, and the maternal breast serves as a "natural biological object to which the infant's mouth relates" (Moore & Fine, 1990, p. 73). Rather than emphasizing the erotization of the mouth and oral mucosa, however, Fairbairn focuses on the object relational idea of *incorporation*. Such "taking in" contributes to a gradual internalization of the breast. This is of course the developmental stage in which *primary identification* occurs, the fusion of the neonate with a maternal object from which she or he has not yet achieved differentiation (Moore & Fine, 1990, p. 73). Like the articulation of the stages of the libido, Fairbairn also postulates a division of the stage of infantile dependence into an *early oral* (preambivalent) *phase* and a *late oral* (ambivalent) *phase*. In the early oral phase, the mother's breast is treated as a part-object, whereas in the late oral phase, mother is a "whole-object treated as a part-object" (Grotstein & Rinsley, 1994, p. 337).

Stage II: Quasi dependence

Fairbairn hypothesizes an extended *transitional* stage situated midway between the stage of *infantile dependence* and that of *mature dependence*, which he terms the stage of *quasi dependence*. In this stage the differentiation of the infant's self from objects is initiated and progressively elaborated, and an inner world is gradually formed that consists of internal representations of these objects. As the object is "taken in," it is treated as bodily contents, and its "bad" parts are expelled (Moore & Fine, 1990). As noted earlier, however, Fairbairn regards such internal object representations as compensatory in nature, a substitute for whatever "sense of security and continuity" might be absent in the real relationships with the parents (Greenberg & Mitchell, 1983, p. 161). Viewed within such a framework—with its emphasis on the object-seeking nature of libido—individual psychic survival *depends upon objects*; therefore, the situation of greatest danger, one that might be termed emblematic of this stage, is the fear of separation or of object loss. Accordingly, the "central conflict of the entire transitional phase ... is between the developmental urge toward mature dependence and richer relations, and the regressive reluctance to abandon infantile dependence and ties to undifferentiated objects (both external and internal)" over the prospect of losing contact with the object (Greenberg & Mitchell, 1983, p. 162).

Stage III: Mature dependence

This stage is marked by the achievement of full differentiation of self from object and a capacity for mutuality, for "give and take," in human relationships. As Fairbairn defines it, maturity is attained only by the child's "renunciation of compulsive attachments to objects based on primary identification and merger" and an analogous repudiation of attachments to the child's compensatory internal objects—in his estimation, a momentous and enormously challenging step, one that is probably never fully complete (Greenberg & Mitchell, 1983, p. 161). In order for such renunciation to occur, a child must feel "loved as a person in his own right" but also experience her or his own expressions of love as "welcomed and valued" by others (p. 161).

As chapter 2 will underscore, Fairbairn's theory of development and his ideas regarding attachment bear a fundamental similarity to Bowlby's formulations and seem in essential respects to be compatible with them. Although both theorists were influenced by the work of Melanie Klein, each "abandoned Klein's efforts to preserve classical drive theory," instead seeking to challenge and redefine "the basic principles within which classical theory operates" (Greenberg & Mitchell, 1983, p. 184). Both theorists were also critical of the physicalist tradition that undergirds classical theory, viewing it as inadequate and anachronistic (p. 184). However, Fairbairn's radical notion that biological impulses do not have primacy but instead arise in consequence of the *frustration of relational needs*, though bearing a superficial similarity to Bowlby's views, is not truly equivalent.[15] As Fonagy and Target note, in Bowlby's theory, the "goal of the child is not the object, e.g., the mother [an underlying premise of Fairbairn's theory]. The goal that regulates the system is initially a physical state, the maintenance of a desired proximity to her," a goal that is only later "supplanted by the more psychological goal of a feeling of closeness to the caregiver" (2003, p. 233).

Michael Balint

Michael Balint's theoretical contributions, though not as celebrated as either Winnicott's or Fairbairn's, are also considered important for their emphasis on what Balint terms unconditional or *primary object love*. Balint, who had trained with Ferenczi and remained a close follower, is credited with further developing his mentor's early work in such areas as early maternal deprivation and its clinical and transferential sequelae, and in simultaneously striving to reconcile these ideas with those of mid-twentieth-century mainstream psychoanalysis (Greenberg & Mitchell, 1983). Balint, unlike Fairbairn, does not go so far as to reject classical drive theory, arguing that libido possessed two "fundamental tendencies—that it is *both* pleasure-seeking and object-seeking" (Greenberg & Mitchell, 1983, p. 183). However, at other times he conceives of "the pleasure-seeking aims of libido" much as Fairbairn does, as arising from frustration in the child's efforts to procure emotional supplies from the object. Nevertheless, he asserts that primary object love can be neither subsumed by nor otherwise "linked" to the Freud/Abraham model of libidinal stages, arguing that the idea of primary object love cannot be conceived in oral, anal, genital terms but rather that it "is something on its own" (Balint, 1952a, p. 85).

Much like his middle-tradition peers, Balint believed object relations to be present from the moment of birth. He is critical of the classical concept of primary narcissism, which, he concludes, asserts that the "individual is born having hardly any or no relationship with the environment" (Balint, 1968, p. 66). He writes:

> Primary narcissism is a very curious notion, full of meaning and yet very poor. If we accept it, the very earliest state of the intrauterine mental life can be characterised as follows: the infant has no knowledge as yet of the external world, does not even perceive it; it has subjectively no relation to the objects and persons of its environment and thus no desires orientated towards the world; it experiences only increase and disappearance of its needs, but does not yet connect them with the external world; the observable emotional phenomena, such as crying, whining…are merely abreactions; as the infant does not yet perceive any external objects, it can have no libidinous object-relations as yet; of its libido nothing has yet been turned outwards.
>
> (Balint, 1952a, p. 103)

Balint's objections are multiple, however. In the first place, he criticizes Freud's methodology, which he considers to represent a hypothesis based upon theoretical extrapolation—no more, no less—a critique he shares with Bowlby. He is critical also on the grounds that direct empirical observation of infants, admittedly a fledgling science in the first half of the twentieth century, had demonstrated that "reactions of infants to libidinous environmental influences can be demonstrated indisputably as early as the first week of their life and certainly in the first month" (Balint, 1952a, p. 104).[16] Balint further asserts that *absolute* narcissism is in itself impossible and, using as an example the difficulty in reaching a transcendental meditative state, observes that even a narcissistic *attitude* is extraordinarily difficult to achieve. Moreover, he believed that primary narcissism implies a state of indifference about the world, and yet infants who are theoretically in a state of primary narcissism express nearly unceasing requirements for attention and emotional supplies from their caregivers.

Balint instead proposes that the "relationship with the environment exists in a primitive form right from the start" and that the desire to be loved is inborn (Fonagy & Target, 2003). He characterizes the infant's earliest object-relatedness as "passive" in nature, suggesting that its aim is simply to "be loved and satisfied, without being under any obligation to give anything in return" (Balint, 1952a, pp. 98–99). In Balint's conception, narcissism represents one of two *detours* from this goal: failing sufficient gratification from primary objects, infants will, as a compensatory measure, love and gratify themselves. A far more adaptive detour, of course, is the individual's willingness to conform to a partner's wishes in order to receive love and gratification, what Balint terms "active" (versus "passive") object love (p. 99). Within this framework, then, narcissism is *never* actually primary but is a reaction to or protection against a "bad" or nongratifying object.

Balint, like Bowlby, Winnicott, Fairbairn, and other object relations theorists, was also interested in the relationship of early traumata to later psychopathology, particularly pathology he identified as being rooted in infantile experience with the primary objects. In Balint's view, traumatic breaches in the earliest relationship between infants and caregivers may give rise to what he terms the *basic fault* (Balint, 1968), a structural rending of the psyche. Balint is careful not to describe the basic fault as "a situation, position, conflict, or complex"; rather, he views it as a *level* of intrapsychic experience, the specific characteristics of which are these:

(a) All the events that happen in it belong to an exclusively two-person relationship—there is no third person present; (b) this two-person relationship is of a particular nature, entirely different from the well-known human relationships of the oedipal level; (c) the nature of the dynamic force operating at this level is not that of a conflict; and (d) adult language is often useless or misleading in describing events at this level, because words have not always an agreed conventional meaning.

(Balint, 1968, pp. 16–17)

According to Fonagy and Target (2003), the basic fault may be legitimately considered to constitute the developmental basis for personality disorders. Phenomenologically speaking, individuals exhibiting a basic fault have the "underlying feeling that something is not quite right about" them (p. 138), for which they seek out various environmental remedies. Ultimately, many such patients enter psychoanalysis or other forms of treatment, Balint believed, principally seeking to heal these basic disjunctions in the structure of the self. In his work with such patients, Balint experimented with various clinical approaches that were intended to "recapture missed developmental opportunities" as well as to reclaim dissociated parts of the self (Mitchell & Black, 1995, p. 136).

Balint's interest in the relationship of early experiences with the primary objects to a child's characteristic ways of managing anxiety led him to hypothesize two basic defensive strategies, *philobatism* and *ocnophilism*. Philobatism, writes Balint, is intended to characterize the "pleasure and activities" derived from reliance on one's own skills and resources in a situation involving a basic threat to one's sense of security (Balint, 1959). Balint's model for such a strategy of defense is that of the acrobat, the thrill of whose performance lies in separation from the security of "mother earth." If the philobat dislikes attachments to object, preferring instead the spaces between them (Fonagy & Target, 2003), the ocnophile, by contrast, is intensely dependent on and invested in objects. The world of the ocnophile, writes Balint, "consists of objects, separated by horrid, empty spaces. The ocnophil [*sic*] lives from object to object, cutting his sojourns in the empty spaces as short as possible. Fear is provoked by leaving the objects, and allayed by rejoining them" (1959, p. 32). At first blush, the ocnophile's solution to the problem of anxiety over separation or object loss seems more primitive and less adaptive than the philobat's acceptance of the inevitability of separation and of the separate existence of objects. The philobat has indeed accepted reality and, moreover, has learned to rely on skills and internal resources to cope with such frustrations and anxieties. However, Balint asserts that both attitudes—not the ocnophile's alone—have the potential to be "pathological"; that is, one may be anxiously clinging to one's love objects "in abject fear that they may change" (ocnophilia) or adopting an attitude of supreme confidence that either new objects will always be readily available or old ones will have remained unchanged upon one's return (philobatism).

It is tempting, though perhaps potentially misleading, to recast Balint's ideas about the basic fault in attachment theory terms. As we recognized in our discussion of Fairbairn, it may also be possible to view Balint's framework as adumbrating Bowlby's theory of the representational or internal working model. In effect, philobats might be seen as having acquired a representational model consistent with secure attachment experiences, while ocnophiles could be seen to operate out of a representational framework reflecting anxious, or even ambivalent or disorganized, attachment experiences. (One problem with this ostensibly good "fit" between the two concepts, mentioned previously, is that Balint would be loath to characterize either philobatism or ocnophilism as necessarily adaptive or pathological, although the representational models in Bowlby's framework are far more readily located along a continuum of adaptiveness/maladaptiveness).

Contributions of Ian Suttie and Imre Hermann

Though the work of Suttie and Hermann is less well known than that of other middle-tradition theorists, no summary of British object relational views on infant-mother attachment could be considered complete without some consideration of these two authors.

Ian Suttie, whose death at an early age seemed to plunge his work into relative obscurity, is nevertheless credited with one of the earliest challenges to the classical theory of motivation and libidinal stages. Writing in the mid-1930s, Suttie argued that infantile attachments to one's mother, rather than constituting "merely the sum of infantile bodily needs and satisfactions," might instead reflect a "need for company" and a primal effort to avoid the anxiety associated with isolation (Suttie, 1935, p. 16). Suttie regarded as "indisputable" that

> a need for company, moral encouragement, attention, protectiveness, leadership, etc., remains after all the sensory gratifications connected with the mother's body have become superfluous and have been surrendered. In my view *this is a direct development of the primal attachment-to-mother* [emphasis added], and, further, I think that play, co-operation, competition and cultural interests generally are substitutes for the mutually-caressing relationship of child and mother.
>
> (Suttie, 1935, p. 16)

Suttie believed that infants begin life with a nonerogenous attitude of be-
nevolent or loving attachment to their mothers, which relationship serves
as a basis for all later forms of object love. Far from classical conceptions
of infantile narcissism or of the libidinization of the infant's own body, Suttie held that the infant's bodily self acquires importance inasmuch as it also
represents the object of maternal interest "and the first plaything shared with
her" (Suttie, 1935, p. 37). In Suttie's view, motives for tenderness and companionship only later unite with the individual's appetite for sexual expression
in mature object love, a position that is, of course, at considerable variance
with Freud's conception of the development of genital sexuality. For Suttie, the instinct for self-preservation drives the infant's longing for and attachment to its mother, and this self-preservative dependency on others "is
never completely outgrown, but persists as a need for companionship *apart
from the organic satisfactions that may be derived therefrom*" [emphasis in
the original] (Suttie, 1935, p. 259).

Perhaps not surprisingly, Suttie's theory of psychopathology is closely
tied to any factor that might interfere with the exercise of the maternal function—that is, anything that has the potential to disrupt the normative developmental processes by which infants become socially mature and independent of the mother. In fact, Suttie asserts that specific disturbances in
maternal character-formation can be linked to the infant's development of
later psychopathology: "fixation[s], regressions, depressions, jealousies and
antagonisms," which, in turn, constitute the basis for mental illness. Psychotherapy represents an attempt to reduce the dislocations of such thwarted attachments—the infant's "love life"—and to "free interest for social purposes"
(Suttie, 1935, p. 259).

Imre Hermann, much like his colleague Michael Balint, was powerfully
influenced by Ferenczi's ideas. Although he published a series of papers in
the psychoanalytic journals of his era, Hermann, unlike the other theorists
whose books and other publications we have summarized, never produced
a major work. Indeed, it was most likely Michael Balint's high valuation of
Hermann's ideas, cited in such works as *Primary Love and Psychoanalytic
Technique*, that has made his work more enduring and guaranteed a place of
some importance in the history of psychoanalytic ideas. Hermann's theory
rests on two significant observations: (1) that infant primates cling to the
bodies of their mothers throughout the first months of extrauterine life and
(2) that human infants are prematurely separated from the bodies of their
mothers. Human infants desire to live as a part of a dual unity with their

mothers, and insofar as the realities of civilization supervene to make this impossible, they will develop "a number of instinctual substitutive symptoms," such as the sleeping position, reflexive adaptations (e.g., the Moro reflex), sucking, and, of course, the general tendency to respond to external threats by clinging to the mother or her substitute (Balint, 1952a). The infant of whom Hermann wrote was, significantly, actively engaged in behavior expressly designed to elicit responses in the maternal object, comparable in important respects to patterns observed in nonhuman primates. There is, therefore, comparatively little importance attached in Hermann's theory to such notions as infantile passivity, autistic-like states, objectlessness, or primary narcissism, ideas that, as we have suggested, are associated both with classical theory and later with the views of developmentalists such as Margaret Mahler.

Hermann also claims that clinging is the developmental precursor of a range of object relational phenomena, both normal and pathological. Stroking, tenderness, and caresses may follow the "attenuation" of the tendency to cling; similarly, sadism and masochism might be traceable to pathogenic frustrations in the infant's instinct to cling (Balint, 1952a). A variant of clinging, Hermann offered, is also assumed to be present in the erotic embrace. At the same time, Hermann, notes Bowlby, "was reluctant to regard [clinging] as an object relationship, so it would probably be incorrect to say that he subscribed to the theory of primary object clinging" (Bowlby, 1969, p. 371).[17]

This chapter has explored the work of a number of psychoanalytic writers, all of whom have developed theories to account for the earliest relations between mothers and infants. Inasmuch as each of the theorists whose ideas we have considered was also actively engaged in ongoing clinical work, developmental issues are, in virtually every case, considered *pari passu* with those involving the origins of later psychopathology—in particular, the ways in which such pathology may be associated with infantile life and with deficiencies or pathogenic features of the infant's early environment. What Mitchell and Greenberg have referred to as Bowlby's "broad reformulation of all the central features of personality development and psychopathology" (1995, p. 137), while no less revolutionary on this account, appears to have been influenced by ideas emerging from the fertile intellectual environment of post–World War II Europe and, more specifically, the British psychoanalytic community. Ferenczi's influence, to the degree it may have existed, probably resided in his late effort to understand pathogenesis as a process invariably affected by the subject's experiences with real, external objects, a viewpoint that was certainly consonant with Bowlby's emerging ideas about the origins of psychopathology. Bowlby was also taking issue with the ideas of his former mentor, Melanie Klein, whose theoretical premises about human development and psychopathology he had found so deeply troubling. (In this, Bowlby adhered to a time-honored tradition in psychoanalysis— that of theoretical secession—a path trod by many other great psychoanalytic thinkers, from Carl Jung to Otto Rank.)

As we have suggested, infant development, as conceived by middle traditionalists such as Winnicott and Fairbairn, reveals certain obvious conceptual parallels with Bowlby's theory of attachment. Like Bowlby, each attributed a great deal of significance to the notion of an infantile tie to the world of objects, and each tended to imbue real-world object relations with a significance at least equal to that of internalized object relations (indeed, in Fairbairn's case, internalized object relations were compensatory for what was unavailable in the external object world). Balint, too, emphasized the overriding importance of the *actual* relationship between infants and their environment. On balance, however, Balint's efforts were in the direction of augmenting and reshaping rather than rejecting the basic premises of Freudian libido theory. His solution—to suggest that libido might comprise both pleasure-seeking *and* object-seeking aims—must have struck Bowlby as both less agreeable and less serviceable a framework than, for example, Fairbairn's radical redefinition of drive. Finally, Bowlby seems to have been taken with the ideas of Suttie and Hermann, both of whom also emphasized the nonerogenous aspects of infant-maternal relations. Hermann, in particular, seemed to draw heavily from ethological ideas, a position that foreshadows Bowlby's own strong inclination to ground components of his attachment theory in infrahuman research.

Bowlby's Theory of Attachment | TWO

The landmark contributions of John Bowlby, the "father" of modern attachment theory, evolved over time, culminating in the publication of his three seminal publications, *Attachment, Separation,* and *Loss,* between 1969 and 1982. Because of his reliance on biology, evolutionary theory, and animal studies, and because he challenged the prevailing dynamic conceptions for the earliest relations between infants and mothers, Bowlby became alienated from the psychoanalytic establishment of his day.

Bowlby's early papers on such topics as separation, the nature of infantile attachment, and grief and mourning in childhood reveal his most important ideas. Having discussed the contributions and influence of his psychoanalytic predecessors and middle-tradition peers on the development of his thinking, we will now turn to the important influences on Bowlby from the areas of biology, evolutionary theory, cognitive theory, and ethology, as well as the contributions of Bowlby's assistant, the social worker James Robertson, and the Uganda and Baltimore studies of Bowlby's most famous collaborator, Mary Ainsworth, whose experimental methods enabled her to test Bowlby's ideas empirically and opened the way for the rich body of attachment research that followed.

John Bowlby and the Origins of Attachment Theory

John Bowlby was born in 1907 to a prominent family in England. The boy's relationship with his parents was distant. He and his siblings were cared for by a series of nannies, and at the age of eight he was sent to a boarding school with his older brother; he later reported that he felt very unhappy there. These early family experiences may have shaped Bowlby's later interest in the impact of upbringing and early environment on children. He later decided to study medicine in Cambridge, but he became interested in working with children and left his studies for a year in order to volunteer at two different institutions for maladjusted children. His relationships with, and observations of, two children in these institutions clearly influenced the course of his future theories. One of the children was an isolated, withdrawn child who was expelled from his former school for theft, and the other was an anxious boy who was very attached to Bowlby and followed him around. Working with these children alerted Bowlby to the effect of maternal deprivation on the development of children (Karen, 1998).

After his year as a volunteer, Bowlby resumed his medical studies, and later he decided to become a child psychiatrist and pursued analytic training at the British Psychoanalytic Institute, where Melanie Klein was a formidable influence. He entered into personal analysis with Joan Riviere, a follower of Klein, with whom he remained for seven years in an apparently unsuccessful analysis, principally because of Bowlby's critical attitude toward psychoanalysis (Karen, 1998). Even so, Bowlby did absorb many ideas from Klein through his analyst and, later, through Klein's supervision of his work. From Klein, Bowlby adopted an object relations approach, along with an emphasis on early child development. In 1936 Bowlby joined the staff of the London Child Guidance Clinic, where his social work colleagues had a significant impact on his thinking, apparently a greater impact than that of his teachers and supervisor at the psychoanalytic institute (Bowlby, 1988).

Charles Rycroft described Bowlby as "a nineteenth-century Darwinian liberal" who was "blunt and forthright" (Grosskourth, 1986, p. 402). For example, Bowlby's feistiness and independent spirit put him into direct conflict with Klein, who could not tolerate any divergence from her own thinking. His interest in real-life relationships and scientific observations contrasted sharply with Klein's focus on the child's inner fantasy life. In 1936, while working at the London Child Guidance Clinic, Bowlby became concerned about behavior disturbances among children raised in institutions. He felt that such children were unable to love because they had not had the opportunity to form a solid attachment to a mother figure early in life. As he noted later, "It is the difficulty of developing new libidinal relationships where none have previously existed or in circumstances traumatic for those already in being, which appears to be critical in the development of the affectionless and delinquent character" (Bowlby, 1944, p. 111). Bowlby attributed this behavior primarily to maternal deprivation and separation. In England during World War II, many families lost fathers who went to fight at the front, and those family members who remained suffered great financial difficulties. Consequently, many parents left their infants, either temporarily or permanently, to be cared for in hospitals and in children's homes. It was also common practice for parents and children to be separated during a child's hospitalization. These were the children that Bowlby studied.

During the war, Bowlby was asked to collaborate on officer selection procedures with other colleagues from the Tavistock Clinic in London. This experience provided him with methodological and statistical expertise that came in handy during his future research studies. After the war, Bowlby became the head of the children's department at the Tavistock Clinic, where he published the first paper on family therapy (Bowlby, 1949), describing how he was able to achieve positive clinical results by interviewing parents about their own childhood experiences in the presence of their children.

In 1948 Bowlby hired James Robertson, a social worker, to help him observe hospitalized children whose parents were not allowed to see them. Unlike Bowlby, Robertson came from a poor family in Scotland. He had worked in the steel mills from age fourteen to age twenty-eight to help support his family, and he was always sensitive to issues of social justice and class distinctions. Robertson and his wife actually went to live in a homeless shelter for two and a half years in order to learn firsthand about the lives of homeless people.

Robertson obtained his formal training in close observation of children at the Hampstead Clinic, where Anna Freud required all the employees to observe and write about the children's behavior. Robertson then spent two years collecting data on children in a long-term hospital ward for Bowlby's research, but eventually he became very frustrated by the resistance of the medical staff, who would not listen to his observations of the children's distress. He consequently decided to make a documentary that would record his observations and thus would have a greater impact on the children's lives. The film was very controversial in the medical community, especially in

Robertson's hospital, where he was barred from further work (Bretherton, 1999). Nevertheless, the movie became quite popular and had a profound impact on medical personnel and child experts, helping to reform hospital policies in pediatric wards throughout the Western world. Robertson became an important, though sometimes unacknowledged, collaborator of Bowlby's; indeed, Robertson's observational research provided the data for many of Bowlby's most seminal ideas. In addition, Mary Ainsworth, whose initial job was to analyze Robertson's studies, was deeply moved by his methods and emulated them in her own later research studies in Uganda and Baltimore.

In 1950, when Ainsworth arrived at Bowlby's research unit, Bowlby was commissioned by the World Health Organization (WHO) to write a report on the mental health of homeless children in postwar Europe. This study followed Spitz (1945) and Goldfarb (1943), as well as earlier reports on the effects of deprivation on young children. Bowlby's WHO report: *Maternal Care and Mental Health* (Bowlby, 1951), was published and translated into fourteen languages. A second revised edition was titled *Child Care and the Growth of Love*, that included chapters by Mary Ainsworth (Bowlby, 1970). Although Bowlby's ideas were still couched in psychoanalytic terminology, they were new and controversial for the time. According to Bretherton (1999), rather than viewing the child's development in terms of Freud's structural theory of the mind (id, ego, superego), Bowlby hypothesized that children internalize their moral values and cognitive capacities from their mothers and that these become their "internal working models." Although Freud had emphasized the father's moral authority as being paramount in the development of the child's superego, Bowlby gave a more prominent role in moral development to the mother (Bretherton, 1999). He also emphasized the reciprocal nature of the child's relationship with the mother (or a substitute caretaker) and the role of social networks, economics, and health factors as crucial environmental conditions for the development of such relationships. He called for social institutions to provide support for parents, aligning himself with basic principles of social justice: "Just as children are absolutely dependent on their parents for sustenance, so in all but the most primitive communities, are parents, especially their mothers, dependent on a greater society for economic provision. If a community values its children it must cherish their parents" (Bowlby, 1951, p. 84).

In line with the social beliefs of the 1950s, Bowlby believed that maternal, rather than paternal, care in early childhood was imperative for healthy child development. He continued to learn and absorb new knowledge from many different sources throughout his lifetime. Consequently, the basic principles of attachment theory reflect an integration of ethology, behavioral and cognitive theory, developmental psychology, evolutionary theory, and psychoanalysis. He contributed the essential empirical foundation for future understanding of children's relationships with their caregivers and the impact of disruptions caused by separation and loss on children's behavior.

Influences: Darwin, Spitz, Lorenz, and Harlow

From Charles Darwin's evolutionary theory, which had become popular and influential at the time, Bowlby learned that the impetus toward biological survival was primary in all species. During his observations of children, he concluded that the only way a human offspring could survive was through a process of adjustment and adaptation to its environment. In this thinking, he was also influenced by Heinz Hartmann's theory, which emphasized coping and adaptation as important ego functions in child development. Through Hartmann's work, the child's interactions with the external environment became more important, and the ego, representing the child's interface with society, became the focal point of inquiry (Hartmann, 1956).[1] Basing his conclusions on evolutionary theory, Bowlby believed that anxiety is caused by both internal and external threats, rather than by internal conditions alone (as Freud believed). While Freud was also interested in Darwinian ideas, which differentiated between primitive and more evolved forms of life, he went in a very different direction. Freud developed a theory of the mind, using evolutionary principles to explain its internal structure, which he divided into three levels: the id, the ego, and the superego. Bowlby, however, was more interested in behavior related to the external environment, and how people adapt and survive in dangerous situations. From earliest human history, he noted, fear is a major component of anxiety. This anxiety includes fear of darkness, isolation, loud noise, and strangers, all of which are associated with increased risk of danger. Thus he regarded such environmental anxieties to be a function of evolutionary history (Bowlby, 1973). In this way, Bowlby used evolutionary theory as a scientific basis for his attachment theory.

Bowlby was also influenced by earlier observations of infants by René Spitz, an American psychoanalyst who had recorded his observation of institutionalized children (Spitz, 1945). In his film, *Grief: A Peril in Infancy*, Spitz showed young children at different stages of hopelessness and depression in a Mexican foundling home. Although the children received good nutritional and medical care, the home did not have adequate staffing and the harried workers did not have time to play with the children or hold them. In this movie, Spitz clearly showed that mere physical survival was insufficient for a human baby to thrive. The infants seemed underweight, anxious, and depressed, and they clearly failed to thrive. Spitz compared these babies to others at a prison nursery in New York State, who were visited regularly by their mothers and who did seem to thrive. Spitz's work was groundbreaking for the time, and he became the major spokesperson in the United States against maternal deprivation. His observations formed the basis for the notion that attachment is based first and foremost on the child's need for physical affection and emotional nurturing rather than on the need for food.

From studies with human babies, Bowlby moved to the natural world and to studies with animals. He was deeply influenced by Konrad Lorenz's work on the imprinting of offspring on their mothers. In a famous experiment, Lorenz observed that recently hatched ducklings would follow him, the first moving object that they saw, despite the fact that he neither resembled a mother duck nor behaved like one. This experiment had a deep impact on Bowlby, who viewed it as an indication of how powerful the need for attachment is in earliest life, even with a substitute maternal figure that does not provide feeding. If the ducklings, however, did not encounter a moving object within a specific period of time, the instinctual behavior was extinguished, and normal bonding did not take place. From this, Bowlby hypothesized that, like animal species, which are genetically "hardwired" to respond to certain signals and intergenerational rituals, human babies, too, have innate relational behaviors, such as sucking, clinging, crying, and smiling; if attachment needs are not met early on in life, a child's development will be seriously disrupted. Bowlby's theory, that a child's most important need is for emotional bonding with another at the earliest stage of life, contrasted with the Freud/Abraham model of libidinal stages, in which the infant's earliest need is an oral one, biologically driven though exclusively focused on obtaining mother's breast milk.

Bowlby was also influenced by Harry Harlow's experiments with baby rhesus monkeys (Harlow, 1958). Harlow, a psychologist who worked at the University of Wisconsin, observed that many of his experimental monkeys died of disease. In an effort to find the solution to this problem, he separated his infant monkeys from their mothers after birth and raised them in complete isolation. He observed that the infant monkeys became attached to the gauze diapers that covered the floor of their cages and furiously protested when the staff tried to remove them. Other baby monkeys became attached to a wire mesh cone covered with terry cloth and placed in their cage. To examine this behavior further, Harlow created two wire models that he called "surrogate mothers." One model was a block of wood covered with terry cloth; it had a face, and a lightbulb placed behind it generated heat. The other model was made only of wire mesh, but also had a face and a lightbulb. For four of the monkeys, the cloth-covered model was fitted with a feeding nipple. For the other four the wire mesh mother had the nipple. Regardless of which model did the actual feeding, the monkeys spent almost all their time, sixteen to eighteen hours a day, clinging to the cloth mother. They then began to use the cloth mother as a secure base for exploration of their environment and as a refuge, running to it when strangers entered the room. Harlow's experiment was the first methodologically sound, scientific experiment offering proof that affectional ties are not based on nursing. Bowlby concluded from this experiment that the need for attachment and emotional nurturing is even more powerful than the need for food—not only in mammals but in human babies as well.

Influence of Behaviorism and Cognitive Theory

Bowlby was interested in providing a scientific basis for his observations and, later in life, sought to find behavioral and cognitive explanations and to revise the prevailing psychoanalytic theories of development. This approach is apparent in his earlier emphasis on behavioral observations, his stress on the physiological primacy of the attachment drive, and later his theory of internal working models, itself influenced by Piaget's cognitive developmental model. The emphasis on behavioral and cognitive theories intensified when Bowlby's collaborators and followers turned increasingly to pure research rather than to clinical data to develop attachment theory further (see, for example, Ainsworth, 1989; Main, 1991; Sroufe, 1988). Yet another factor contributing to the influence that Piaget's empirical studies of infants' cognitive and emotional development exerted over Bowlby was through his participation in the Psychobiology of the Child Study Group. This group, to which Bowlby belonged from 1953 to 1956, also included the likes of Erik Erikson, Konrad Lorenz, and Margaret Mead. Bowlby believed Piaget's focus on exploration and mastery and his own emphasis on attachment instincts to be complementary. Attachment behavior, or the need for proximity to the caregiver, was activated because of fear and threat, and mastery and exploration were activated when the child felt secure. Ainsworth clearly observed these behaviors in her Uganda and Baltimore studies (Ainsworth, 1963; Ainsworth & Bell, 1970). Mahler also observed them in her work with infants, as did Harlow in his experiments with rhesus monkeys. Bowlby believed that parents who are nurturing and attuned to an infant's needs enable the child to feel securely attached and, at the same time, to be curious about the environment and to engage in exploratory behavior, thus developing a sense of competence. Unlike social learning theorists, who saw dependency as a pathological trait, Bowlby differentiated attachment, which he saw as a normal and healthy need of both children and adults, from dependency.

Controversies with Psychoanalysis, the Women's Movement, and the Social Work Establishment

During the time of Bowlby's work, very little was written about the influence of children's relationships with caregivers on their development. Although Freud and Klein both adhered to the genetic perspective—that one's earliest experiences shaped subsequent development—neither they nor their followers seemed interested in examining early relationships. This shift came about after Freud abandoned his "seduction theory" and chose to develop the structural theory of the mind instead, privileging fantasies and internal psychic structures over real experiences in the social environment. Bowlby, in contrast, gradually moved away from the psychoanalytic theories of his time. His direct observations of children's behavior convinced him that Freud and Klein were on the wrong track. His focus was the relational and interpersonal, rather than the intrapsychic. He saw the desire for bonding and attachment as primary, unlike Freud and Klein, who believed that the sexual and aggressive drives are paramount.

Bowlby was trained and supervised by Melanie Klein during 1938–1939, but he soon found that his observations of children's behavior conflicted with her theoretical constructs. While Klein was interested in building a theory that would explain children's inner drives and conflicts, Bowlby wanted to observe real-life relationships between children and their caregivers. In one case, Klein forbade him to interview the anxious mother of a three-year-old patient of his, and he was not allowed to offer her any help. Bowlby later learned that she was admitted to a mental hospital. When he informed Klein of this development, she was concerned only with the interruption of the treatment. Indeed, Bowlby recounted that Klein considered the mother's admission "a nuisance ... [since] we shall have to find another case" now that the child's mother could no longer bring him to treatment (in Grosskourth, 1986, p. 402). Bowlby concluded that for Klein only internal relationships within the child's psyche mattered; the child's real relationship with his/her mother was completely unimportant. From the beginning, Klein's personality and theories were at odds with Bowlby's. Whereas he observed that children suffered depression because of bereavement, Klein viewed depression as having its origins in internal guilt.

Bowlby was not alone in observing infants at the time; the Hampstead Clinic had already published clinical accounts of infants' behaviors. These case histories, however, were not systematically studied, and Anna Freud, who was deeply influenced by her father and highly invested in maintaining and bolstering Freud's drive theory, attributed the infants' behaviors to defensive structures of the ego. Bowlby, on the other hand, believed that the most important human motivation is the need for affectional bonds with others, and he considered the mother's behavior an important aspect of the infant's attachment responses. As stated above, he was more interested in the interactive process between mother and child than in the world of fantasy and internal drives developed by Freud and Klein (Mitchell, 2000).

While Bowlby did study with Klein, he began to disagree with her belief that aggression, which she linked to the "schizoid position" and guilt, which she associated with the "depressive position," possess elemental significance. Bowlby also differed with her theory that emotional problems in children originate in fantasies stemming from internal conflicts between the aggressive and sexual drives. Instead, his understanding was that the infant's behavior is based on the caregiver's presence and responsiveness. Once, during a meeting of the British Psychoanalytical Society, Bowlby declared, "But there is such a thing as a bad mother!" (Mitchell, 2000, p. 84). Bowlby believed that children are greatly influenced by their physical, as well as emotional, need for an actual bond with a real attachment figure and that that is their prime motivation not only throughout infancy but also throughout life. He thus began to look for supporting data outside the realm of psychoanalytic theory, in other social and behavioral fields, such as ethology, evolutionary theory, developmental psychology, behaviorism, and cognitive theory.

Another point of contention was the issue of children's grief reaction to loss and separation. Bowlby had noted that most of the psychoanalytic writers of his time perceived grief to be a depressive illness or a pathological response to loss. He, on the other hand, differentiated between healthy mourning and pathological mourning. In his second volume (Bowlby, 1973), he observed that for Freud, the process of mourning is primarily internal; the mourner detaches from the lost person, turning inward to grieve for an internal representation of the lost object, and eventually, in a healthy grief process, is able to move on to develop new attachments. Klein's conception was somewhat different, inasmuch as she believed mourning stems from either the fear of retaliation (schizoid position) or the sense of guilt (depressive position). Bowlby, however, believed that anxiety is directly related to grief and mourning stemming from a *real* loss, generally that of a parent. As noted previously, Bowlby took exception to the prevailing psychoanalytic view that children are incapable of real mourning. Moreover, he asserted that mourning in childhood becomes pathological only when children are institutionalized and have not been provided the opportunity to engage in normal bonding with their parents. He observed, "There is no experience to which a young child can be subjected more prone to elicit intense and violent hatred for the mother figure than that of separation" (Bowlby, 1960, p. 24). He noted that children as young as two can experience real grief for the loss of a parent and can be helped to resolve it.

The reception given to Bowlby's first paper at the British Psychoanalytic Association, "The Nature of the Child's Tie to His Mother" (1958), was intensely critical. In the paper he applied ethological principles, based on Lorenz's imprinting experiments with ducklings, to infant behavior. He also compared the infant's need to maintain a primary attachment to a caregiver to the behavior of monkeys, citing Harlow's experiments. Using examples from the natural world, he replaced Freud's drive theory, which he viewed as unscientific, with an ethological-evolutionary perspective. The psychoanalytic community at the time saw this approach as dangerous and unacceptable, and Bowlby was criticized not only by the Kleinians but also by Winnicott and Anna Freud. Bowlby's next paper, "Separation Anxiety," published in 1959, also generated criticism. In it, Bowlby presented Robertson's observations on how young children respond to being without their mother in the hospital. In both papers, Bowlby also challenged Freud's theory of libidinal needs in children and continued to use data from the animal world to compare with children's attachment behaviors. He wrote: "In very many species of bird and mammal the young show signs of anxiety when removed from their parents.... Since it resembles closely ... what we see in humans and seems almost certainly to be homogenous, it is instructive to examine it" (Bowlby, 1960, p. 100). Even Winnicott, whose theories Bowlby respected, wrote to Anna Freud: "I can't quite make out why it is that Bowlby's papers are building up in me a kind of revulsion" (Grosskourth, 1986, p. 406). While many analysts of the time saw Bowlby's theories as simplistic and anti-psychoanalytic, Bowlby himself was confident of his ability to use scientific methods and statistics. Later on, however, flaws were found in his methodology, as well as in that of Spitz, for their failure to differentiate cultural, ethnic, and socioeconomic variables in the children's samples (Karen, 1998).

Despite his controversial position within the psychoanalytic community, in many of his papers Bowlby gave credit to his colleagues, including Freud, Anna Freud, Klein, and Winnicott. He admitted, for example, that Melanie Klein had provided him with training in object relations theory and that some of Freud's theories about mourning and melancholia were correct. However, unlike other object relations theorists such as Margaret Mahler (whose work will be discussed more thoroughly in chapter 3), Bowlby emphasized behavior, environment, and an actual attachment to another rather than the internalized object (or the concept of object constancy). He also suggested that attachment behavior persists throughout life, not only during infancy and childhood. He believed that with the danger of imminent loss, the child will continue to do anything to forestall such loss rather than detaching from the lost object and turning inward, as Freud had maintained in *Mourning and Melancholia* (1917). Bowlby and Robertson both observed that children who either had lost their mothers or had been separated from them suffered protracted distress (Bowlby, 1973). He concluded that children's cognitive development, and their understanding of object relations, begin much earlier than theorists had commonly held (Bowlby, 1980).

Bowlby's theories also proved controversial among social workers and child care workers, who believed that the material attributes of the home, such as good nutrition, hygiene, and proper clothing, are more important that the emotional quality of the relationships within the home. He encouraged social workers and child care workers not to remove children from parental homes where they received love, even though their material needs may have been neglected. A final criticism that Bowlby elicited, in this case from the women's movement, resulted from his more or less exclusive emphasis on the role of mothers rather than that of fathers. In his view, the father has a minimal role in young children's upbringing. Instead, he stated, the mother has the primary and practically the sole responsibility in raising the young child. Bowlby believed that if the child does not receive appropriate nurturing in the first two years, those developmental milestones that have not yet been reached are lost forever. Because of his views in this regard, the feminist movement of the time saw him as advocating that women stay at home and give up their professional aspirations (Karen, 1998).

Bowlby's Papers and His Three-Volume Opus: *Attachment* (1969), *Separation* (1973), and *Loss* (1980)

Bowlby's empirical study involved recorded observations of forty-four children from the London Child Guidance Clinic, where many of his subjects had been engaged in antisocial behavior such as stealing and aggression (Bowlby, 1944). From 1936 to 1939, he collected data on these boys, whose ages ranged from six to sixteen. The children, whom Bowlby termed "affectionless," had been accused of stealing and displayed behaviors ranging from depression to hyperactivity and detachment. Bowlby explained in his paper that the cause of theft and aggressive behavior lay in the child's attempts to get something that represented his mother's love: "The food they stole was no doubt felt to be the equivalent of love from the mother whom they had lost, though probably none was conscious of the fact" (Bowlby, 1944, p. 121). The children's mothers were found to have disturbed attitudes and behaviors, such as violence, anxiety, mental illness, and alcoholism. Bowlby's perspective was that the children were expressing their need for love, and their anger over its absence, through their aggressive and delinquent behavior. He suggested that they were difficult to work with because they had developed a tough exterior in order to protect themselves against further rejection and loss (Bowlby, 1944).

In 1948 the World Health Organization (WHO) commissioned Bowlby to do a study on the psychiatric problems of homeless children. In 1950 he started to gather data from social workers and child psychiatrists in France, Sweden, Switzerland, Holland, and the United States, and a short time later he published the *Maternal Care and Mental Health* (1951) report. He found that professionals, despite living in different countries, made very similar observations: that babies abandoned by their mothers and subsequently institutionalized, suffered developmental deficits and a greatly diminished capacity to relate to others. Many of these children were incapable of form-ing meaningful or lasting relationships. On the basis of his findings, Bowlby started to advocate that mothers, despite their poverty, receive as much sup-port as possible in order to keep their children. Bowlby's report had a signifi-cant impact on international public policy, particularly in adoption, social work, and hospital practices. It also contributed to a new understanding of the causes and prevention of child delinquency (Karen, 1998).

In his next paper, "The Nature of the Child's Tie to His Mother" (1958), Bowlby used findings in ethology to show that both animal and human off-spring have a need to be close to their mothers and this need for proximity supersedes the need for feeding. He compared human babies to the duck-lings in Lorenz's experiment, who followed whatever object they saw first after hatching, whether or not that object was capable of meeting their needs for sustenance.

James Robertson, one of Bowlby's major collaborators, was the first to identify three stages of emotional response to the child's separation from his or her mother. He called the first *protest*, or behaviors including crying, cling-ing, and screaming. The second was *despair*, or listlessness, and loss of inter-est in surroundings and food. The final stage was *detachment*, during which the child started to interact more with the environment and other caregivers, but no longer responded to the mother when she came back (Robertson, 1953). Robertson's influential film *A Two-Year-Old Goes to Hospital* chroni-cled the dramatic shift exhibited by two-year-old Laura from the time of her hospitalization for an elective surgery until her discharge eight days later. So compelling was Robertson's documentary that it convinced many nurses, social workers, doctors, and other health professionals of the profound ill ef-fects of separating children from their mothers during hospitalization.

The first of Bowlby's three volumes, *Attachment* (1969), was based on his own research and the data available at the time and focused on normal attach-ment behaviors and their origins. In his second volume, *Separation* (1973), he looked at the infant's response to separation, and in his last volume, *Loss* (1980) he discussed both infant and adult responses to grief and mourning.

In the first volume, Bowlby was just starting to formulate his attach-ment theory and was not yet completely clear about whether attachment included the infant's needs for emotional bonds as well as desire for prox-imity based on physical survival. Because he was intent upon basing his re-search on scientific methods, he decided to use behavioral measurements and observations to gauge attachment behaviors in children, formulating his emerging theory solely on the basis of biological needs. These early formulations became further refined in the 1970s through the work of Ainsworth (Ainsworth, Blehar, Waters, & Wall, 1978). Ainsworth eventually understood that physical separation was not the primary event in what she termed "the Strange Situation"; rather, the infant's emotional response to the mother's unpredictable behavior was the fundamental component.

In his second volume, Bowlby expanded his understanding of attachment behavior to include the caregiver's accessibility and emotional responsiveness, which he called "availability" (Bowlby, 1973, p. 202). He also focused on separation anxiety in children, discussing it on the basis of Robertson's three phases of separation response—protest, despair, and denial or detachment. These studies suggested that the longer the separation lasted, the more detached a child was likely to become from a caregiver after that caregiver's return.

During protest and despair, children were still very much preoccupied with the caregiver. Once detachment set in, however, they lost interest. Bowlby compared these three stages to principles of psychoanalytic theory, with protest equivalent to separation anxiety, despair equivalent to grief and mourning, and detachment equivalent to defense, especially repression. Unlike Klein and Freud, who attributed separation anxiety to internal causes, Bowlby attributed it simply to the mother's physical departure. He compared this human behavior to the behavior of animals—Harlow's monkeys, for example—and emphasized Darwinian evolutionary theory in its focus on adaptation to the environment. He also referred to Bandura's learning theory (1971) and the role of learned fears and human behavior.

In his third volume, *Loss*, Bowlby addressed the grief and mourning process in both adults and children. He suggested that the three different patterns of attachment, as described by Ainsworth's "Strange Situation" experiments, were determined by the range of past interactions with the caregiver and his or her accessibility to the infant. In his discussion of the grief and mourning response in children, Bowlby emphasized that the ultimate goal was to maintain an affectional bond with the attachment figure and that the child would continue to protest, cry, and express distress in order to preserve this bond. Even children who did not protest and seemed to be independent, he believed, only repressed or concealed their feelings of grief. By the time Bowlby wrote this third volume, he had become increasingly influenced by cognitive psychology, including the information-processing model of neural and cognitive functioning. Consequently, he continually stressed that he, unlike psychoanalytic theorists, had relied on psychosocial conditions and empirical studies to arrive at his theories.

More recently, a shift has occurred in attachment theory, broadening the perspective from focusing solely on infant behavior to considering a wider range of applications, including (1) internal representations in infant and parent, (2) increasing concern within the psychoanalytic community on systematic observation and empirical research, (3) the development of intersubjective and relational paradigms in psychoanalysis, and (4) a growing recognition within the attachment research community of the limitation of a purely cognitive scientific approach, and efforts to make it more broadly relevant to clinicians (Fonagy, 1999, p. 18). Fonagy also emphasizes that attachment theorists such as Mary Main and others who have followed have focused more on internal development than solely upon behavioral observations. Furthermore, attachment research provides a sound empirical underpinning to psychodynamic theory and practice, particularly in the application of current relational and intersubjectivity theories. The growing interface between different fields of research, theory, and clinical practice has made attachment theory progressively more relevant to social work practice. Another important development is that we can now apply our understanding of how attachment disruptions affect both child development and adult personality to the treatment of diverse clienteles.

Bowlby's Theory of Mental Representations

Bowlby's theory of mental representations was an early attempt to explain the impact of attachment experiences on internal object relations. In his understanding of cognitive development, children develop certain expectations for their caregiver's behavior on the basis of past experiences with that caregiver. This developmental schema was also greatly influenced by Piaget's cognitive and social development model, but Piaget's cognitive schema could not fully account for Bowlby's theory of mental representations. Bowlby believed that the child's internal schema of relationships with caregivers does not represent objective reality and in fact is frequently distorted by attachment deficits (e.g., abuse or neglect) that in turn lead to the development of defenses. In other words, children who have experienced abuse or neglect may develop a rigid defensive structure that remains with them, conferring a distorted template for all subsequent relationships, regardless of whether the children later receive love and nurturing. While securely attached children are more flexible in their ability to adapt, abused or neglected children often find it difficult to change their responses in new situations. Bowlby also noted that many anxiously attached children are delayed in their cognitive development and thus have additional difficulty in reevaluating their distorted internal models.

Finally, Bowlby believed that children frequently change their perceptions of their parents' behavior depending on what they feel their parents want or ask of them. One study, for example, done during Bowlby's time, found that children who witnessed a parent's suicide had no memory of the event; instead they adopted a more acceptable explanation furnished by the surviving parent, who either was unable to tolerate the traumatic experience or wanted to protect the child from it (Karen, 1998). This study demonstrates that parents have a powerful influence on the nature of the child's internal representations; the children's internal experiences are subjective, evolving out of a complementary relationship with their parents rather than constituting an accurate representation of an objective reality. Moreover, it may be that children's ability to integrate traumatic events is more limited at early developmental stages, so that a version of events that is not threatening to their psychological cohesiveness is internalized instead of the reality of the situation.

Bowlby's theory of internal working models represents the link between his ideas about attachment and object-relational thinking. The theory of internal working models emphasizes the complementarity of mother and infant roles, further noting the mechanism through which such interchanges between mother and child affect the baby's later relational styles and expectations of others. Thus the mother's responses to the baby, whether attuned, rejecting, or intrusive, determine the baby's self-representation as, for example, lovable or bad. Bowlby's theory of internal representations served as an early prototype for later studies that focused on the mutual influence between parents and children, such as those of Stern (1985). Ainsworth and her colleagues' study of attachment difference (1978) and Main and Goldwyn's study of the impact of adults' early attachment style on their children (1984) are other examples. On the basis of this more complex model, differences between secure and insecure attachment styles could be identified, and it became possible to study individual differences in attachment behaviors. Complementary roles of children and caregivers, specifically with regard to how specific parental behaviors affect the child's sense of self, could be clearly explained. In children who develop an insecure attachment style, for example, a working model of rejection and criticism leads to a sense of being unlovable, flawed, and unworthy.

Ainsworth's Contributions to Attachment Theory

History and Early Studies

Mary Salter, later Ainsworth, was born in Ohio and was reared in Toronto, the eldest of three daughters from a middle-class family. Although her material needs were met, Ainsworth's emotional environment appears to have been lacking, and she grew up with feelings of insecurity and self-doubt. This early experience seems to have influenced the direction that her career would take (Karen, 1998). At the University of Toronto in 1929 she met her first mentor, William Blitz, who taught abnormal psychology and developed a "security theory," linking children's sense of inner security, curiosity, and desire to explore their environment to the emotional relationship with their parents. On the basis of this theory, Ainsworth later coined the phrase "a secure base" (Ainsworth, 1983).

Ainsworth served as a military officer during World War II, in the Canadian Women's Army Corps. After the war she became a faculty member at the University of Toronto, married, and then accompanied her husband abroad. While in London, she started to work with John Bowlby as a research assistant and participated in analyzing James Robertson's raw data, which concerned his observation of hospitalized children. Ainsworth was impressed with Robertson's observational methods, and she soon applied them to a research project that she herself conducted in Uganda.

Ainsworth's Empirical Studies

In 1953 Ainsworth left the Tavistock Clinic and moved to Uganda, where her husband obtained a position at the University of Kampala. While there, she decided to do observational research on infant-mother interactions. From several neighboring villages, she recruited twenty-six families with unweaned babies ranging in age from one to twenty-four months. Though she did not speak the Ugandan language, she learned the essential phrases and took with her a local interpreter, a Ugandan woman who was educated in the United

States and served as Ainsworth's sole assistant during the data collection phase of the project. Ainsworth's research consisted of observing mothers' and babies' interactions during two-hour visits conducted every two weeks over a period of up to nine months. The visits took place in the family's living room, where the women and children spent most of their time. The families had no electricity or running water and were either Muslim or Christian. Ainsworth obtained her sample by talking to the chiefs of the villages, who were initially suspicious but later helped her to arrange meetings with the local villagers. Ainsworth, who had very limited funding for the project, rewarded her participants with transportation to medical clinics and with dried milk.

Ainsworth was interested in investigating the onset of attachment signals and behaviors of the infants toward their mothers, and she recorded when such signals and behaviors occurred (Ainsworth, 1963, p. 67). She noted that the babies' behaviors with their mothers differed considerably from their behavior with others, regardless of who fed them. She quickly determined that Bowlby's assertion that attachment behavior had nothing to do with feeding was accurate. She observed, for example, that the babies would cry when picked up by others but would immediately stop crying when picked up by their mothers. The infants' behavior also included different vocal signals and smiling responses to their mothers. Ainsworth soon identified three infant attachment patterns: securely attached infants, who cried little and seemed content to explore in the presence of their mothers; insecurely attached infants, who cried frequently, even when held by their mothers, and explored little; and not-yet-attached infants who expressed no special behavior with their mothers. She also observed that attachment quality was significantly correlated with maternal responsiveness and that babies of attuned mothers tended to be securely attached, whereas babies of less responsive mothers were more likely to be insecure.

Ainsworth hypothesized that attachment consists of a five-phase developmental sequence. The first, the undiscriminating phase, when the baby has few social responses, is followed by a phase of differential responsiveness, when the baby first shows signs of knowing and preferring the mother; in the third phase the baby is able to respond differentially from a distance, crying when the mother leaves the room and smiling when he sees her return. During this third phase, the onset of separation anxiety signals the beginning of attachment bonds. In the fourth phase the baby shows more initiative, demonstrated by approaching and scrambling over the mother, crawling after her, and beginning to leave her to explore. At around six to eight months, uneasiness with strangers becomes more apparent, heralding the beginning of the fifth and final phase, stranger anxiety. At this phase babies who initially had seemed friendly to Ainsworth and her interpreter would try to avoid them or become tense when the researchers came over to them. These phases appeared to coincide in certain respects with Mahler's separation-individuation paradigm. But whereas for Mahler the critical developmental process was physical separation and increasing psychological individuation from the mother, for Ainsworth it was a more mature stage of attachment.

In her observations, Ainsworth noted that the mother's material care for the infant was not in itself sufficient to help the child develop a secure attachment. It was the relational quality of the care and the mother's behavior and emotional well-being that made the difference. One baby's mother, for example, seemed to meet all his feeding needs and held him in proximity to her body almost all day long. However, Ainsworth noted that the baby displayed insecure and clingy behavior and eventually lapsed in his physical and cognitive development. Further observation revealed that the baby's mother was highly anxious and depressed and seemed overwhelmed with all her responsibilities.

Ainsworth moved to Baltimore in 1956, again following her husband's career. She obtained work as a part-time clinician at Sheppard Pratt Hospital and taught courses at Johns Hopkins University. She started a second observational project, in which she enrolled twenty-six Baltimore families who were recruited before the birth of their babies. Each family received a total of eighteen home visits, beginning within the baby's first month and ending at fifty-four weeks. Each visit lasted four hours to ensure the mothers' comfort level with the researcher, resulting in approximately seventy-two hours of data collection per family (Ainsworth et al., 1978). Ainsworth and observers who worked with her identified significant individual differences in how well attuned mothers were to their infants' signals. Some mothers had difficulty in adjusting their behavior and pace to the baby's cues. Ainsworth and her team observed that these mothers' babies tended, in response, to struggle, choke, and spit up. For other mother/baby dyads, the feeding experience seemed to be more pleasurable and harmonious. The mother's expressions, whether smiling or unsmiling, seemed to have a powerful impact on the nature and length of interactions with their babies, pointing toward results in later experiments on the reciprocal interactions of infants and caregivers (Beebe & Stern, 1977; Stern, 1985).

Some minor cultural differences in the mothers' and babies' responses to each other were apparent; for example, the Baltimore babies hugged and kissed their mothers, whereas the Ugandan babies clapped when greeting their mothers. In addition, the Baltimore babies became less upset than the Ugandan babies did when their mothers left the room, and they showed less stranger anxiety, which Ainsworth attributed to the fact that they were more accustomed to seeing their mothers depart and return and also to their mothers' spending less time with them. In other respects, regardless of culture, the Baltimore experiment essentially replicated the results of the Ugandan study. Ainsworth found that the mother's responsiveness predicted the infant's later behavior. Infants whose mothers provided attuned responsiveness during the first three months cried less later on and sought less contact at ten to twelve months; however, when contact did occur, it was more satisfying and affectionate (Bell & Ainsworth, 1972).

In order to measure more accurately whether attachment behaviors had a universal basis, Ainsworth decided to develop a controlled laboratory experiment in which the environmental conditions were equal for all the babies. The experiment, set up at Johns Hopkins University in Baltimore, served as a prototype for many later developmental studies. At the time, however, very few researchers were interested in investigating children's early development, and Ainsworth's studies represented a milestone in child development research.

The Strange Situation

While Bowlby developed the initial hypotheses on attachment behaviors, based on his own and others' observations of children in hospitals and homes, Ainsworth was the first to design a systematic experiment to identify specific differences in children's attachment behaviors. She called her experiment "the Strange Situation." This research study took place during the sixties and seventies, when behaviorism and learning theory were the prevalent paradigms in the United States, drawing from the work of Edward Thorndike, Ivan Pavlov, and B. F. Skinner. Attachment theory, with its emphasis on emotional ties and internal life, did not lend itself to direct observation or quantification, and therefore it was not taken seriously among psychologists and researchers (Karen, 1998). This controversy between behaviorists and attachment theorists was most clearly demonstrated in differing beliefs about the upbringing of children. Early behaviorists believed that children should not be picked up when they cried unless they needed to be fed or changed, since that behavior on the part of a caregiver would reinforce their crying. Attachment theorists, on the other hand, believed that it was important to respond to children's signals of distress in order to provide for their emotional needs. While Ainsworth as well as Bowlby agreed that behavioral theories might offer explanations for certain aspects of human development, they believed that attachment existed and developed because of innate instinctual needs and that it had nothing to do with learned behavior influenced by rewards or punishments (Karen, 1998). For Skinner, children's "dependent" behavior came about because mothers responded to their crying and therefore conditioned them in a negative way. In behavioral theory, more generally, the mother's caretaking role was equated with other bodily needs, such as eating and sleeping. The child's emotional needs were not mentioned.

During Ainsworth's Strange Situation experiment, mother and infant were brought into an unfamiliar room filled with toys, a stranger entered, and the mother soon left the room, leaving the infant alone with the stranger. The mother subsequently returned, pausing to allow the infant a chance to respond to her return. After a time, the stranger departed, and shortly thereafter the mother again left the infant; this time the infant was left alone in the room. The mother then returned a second time and picked the infant up. During the session, then, the infant was exposed to four different situations involving separation and reunion: with the mother, with the mother and the stranger, with the stranger, and alone in the room. The Strange Situation therefore allowed Ainsworth and her collaborators to observe the infant's behavior during a variety of experiences (Ainsworth et al., 1978). Ainsworth spent much of the remainder of her career analyzing this enormous body of data and publishing her findings, as well as training and supervising others who have continued her work.

On the basis of Strange Situation data, researchers initially identified three patterns of attachment style: secure, insecure-avoidant, and insecure-resistant (or ambivalent). A fourth pattern, the disorganized attachment style, was subsequently discovered by Mary Main and will be discussed in chapter 4.

Secure attachment

The majority of infants in the experiment exhibited a secure attachment pattern. Initially, the infant was distressed when left alone with a stranger, but when the mother returned, the baby made eye contact with her and came up to her to greet her. The baby was quickly reassured and returned to his or her exploratory play. These infants seemed to use their mothers as a "secure base," from whom they derived a sense of safety and autonomy, thus fostering both curiosity and the physical exploration of their environment. Ainsworth noted that the mothers of these infants consistently exhibited an attitude of attuned responsiveness and that there was a sense of harmony and cooperative behavior between the mother-infant pairs.

Insecure-avoidant attachment

During the Strange Situation the avoidant infant appeared uninterested in the mother or her whereabouts. The infant did not seem distressed by her leaving and was indifferent to her return. Instead, the baby tended to focus on the toys and play with the stranger in the room. Ainsworth and her collaborators concluded that this behavior was associated with the mother's rejecting behavior, her anger at the baby's demands, and her lack of cuddling or soothing of her baby. These mothers also exhibited controlling and intrusive behaviors, such as trying to supervise the infant's play. These infants' avoidant behaviors seemed to be designed to minimize their attachment needs and behavior, and consequently to avoid the pain of rejection and/or the frustration of intrusion.

Insecure-resistant (ambivalent) attachment

Ainsworth and her colleagues observed that the resistant infant, unlike the avoidant one, seemed to be intensely preoccupied with the mother. This baby became highly distressed when the mother left and was not comforted on her return. The infant's behavior seemed angry and resistant, as well as clingy. The baby protested if the mother did not pick him up, and then when she did pick him up, he resisted and pushed her away. Ainsworth thought that this pattern was associated with a maternal lack of responsiveness or inconsistent attunement, including the mother's being withdrawn, depressed, or insensitive to her infant's needs. The resistant infant's behavior seemed to be a way of trying to obtain the mother's attention and proximity, whereas the avoidant infant's behavior seemed designed to minimize contact with the mother (Allen, 2001).

These distinct patterns of attachment behavior paralleled Bowlby's conception of internal working models. The infants had internalized their experiences with their mothers, and these internalized models in turn dictated their expectations and responses to the mothers' future behavior, as well as to the behavior of others. Ainsworth's findings were crucially important to the understanding of child maltreatment, infant mental health, and the impact of early interactions on later personality development and patterns of interpersonal behavior.

Applications of Attachment Theory to Social Work Practice

Bowlby was interested in creating a scientifically based theory that would contribute to general developmental psychology and research. Beyond this initial objective, however, his observations and Ainsworth's later experiments contributed to a greater understanding of the impact of early interactions between infants and caregivers and led to further developments in clinical practice with children, adolescents, and adults. Bowlby's and Ainsworth's work reinforced Sullivan's interpersonal theory, which subsequently influenced current relational thinking (Mitchell & Aron, 1999). We have already described how their work gave greater credence to Winnicott's constructs of the true and false self (Winnicott, 1960a, 1965), as well as to Fairbairn's object relations theory (Fairbairn, 1952), which had been used to examine the traumatic impact of childhood abuse on the bonds between parents and children.

In relation to social work practice, attachment theory contributed greatly to the field of child welfare, to clinical practice with adult survivors of childhood abuse, and to a greater understanding of the dynamics of domestic violence. With its emphasis on the importance of the environment in human development, Bowlby's attachment theory also conforms well to social work's person-in-environment perspective. Since the early 1990s, efforts have been made to integrate attachment theory with psychodynamic practice paradigms, as feminist, relational, and intersubjective theorists have gained influence. These theorists used the sound empirical basis of attachment research as the scientific foundation for their dynamic concepts, demonstrated through quantitative research methods. One example of this application is the development of several attachment instruments for children and adults, including Main's Adult Attachment Interview, which will be discussed in chapter 4. Bowlby's and Ainsworth's work made a significant contribution to the understanding of the behavior of those children whose attachment bonds had been disrupted because of parental death or as a result of childhood abuse or neglect. These pioneering studies formed the basis for further investigations into the implications of insecure early attachments for child development, adult behavior, and the capacity to create and maintain relational bonds with others. Bowlby's and Ainsworth's research also helped to clarify the notion of intergenerational transmission of trauma and the development of mental disorders, including personality disorders (Blatt & Levy, 2003). More recently, an even stronger link has been forged between attachment research and clinical practice, with the development of clinical methods emphasizing both treatment and prevention, applied to such domains as child welfare, trauma and eating disorders, and personality disorders (Farber, 2000).

Attachment theory is a natural fit with social work theory and practice. It directly concerns areas that are traditionally served by the profession and provides the empirical groundwork for extant models of social work practice. Finally, attachment evaluation instruments are of great value in the study and measurement of early development, relationships between children and caregivers, and treatment outcomes.

Contemporary Psychoanalytic Perspectives on Attachment | **THREE**

Bowlby's theoretical conception of attachment represented a highly original and substantively unique paradigm for understanding the psychological and social development of human infants, as well as the short- and longer-term sequelae of failures in attachment. His ideas have also been highly generative, leading to a vast scientific literature that now encompasses several different disciplinary domains. Moreover, unlike many psychoanalytic developmental concepts, Bowlby's attachment theory is regarded by many social scientists as eminently researchable. His ideas also reflect the influence of his psychoanalytic predecessors and the British object relations tradition with which he identified. Bowlby's unique contribution appears to have resulted from the combined effect of several factors, foremost among them his systematic and empirical approach to the study of attachment, his willingness to challenge existing psychoanalytic ideas, and his ability to synthesize and integrate research and theoretical models from fields outside of psychoanalysis (most notably ethology). Nevertheless, despite increasing popularity, Bowlby's ideas about human development are not universally embraced by dynamically oriented clinicians, who may favor other theoretical frameworks to explain developmental phenomena or psychopathology, or perhaps both. How are we to understand Bowlby's ideas about attachment, separation, and loss in light of other psychoanalytic developmental theories?

To address this issue we will explore the "goodness of fit" between attachment theory and four important contemporary psychoanalytic frameworks for understanding human development. Selected because each offers a unique vision of development, the four are Harry Stack Sullivan's *interpersonal model*, Margaret Mahler's *separation-individuation theory*, Erik Erikson's *epigenetic model*, and Heinz Kohut's *psychology of the self*. Each will be examined in detail, with particular attention to controversies and points of convergence.

Sullivan and the Interpersonal Model

Harry Stack Sullivan (1892–1949), an American physician best known for his pioneering work in the psychiatric treatment of schizophrenic and other highly disturbed individuals, is generally credited with having founded the school of interpersonal psychoanalysis as well as having formulated its most important developmental and clinical ideas. While a medical student at the University of Chicago, Sullivan was greatly impressed by such important social scientists as sociologists George Herbert Mead and Robert Park and cultural anthropologist Edward Sapir; he was also influenced, though less directly, by John Dewey, and more arguably, by the social work pioneer and Hull House founder Jane Addams (Perry, 1964). Sullivan has been linked, more generally, with the American pragmatist school of philosophy; indeed, Sullivan's biographers have argued that his unique approach to clinical work reflected an enduring commitment to this intellectual tradition (Brandell & Perlman, 1997; Chapman, 1976; Mullahy, 1970; Perry, 1964, 1982).

Sullivan's influence during the 1940s and 1950s was considerable. Such important theorists as Frieda Fromm-Reichmann, Erich Fromm, and Clara Thompson, who, with Sullivan, are now considered architects of the *interpersonal-relational* tradition in psychoanalysis, were among those in his intellectual debt. However, Sullivan had never trained as a psychoanalyst, and despite the originality of his views regarding development and psychopathology, as well as a distinctive approach to psychotherapeutic treatment resulting from these ideas, his work remained somewhat outside the mainstream of American psychoanalytic thought and was virtually unknown elsewhere—that is, until the publication of Greenberg and Mitchell's epic volume on object relations theory in the early 1980s (Fonagy & Target, 2003; Greenberg & Mitchell, 1983). Since that time, Sullivan's ideas have achieved greater acceptance among psychoanalysts, though perhaps in part because some proponents of Sullivanian theory "have increasingly moved toward integrating Sullivan's thinking with contemporary systems of psychoanalytic thought rather than attempting to maintain his ideas in pure form" (Fonagy & Target, 2003, p. 205).

Sullivan's adherence to two theoretical positions, pragmatism and operationalism, as well as his early experience in treating schizophrenics, seem to have combined to create within him a profound dissatisfaction with traditional psychoanalytic developmental and clinical theories. Despite his great respect for Freud's creative genius, Sullivan expressed dismay over the failure of classical psychoanalysis to operationalize its theoretical precepts. Even such a fundamental psychoanalytic concept as the unconscious was, in Sullivan's view, problematic inasmuch as it could be neither observed nor measured and was therefore destined to remain wholly hypothetical. Sullivan also objected to Freudian theory on clinical grounds, believing that traditional psychoanalytic thinking had failed to adequately explain psychosis and other forms of severe psychopathology and, furthermore, that it did not offer a particularly useful approach to working clinically with such patients. At the very heart of Sullivan's critique of Freud was an elusively simple belief, one cited by psychoanalytic historians as the basis for designating Sullivan as a pioneering exponent of the "relational/structure" model: "The field of Psychiatry is the field of interpersonal relations—a personality can never be isolated from the complex of interpersonal relations in which the person lives and has his being" (Sullivan, 1940, p. 10).

Sullivan also endeavored to create an entirely new interpersonal "vocabulary," intended to supplant the more abstract and less empirically anchored conceptual language of classical theory. Critics, however, have noted that the formulations of Sullivan's interpersonal theory "are not significantly different epistemologically from those of other psychoanalytic schools" (Singer, 1998); that the language of interpersonal theory was highly idiosyncratic and confusing, composed of terms that Sullivan himself had invented to describe various mental phenomena; that interpersonal psychoanalysis lacked a unified, integral theory; and even that interpersonal psychoanalysis was not especially original, merely representing "an attempt by Sullivan to recast the intrapsychic language of Freud into interpersonal terms" (Joseph Kepecs, M.D., personal communication).

It is beyond the scope of this chapter to fully address such criticisms. Nor can we undertake a thorough discussion of Sullivan's clinical formulations. Rather, we shift our focus to Sullivan's model of human development, the most detailed exposition of which probably appears in *The Interpersonal Theory of Psychiatry*, a posthumously published edited collection of lectures given by Sullivan in the mid-1940s (Sullivan, 1953). As noted above, an overarching theme in Sullivan's work is that human infants are born into a relational milieu and that relational configurations evolve out of actual experience with others. Sullivan repeatedly stressed the assertion that human beings can be understood only within the "organism-environment complex"[1] and are thus incapable of "definitive description in isolation" (Sullivan, 1930, p. 258). Accordingly, Sullivan's developmental model places supreme importance on the interpersonal field in tandem with the efforts that children—and later, adults—devise to maintain relatedness with significant others in their environments. Sullivan's developmental schema, formulated as a series of "heuristic stages," consisted of infancy, childhood, the juvenile era, preadolescence, early adolescence, late adolescence, and adulthood or maturity; our focus will of necessity be limited to the earlier stages of development.

In infancy, Sullivan wrote, human beings possess innate physiological and emotional needs that require satisfaction, but their gratification depends upon the capacity of another individual, the mother, to experience the infant's tensions as her own and to act upon this experience (Fonagy & Target, 2003). Such complementary interactions are experienced as "tenderness" by the infant and establish a sort of interactional or interpersonal template for all subsequent experiences; ultimately, these serve to generate a *need for tenderness* in the infant. Sullivan believed that the infant's need for tenderness actually consists of a group of tensions for the most part derived from disequilibria involving the "physicochemical universe" existing both within and outside of the infant, and requiring interpersonal involvement. He also included one need that was not physicochemically induced, the *need for contact*, which reflected just what the term implies, a basic human need for "manipulations by and peripheral contact with" caregivers that is independent of the infant's other tensions (Sullivan, 1953, p. 40).[2]

Sullivan theorized that infants begin to develop what he termed *personifications* early in their development. In the Sullivanian universe, a personification is defined as the representation of an infant's experience of others in the caretaking environment. Personifications often do not correspond closely to objective reality; they are most usefully thought of as "personal, idiosyncratic phenomenological representations" of self and others (Singer, 1998, p. 77). Thus, personifications are of two basic types—*self* and *other*—and acquire a predominantly positive ("good") or negative ("bad") valence depending on experiences of relative satisfaction or dissatisfaction. For example, the experience of nursing (at either bottle or breast), arguably a prototype for all subsequent interpersonal encounters in early development, initially results in the infant's personification of the nipple as either good (satisfying) or bad (frustrating). Gradually, via the repetition of many such experiences, and in consequence of the developing infant's capacity for perception and prehension, the nipple is integrated into a more expansive and multifaceted experience of the organism that *provides* the nipple—the infant's mother. When these experiences are gratifying, they lead to a personification of mother that is predominantly positive, and that may also include others (father, older siblings, and so forth) who, in addition to the mother, later become associated with the good feeding experience. Inversely, feeding experiences that evoke the infant's frustration and the human figures associated with such experiences are elaborated into a personification of the "bad" nipple/mother.

In this same example, the infant's personifications of the *self* are also closely connected to experiences with the "good" or "bad" nipple/mother. Sullivan assumed that infants are both highly egocentric and incapable of making discriminations between self and others in early development.[3] Consequently, the infant makes an assumption that she or he has performed some action or otherwise brought about the *good mother* personification; in effect, it is on account of something the infant "believes" she or he has done that evokes the good, satisfying nipple—an inner experience that Sullivan termed the *good me*. The same sort of association obtains when the nipple is nongratifying or otherwise anxiety-generating—once again, it is something in the nature of the infant's behavior, a *bad me*, that has brought about this negative experience of the mother-infant dyad rather than independent actions taken by the mother herself (Singer, 1998).

Such primitive mental operations are further described by Sullivan as examples of *parataxic thought*, a primitive mode of cognition (much like the Freudian primary process) in which logical processes are largely absent and (oftentimes) erroneous connections are made on the basis of temporal contiguity or spatial sequencing rather than more formal reasoning using deductive or inductive processes. Frustrating or negative experiences with one caregiver resulting from that particular individual's limitations or unempathic responses to the infant not only may be incorrectly experienced as a shortcoming of the infant's but may in the future become generalized to other caregivers. Within a clinical context, it then becomes possible to understand the templates forged from early parataxic distortions as forming a basis for transference phenomena, though in a later, somewhat more evolved form (Singer, 1998).

In addition to "good" and "bad" self/other personifications, Sullivan also proposed a third variety, one associated with profoundly painful or terrifying interpersonal encounters. Such experiences, in Sullivan's view, might evoke qualitatively different representations of self and other, personifications that he called the "not me" and the "evil mother." Although Sullivan believed "not me" and "evil mother" personifications to be universal, these representations are much less important or influential in normal or neurotic individuals than in those who suffer from schizophrenia or other severe psychopathology.

Interpersonal theory posits two kinds of motivation. The first, as intimated above, involves the gratification of bodily and emotional needs, including sexuality and intimacy. A second kind of motivation is associated with the experience of anxiety, as well as with those defensive maneuvers—which Sullivan called "security operations"—intended to alleviate such anxiety. Sullivan's premise is that both kinds of motivation need satisfaction and that the subject's strivings for security are comprehensible only within an interpersonal context. Indeed, in Sullivan's formulations, the intrapsychic emphasis of classical psychoanalytic theory, as well as Freud's later (1926) model of anxiety, have little utility or explanatory power. Whereas Freud understood anxiety relative to a hierarchy of danger situations (loss of the mother, loss of the mother's love, castration, and guilt), situations that may or may not be closely connected with interpersonal interactions, Sullivan emphasized mental distress, psychic pain, or upset activated in an interpersonal milieu. Furthermore, in Freud's final theoretical model, the function of anxiety as a *signal* of internally arising danger as well as the inextricable link between the drives and reality in the production of anxiety is underscored (Holzman, 1998). In Sullivan's theory, however, it is the caregiver's failure to manage or contain her or his anxiety or other distressing affects that *educes* anxiety in the infant. Perhaps foreshadowing ideas popularized by Heinz Kohut, Sullivan located the earliest experience of what might be called "empathy" in such experiences of "emotional contagion or communion" that "subtend the relationship of the infant with other significant" individuals (Sullivan, 1940, p. 17).

Sullivan's ideas are not truly compatible with those of Bowlby, although certain similarities are unmistakable. True, Sullivan's emphasis on the interpersonal matrix and his focus on the primacy of the infant's physiological needs seem more or less consonant with Bowlby's emphasis on attachment. Both theorists believed it impossible to understand human development on the basis of the libidinal-stage model; neither accepted the relatively scant role accorded to the environment and to the influence of caregivers on the infant's psychosocial development by traditional psychoanalysis; and neither accepted the rather limited role that classical formulations attributed to factors outside the infant in the production and/or management of anxiety. On closer examination, however, several significant differences emerge.

For example, Bowlby and Sullivan are not in agreement as to the importance of *actual physical separation* in the production of anxiety in the infant. Sullivan tended to locate anxiety, per his concept of *empathic linkage*, in the caregiver; in his view, it was ultimately a failure on the part of the care provider that led to the experience of anxiety in the infant. Although Sullivan believed that loneliness could be a devastating experience for adolescents and adults, he asserted that it was not an experience phenomenologically available to infants and young children (Sullivan, 1953). Indeed, in his critique of Sullivan, Bowlby suggests that Sullivan may never have fully grasped the importance of separation anxiety (Bowlby, 1973, p. 396). Bowlby was also critical of Sullivan's claim that "no action of the infant is consistently and frequently associated with the relief of anxiety" (Sullivan, 1953, p. 42), believing that Sullivan had overlooked the most obvious challenge to his assertion—the infant's relief when she or he is able to clutch the mother. Finally, Sullivan had maintained that self-appraisal in children is originally modeled after the way in which they are viewed by the significant adults in their lives, an idea that is firmly anchored in the Sullivanian theory of self/other personifications and that presupposes a more or less passive acceptance of such appraisals by the child. Bowlby's concept of internal working models, however, holds that children "not only passively accept" the views of others but also *actively* arrive at sometimes radically different appraisals of themselves or of others (Bowlby, 1980, pp. 234–235 n).

More-recent distillations of the Sullivanian theory, which has become rather intimately associated with the emerging relationalist perspective in contemporary psychoanalysis, highlight yet another, even more fundamental, difference between these two traditions. As Fonagy has observed,

> relational theories, in part as a consequence of their historic origins, *tend to repudiate the biological* [emphasis added] in thinking about motivation and

human nature. The adult human organism is not thought to be understandable in terms of other sorts of organisms, bestial or infantile, but has its own distinctive nature. It is not "driven" by "special" drives, but is the agent of many kinds of activities, all of which are devoted to the general project of creating, recreating, and expressing itself within its relational context.

(2001, p. 131)

Attachment theory, of course, is either confirmed or refuted on the basis of both its biological foundations and its integration within a natural sciences context (Bowlby, 1981; Fonagy, 2001). Sullivanian interpersonal theory and its contemporary relationalist counterpart, however, are "more at home with postmodern deconstructive ideas" than they are with Bowlby's efforts to link brain and behavior and what Fonagy has referred to as the "reductionism of the biological context of attachment" (Fonagy, 2001, p. 32).

Mahler's Theory of Separation-Individuation

Margaret Mahler (1897–1985), who, like D. W. Winnicott and Melanie Klein, made a mid-career transition from pediatrics to psychoanalysis, was originally less focused on normal development than on arriving at a more satisfactory explanation for the development of psychotic disorders in children. Her early work with autistic and schizophrenic youngsters throughout the 1940s and 1950s, however, gradually led her to consider the importance of the role played by the human infant's "mediating partner," the mother, not only within the matrix of psychopathology but also in the course of normal development. Mahler's theory is not without its critics, but her ideas regarding separation-individuation have been indisputably influential and are judged to occupy a crucial position in the history of psychoanalytic thought (Greenberg & Mitchell, 1983).

Although Mahler's theory of separation-individuation underwent numerous changes and revisions dating to its earliest distillations in the 1950s (e.g., Mahler, 1954; Mahler & Gosliner, 1955),[4] this discussion is, for the sake of clarity, concerned with the more fully evolved version that appeared in the mid-1970s (Mahler, Pine, & Bergman, 1975). By that time, Mahler had shifted her attention almost completely away from severe childhood psychopathology and was engaged in a project that sought to redefine the essential features of the normal infant's emergence from "formlessness to form"—emphasizing the relationship of child to mother rather than the classical focus on development of the libido.

This final version of Mahler's separation-individuation theory grew from a longitudinal research project involving mother-infant pairs conducted in a nursery setting (the Masters Children's Center in Manhattan). Characterizing infants as essentially nonrelated or objectless at birth (the *normal autistic phase*), Mahler and her colleagues described their gradual emergence via a period of maternal-infant *symbiosis* into four relatively discrete stages of separation and individuation: *differentiation, practicing, rapprochement,* and *development of object constancy.* Throughout this later work, Mahler characterized separation and individuation as complementary though nevertheless phenomenologically distinct processes. *Separation* was defined as the infant's gradual extrication from her or his symbiotic fusion with the mother, while *individuation* consisted of "those achievements marking the child's assumption of his own individual characteristics" (Greenberg & Mitchell, 1983; Mahler, Pine, & Bergman, 1975, p. 4).

The Normal Autistic Phase (Birth to 1 Month)

Mahler believed that in the first several weeks following birth, infants are relatively unresponsive to external stimuli and are largely incapable of making distinctions between inner and outer reality or, for that matter, between the self and the inanimate world. At this early stage of development, Mahler asserted, infants' sleeplike states are disproportionately greater than their states of arousal, and their inner experience is a sort of primitive hallucinatory wish fulfillment in which the principal effort is directed toward the satisfaction of needs and, concomitantly, the achievement of physiological homeostasis (Mahler, 1979b, p. 77). The most essential feature of Mahler's conception of *normal autism* lies in her depiction of the infant at this time as a closed psychological system, metaphorically encapsulated in a "quasi-solid stimulus barrier" or "autistic shell" that prevents penetration by external stimuli (Mahler & Furer, 1968), an idea underscored by Mahler's reference to Freud's (1911) analogy of the bird's egg as a model for autistic satisfaction of nutritional needs. Admittedly, this conception follows a classical psychoanalytic view of neonatal life, as Mahler seemed to anchor her description of this stage firmly in the tension-reduction language of libido theory (Freud, 1911). Infantile experience at this early stage of development is, from an object relations perspective, considered "objectless" (Greenberg & Mitchell, 1983).

The Phase of Normal Symbiosis (1–5 Months)

Symbiosis is a concept derived from biology to describe a close and mutu-ally advantageous association between two organisms. Mindful of the fact that infantile dependence on caregivers is absolute, while that of mothers on infants is not, Mahler nevertheless chose to employ this term in a meta-phorical way. To her, *human* symbiosis refers to a state of fusion between infant and mother in which self and not-self are not yet differentiated and in which there is only the faintest awareness of the distinction between in-ner and outer experience. Perhaps the most essential feature of human sym-biosis, Mahler asserted, is the "hallucinatory or delusional, somatopsychic, omnipotent fusion with the representation of the mother and, in particu-lar, [the] delusion of [a] common boundary" of two individuals who are in reality physically separate organisms (Mahler, 1979b, p. 79). Infants during this developmental phase, however, are already capable of developmental achievements not possible just a few weeks before. There is a dim, though increasing, awareness of the mother as an object existing outside of the self, support for which is adduced in part by the social smile that infants first ex-hibit during this period of development. In addition, the infant now begins to invest libido toward the "periphery"—what Mahler referred to as the "dual unity" of mother and infant—rather than exclusively inward, as was the case during the first several weeks of life. Aided by the maturation of such au-tonomous ego functions as memory, infants begin to organize experience according to what is "good" (pleasurable) or "bad" (painful), and such ex-periences are subsequently stored as memory traces (Greenberg & Mitchell, 1983). It is during this phase, Mahler noted, that infants may be legitimately thought of in more psychological terms, although she nonetheless regarded them as "pre-objectal" during this phase (Mahler, 1979b, p. 79).

The Differentiation Subphase (5–9 Months)

Sometime around four or five months, the first phase of the formal separa-tion-individuation process is ushered in. Mahler used the term "hatching," again borrowing from Freud's bird egg analogy, to describe the momentous psychological growth that occurs at this time. Although keenly interested in examining the mother's face and hair (what Mahler has termed "customs inspection"), differentiating infants are no longer totally dependent on their mothers' bodies; they have begun to creep, crawl, and climb, and they also exhibit progress in the coordinated use of hands, mouth, and eyes (Mahler, 1979b). There is continued growth and maturation of various ego functions, gradually permitting infants to make more reliable distinctions between that which belongs to inner experience and that which is perceived with the sense organs to exist outside the self, a critical developmental benchmark that makes possible increasingly clearer sensory discriminations between self and object. Peekaboo games offer the infant an opportunity to master some of the anxiety associated with the mother's comings and goings. At the same time, there is interest in the visual field beyond the mother, though each new person or object encountered is carefully, even soberly, compared to the mother, a process that Mahler referred to as "comparative scanning." At six to eight months, these emerging skills and capabilities culminate in the infant's ability to clearly and consistently distinguish his or her mother from other figures in the environment, a developmental accomplishment signaled by the appearance of stranger anxiety.

The Practicing Subphase (9–15 Months)

This subphase, Mahler observed, is actually composed of two more or less distinct periods: *early practicing* and the *practicing subphase proper*. The early practicing period, at first coextensive with the latter part of the *differentiation subphase*, is defined by the infant's acquisition of the capacity for quadruped locomotion (crawling, climbing, paddling, and so forth). This important achievement makes possible more sustained forays into what Mahler termed "the extramural environment," the world that exists beyond the mother. It is at this time, she believed, that infants' belief in their own magical omnipotence reaches a peak and contributes to what Phyllis Greenacre called their "love affair with the world" (Greenberg & Mitchell, 1983). Now able to move independently, the infant finds a whole new universe to explore, one that is filled with novelty and excitement. At the same time, the infant periodically seeks the mother out as a "home base" for "emotional refueling," further cementing the unique affectional bond that exists between the two of them. Yet another developmental task of early practicing is the "dramatic growth of the autonomous functions of the ego, a growth which occurs optimally in close proximity to the mother" (Greenberg & Mitchell, 1983, p. 276).

Mahler believed that "psychological birth" is coextensive with a monumental achievement—that of the capacity for upright locomotion. Feeling

exhilaration both because of the seemingly limitless opportunities for exploration afforded by this new ability as well as by the avenue of "escape" it
furnishes from the earlier symbiosis with the mother (Greenberg & Mitchell, 1983), the infant enters the practicing subphase proper. The mother is
still not a fully separate person in the toddler's estimation, even now, and
she continues to be treated as a "home base" for replenishment of the child's
emotional needs. However, Mahler also noted that the mother must be willing to put aside her claims on her child's body at this juncture in the interest
of promoting developmental progress; furthermore, she "must be willing to
allow and even to enjoy [the child's] increasing capacity to operate at a distance from her" (Greenberg & Mitchell, 1983, p. 277).

The Rapprochement Subphase (15–24 Months)

The rapprochement subphase is initiated by the child's beginning awareness
that the mother is in fact a separate person, that she operates independently
of her toddler, and is therefore not always physically available to furnish assistance in the toddler's ongoing efforts to negotiate environmental challenges.
Indeed, one of the hallmarks of the rapprochement subphase is the toddler's
increasing—and at times painful—awareness that she or he is a rather small
person in a big world. During the practicing period, the toddler's burgeoning
sense of separateness was at first a cause for exhilaration, but now the earlier
sense of omnipotence and the ideal self of which it was a concomitant have
been replaced by renewed anxiety over separation. Furthermore, the toddler
is no longer able to pursue goals with the indefatigability and imperviousness
to setbacks that seemed almost to define the practicing period; instead, frustration and distress have taken their place. There is an inherently contradictory quality to the child's behavior during this period; on the one hand, the
toddler of the rapprochement subphase strives to become increasingly independent of the mother and yet "nevertheless insistently expects the mother to
share every aspect of his life" (Mahler, 1979b, p. 39). Spoken words gradually
replace the more developmentally primitive forms of communication, such
as vocalizations and preverbal gestural language, as the toddler strives to find
more efficient ways to convey his or her basic needs, affect states, and more
generally, her experience of the world. At some point midway in the rapprochement subphase, the toddler's loss of the ideal sense of self in tandem
with the shock of discovering that the world is not really his or her oyster
ushers in the *rapprochement crisis* (Mahler, 1979b, p. 39). As Mahler writes,

from around eighteen months on, we observed our toddlers were quite eager to exercise their growing autonomy. Increasingly, they chose not to be reminded of the times when they could not manage on their own. On the other hand, the desire to be separate, grand, and omnipotent often conflicted with the desire to have mother magically fulfill all one's desires—without the need to recognize that help was *actually coming from the outside* [emphasis in the original]. Thus, in a majority of cases, the prevalent mood swung to that of general dissatisfaction and insatiability, and there developed a proneness to rapid swings of mood and to temper tantrums. The period of rapprochement was thus characterized by a sometimes rapid alternation of the desire to reject mother, on the one hand, and to cling to her with coercive, determined tenacity on the other, a behavioral sequence that the word *ambitendency* describes most accurately... a *simultaneous* desire in both directions.

(Mahler, 1979b, p. 161)

Mahler and other adherents of separation-individuation theory believed that successful resolution of the rapprochement crisis was a critical prerequisite for the development of healthy object relations and, moreover, that developmental derailments occurring during separation-individuation could lead to severe psychopathology later in life.[5] Although separation-individuation theory assigns a special role to the mother in promoting healthy individuation in toddlers, the influence of the father is not considered inconsequential. The father is more often on the periphery of Mahler's framework, but he is nevertheless charged with the responsibility of helping to extricate toddlers from their symbiosis with the mother. This is a task that assumes different meanings at various stages of separation-individuation, but it is probably at no time more important than during rapprochement. In James Herzog's estimation, the father not only pulls the toddler out of the maternal symbiosis but also *actively intrudes* on it, breaking up the "intimate, homeostatically-attuned, resonating empathy" (Herzog, 2001). During rapprochement, children develop a beginning capacity for reality testing and become more aware of gender differences, and the father's role as a "member of the family who is not mother but stands in a special relationship to the child" takes on additional meaning (Greenberg & Mitchell, 1983, p. 278).

The Subphase of Object Constancy (24–36 Months and Beyond)

Although Mahler includes this as the fourth and final subphase of her separation-individuation process, this assignation is probably somewhat misleading. In point of fact, object constancy in the course of the normal separation-individuation is first established during the third year of life, although it is most usefully thought of as an open-ended process that continually evolves throughout an individual's lifetime.[6] Nevertheless, it is during this early period that consolidation of object constancy occurs. Mahler thought of object constancy as consisting of two vital and interrelated tasks: the formation of stable images or mental representations of the self and of the other. In effect, she gauged the achievement of true intrapsychic separateness through the child's attainment of a more or less enduring sense of her or his own unique self, in tandem with the capacity to preserve an essentially positive, internally available image of the mother *in her absence* or during other times of distress (e.g., when the child experiences frustration and anger toward her). Such an achievement, in turn, required that *good* and *bad* images of both self and other become unified into self and other representations that possess *both* good and bad qualities.

As mentioned previously, Mahler's separation-individuation theory has been criticized on several grounds. Serious questions have been raised, for example, about the empirical soundness of her designation of the neonatal experience as "autistic," inasmuch as newborns are responsive to bright colors, movement, and, even more significantly, to the human facial gestalt and the human voice. Furthermore, evidence has been presented in support of the existence of capacities for both short-term and long-term memory during the infant's first five months (Meltzoff & Moore, 1989; Rovee-Collier, 1987), as well as for the efforts babies undertake to establish relations between their own actions and events occurring in their physical environments (Bahrick & Watson, 1985). Collectively, such data cast serious doubt on the validity of Mahler's ideas regarding both "normal autism" and "normal symbiosis" (Fonagy & Target, 2003; Lichtenberg, 1987), assumptions that are fundamental to her view of the infant's psychological birth. Nevertheless, Mahler's ideas about separation and individuation have endured, perhaps in part because of their comparatively greater explanatory power—when compared with other psychoanalytic developmental models—in establishing a developmental basis for severe character pathology.

We are far more concerned, however, with the relationship between Mahler's ideas and those of Bowlby and with whether and in what ways they are compatible or incompatible with each other. Interestingly, Mahler's conception of rapprochement and of the rapprochement crisis, with its emphasis on the toddler's simultaneous need for maternal involvement and fear of regressive symbiotic merger, seems to parallel attachment researcher Alan Sroufe's research findings culled from his studies of "the Strange Situation" (Karen, 1998). Sroufe found that the mothers of securely attached children demonstrated the same sort of sensitivity to their toddlers as they had earlier in their children's development, adapting to the requirements of this new developmental epoch by remaining minimally though consistently engaged with the toddlers and offering just enough assistance and information without interfering with the toddlers' quest for autonomous activity. Mahler, of course, had strongly intimated that successful passage through separation and individuation and the attainment of object constancy depended a good deal on the ability of mothers to titrate their involvement, neither withdrawing from the toddlers' growing and at times wholly unreasonable demands nor, on the other hand, infantilizing them in response to their autonomous actions.

Bowlby, however, expressed significant reservations about a basic assumption of Mahler's, which he elaborated at some length in volume 3 of *Attachment and Loss.* At issue was the relationship of the child's mental representations to her or his capacity to sustain separations with emotional equanimity. In Mahler's view, libidinal object constancy was more or less coextensive with the child's capacity to endure brief separations from the mother without experiencing undue distress. In other words, the child's success in tolerating brief separations signaled the attainment of a capacity for internally accessing a positively valenced image of the mother. Bowlby, however, took exception to Mahler's position on two grounds. First, he maintained that the capacity for evocative memory typically antedates the child's ability to sustain brief separations by a year or two, sometimes longer. Furthermore, he emphasized that the representational model that a child develops of the mother is "dependent not only on the maturation of certain cognitive skills but also on the form the child's model of his mother takes, *which is in turn dependent in high degree on how she treats him* [emphasis added]." Such observations suggest that Bowlby was far more explicit than Mahler in acknowledging the role of the environment and of ongoing environmental transactional processes in *shaping* such internal mental representations.[7]

In other, more general respects, however, Bowlby's and Mahler's views might almost be superimposed on one another. For example, Bowlby believed that there was a fundamentally complementary relationship between the infant's attachment behaviors and exploratory activity; that is, once a child had achieved attachment, attachment-seeking behaviors were extinguished and the child could then engage in exploration of the environment. Mahler commented on the very same phenomenon, although using different language, when she observed that an infant in the practicing subphase tended to seek "emotional refueling" from the mother to allay separation fears, after which exploration of the extramural landscape could begin anew (Karen, 1998). Indeed, both theorists stressed the developmental importance of parental encouragement, interest, and support at such times. Bowlby also acknowledged that although for the purposes of theory building, the differences between his formulations and those of Mahler were "of considerable consequence," the therapeutic principles derived from Mahler's developmental scheme were "extremely close" to those Bowlby himself had derived from his theory of attachment (Bowlby, 1980, p. 433).

Erikson's Epigenetic Model

A member of the small inner circle of adherents that formed around Sigmund Freud and his daughter, Anna, in the late 1920s, Erik Erikson (1902–1994) was perhaps most unlike his psychoanalytic peers. He was a talented artist who possessed an equally deep commitment to intellectual pursuits, and early on he developed a keen interest in the study of culture and its influence on the formation of personality, an interest that was further shaped through his exposure to the work of American cultural anthropologists Ruth Benedict, Margaret Mead, and Gregory Bateson. Erikson had also trained as a Montessori teacher, and he was passionate in his love of children, whether he assumed the role of educator, researcher, or psychoanalyst.[8]

Although his contributions to psychoanalysis as a post-Freudian author are both numerous and influential, Erikson was perhaps best known for his developmental theory of *psychosocial and psychosexual epigenesis. Epigenesis* is a term that Erikson expropriated from the field of embryology, where it is defined as "the predetermined sequential development of the parts of an organism" (Holzman, 1998, p. 160). In fetal development, the successive emergence and predominance of each part or organ system culminates in the complex final integration of the infant's physical processes (Mitchell & Black, 1995). Erikson theorized that the ego develops in a homologous fashion, with various capacities and attributes emerging according to a sort of internal organismic timetable, and their subsequent integration into the functioning whole dependent upon the successful completion of the stage of development that has immediately preceded it. Erikson also believed that in such a developmental schema, earlier stages of growth are inherently more vulnerable to environmental disruption than are later ones; furthermore, more profound developmental sequelae would be likely to follow such early disruptions, affecting all subsequent later developmental stages.

Erikson's psychosocial/psychosexual epigenetic theory charted ego development across the entire life span and highlighted social-environmental factors to a greater degree than had any previous psychoanalytic developmental model. His most enduring work, *Childhood and Society*, is perhaps the best illustration of his profound interest in the way individual development is shaped by the influences of culture, or the "interpenetrability of individual and culture" (Mitchell & Black, 1995, p. 143). In this work, the final shape of the individual personality is deemed to be subject to a variety of influences aside from the purely libidinal interests that Freud had identified; such influences were culture-specific and could also involve complex geographical, economic, and social forces only hinted at by earlier psychoanalytic authors.[9]

In Erikson's view, healthy ego development depends upon the mastery of specific developmental tasks and normative crises associated with each of the eight life cycle stages that he identified (see box). Citing the tendency to misinterpret and oversimplify Erikson's complex developmental timetable, some have characterized the "crisis" of each successive developmental epoch as more accurately representing a sort of *dialectical tension*—reinforcing the notion that trust and mistrust, autonomy and shame and doubt, industry and inferiority, and so forth are always in a complementary relation to each other.

> Even though one or another crisis is in the forefront at any particular time, all these issues and tensions are active throughout the life cycle. Each stage is reworked anew by the struggle with subsequent ego qualities, and Erikson envisioned ego development across life cycle stages less in terms of a stepladder and more in terms of a complex set of tensions, progressively unfolding and in constant resonance with each other.
>
> (Mitchell & Black, 1995, p. 148)

Although many writers have emphasized Erikson's unique contributions to our understanding of adolescence and to the stages of adult development—largely uncharted terrain when the first edition of *Childhood*

ERIKSON'S EIGHT-STAGE EPIGENETIC MODEL

1. *Basic trust versus basic mistrust.* Coterminous with the oral phase of Freud's libidinal stage model. The main experiential mode in this stage is oral-receptive. In optimal circumstances, a preponderance of positively valenced experiences with one's mother culminates in basic trust.

2. *Autonomy versus shame and doubt.* Coincides with the anal stage in the Freudian model. The emphasis here is on the child's newly emerging autonomy, which is in turn linked to the increased radius of locomotor activity and maturation of the muscle systems. Success in this phase results in the child's pleasure in independent actions and self-expression; failure leads to shame and self-doubt.

3. *Initiative versus guilt.* Corresponds to Freud's phallic stage. Sexual curiosity and oedipal issues are common, competitiveness reaches new heights, and the child's efforts to reach and attain goals acquire importance. Danger arises when the child's aggression or manipulation of the environment triggers an abiding sense of guilt.

4. *Industry versus inferiority.* Occurs during the latency period in Freud's model; associated with the child's beginning efforts to use tools, his sense of being productive, and his developing ability to complete tasks.

5. *Identity versus identity diffusion.* Ushered in by adolescence and perhaps the most extensively developed component of the Eriksonian epigenetic model. Stable identity requires an integration of formative experiences "that give the child the sense that he is a person with a history, a stability, and a continuity that is recognizable by others" (Holzman, 1998, p. 163). Erikson also enumerated seven aspects of identity consolidation (Erikson, 1959) that are critical codeterminants of success or failure in this stage: (1) time perspective, (2) self-certainty, (3) role experimentation, (4) anticipation of achievement), (5) sexual identity, (6) acceptance of leadership, and (7) commitment to basic values.

6. *Intimacy and distantiation versus self-absorption.* Occurs during early adulthood. The major developmental task is the individual's acquisition of a capacity for healthy sexual and nonsexual intimacy while still retaining a firm sense of personal identity. Should such intimacy be impossible, a "regressive retreat to exclusive concern with oneself" results (Holzman, 1998).

7. *Generativity versus stagnation.* Penultimate phase of the adult life cycle. The adult is engaged in the critical tasks and responsibilities of parenting. Parenthood is not inextricably tied to generativity, however. Just as there are adults who relinquish or are otherwise unable to fulfill parental responsibilities, so too are there childless adults whose generativity involves the pursuit of creative or artistic initiatives.

8. *Integrity versus despair and disgust.* The culmination of ego identity (Erikson, 1959; Goldstein, 1995). Ego integrity reflects a level of maturity signaling the individual's acceptance of the past, particularly past disappointments and mistakes.

Adapted from Brandell & Perlman (1997), p. 58.

and Society appeared—his conception of early childhood is equally radical. While preserving the essential structure of the classical theory of libidinal stages, Erikson's vision of the oral, anal, and phallic stages was transformed by a concomitant emphasis on both the historical and the contemporary influences of culture. In the Eriksonian framework, in marked contrast not only to classical conceptions but also to then-prevailing views of ego psychology, cultural forces were thrust into the foreground, possessing causality and capable of generating meanings of their own (Mitchell & Black, 1995). Although Erikson never disputed the common ground that the erogenous zone/libidinal stage theory offered, he was equally determined to highlight the dialectical relationship that existed between the individual and the culture of which he or she was a part, which he once termed "a psychosocial relativity" (Erikson, 1968, p. 23). Obviously, developmental deviations and psychopathology could also then not be presented in absolute terms. Consider the following passages from *Childhood and Society*:

> It is already in his earliest encounters that the human infant *meets up with the basic modalities of his culture....* The pathology and irrationality of oral trends depend entirely on the degree to which they are integrated with the rest of the personality and the *degree to which they fit the general cultural pattern....* Here, as elsewhere, we must therefore consider as a topic for discussion the expression of *infantile urges in cultural patterns* which one may (or may not) consider a pathological deviation in the total economic or moral system of a culture or nation [emphasis added].
>
> (Erikson, 1950, pp. 60–64)

Erikson also focused to a much greater degree than had Freud on the *nature* of the interpersonal processes that characterized the earliest relations of infants and mothers. Further, his concept of "organ modes" or "modes of functioning" furnished a basis for meaningfully extending psychical aspects of bodily functions. Hungry infants, Erikson wrote, are not only interested in being nursed or fed; they are receptive in many other ways, as well; they "take in" with their eyes, as well as via tactile sensations, anything that feels good. Toddlers, in contradistinction, struggle with the dialectic of "holding on" and "letting go," oedipal-age children with "intrusiveness" and "inclusiveness," and so on (Erikson, 1950, 1997).

Although Erikson devoted somewhat less attention to separation and attachment, one might argue that his ideas in this area are implied in his focus on breast-feeding and weaning and, more generally, in his depiction of the maternal-child relationship during the oral-respiratory-kinesthetic stage, with its psychosocial crisis of basic trust versus basic mistrust. This crisis, which Erikson dates to the second half of the first year, is ushered in by three more or less concurrent developments. The first, he observes, is physiological, consisting of the "general tension associated with a more violent drive to incorporate, appropriate, and observe more actively" and is linked to teething; the second is psychological, involving a gradually accruing awareness on the infant's part of herself or himself as a separate person. The third, however, is "environmental," consisting of the mother's "apparent turning away from the baby" in order to resume various work and/or social activities suspended since the beginning of her pregnancy (Erikson, 1959, p. 60). Although all of these developments are considered normative, Erikson suggests that the sudden physical loss of the infant's mother "without proper substitution" carries with it the risk of anaclitic (infantile) depression as well as the potential for lasting psychological damage.

Bowlby believed, however, that Erikson, despite his tremendous creativity in integrating theories of drives with post-Freudian conceptions of ego and sociocultural forces, seemed intent on preserving both Freud's original erogenous zone framework and with it an apparently irreducible relationship between orality and attachment. The relatedness of infant and mother, which Erikson freely acknowledges to be of such importance in the earliest months of life, is not subject to a secondary drive, but rather is fundamentally linked to orality: "The oral stages then, form in the infant the springs of the *basic sense of trust*" (Erikson, 1950, p. 75). In Bowlby's estimation (Bowlby, 1969), the importance that Erikson attributes to "primary object sucking" in this first developmental period, in tandem with his failure, generally speaking, to account more fully for attachment phenomena within the psychosocial epigenetic theory, places him in a position that is just as untenable as those of Sullivan and René Spitz (another infant developmentalist, discussed earlier). All three, Bowlby notes, are "trapped" by the disparity between "their clinical appreciation of the facts" and their "conventional theorizing" (Bowlby, 1969, p. 374).

Bowlby, however, may not have been completely fair in his dismissive critique of Erikson on the grounds just cited. Indeed, just nine years after the publication of *Childhood and Society*, Erikson appeared to have placed somewhat more emphasis on the *qualitative* aspects of the infant-mother relationship, declaring, "[The] amount of trust derived from earliest infantile experience does not seem to depend on absolute quantities of food or demonstrations of love, but rather on the *quality* of the maternal relationship" (1959, p. 63). Erikson's important and pioneering ideas regarding "reciprocity or mutual regulation," first described in *Childhood and Society* (1950, p. 58), seem to parallel the notion of *interactional synchrony*, a concept attributed to attachment theorists (Isabella & Belsky, 1991). Further, his interest in a life span perspective also represents an important source of convergence with Bowlby's framework. Then, too, there was the recognition Erikson gave to cultural forces, and to the immediate social context of mothering, both of which are resonant with much current thinking in the attachment field (Fonagy, 2001). Finally, Erikson's ideas regarding the longer-term sequelae of trust and mistrust, and specifically trust and identity, are upon closer examination rather close to Main's concept of *coherence*, a central organizing theme in her framework for adult attachment (Fonagy, 2001). Such similarities have led some to conclude that Erikson's ideas, "in both spirit and particulars," demonstrate a consistency "with contemporary research on infant attachment and its roots in interactions with the primary caregiver" (Fonagy, 2001, p. 59).

Kohut's Psychology of the Self

A relative newcomer among the psychoanalytic psychologies that comprise contemporary psychoanalysis (classical psychoanalysis, ego psychology, and object relations theories, among others), the psychology of the self[10] was introduced by the American psychoanalyst Heinz Kohut (1913–1981) in a series of essays and books published between 1959 and 1984. Although originally presented within the existing classical drive theory (Kohut, 1966, 1971), Kohut's ideas about development, psychopathology, and psychoanalytic treatment were gradually expanded and revised, culminating in a distinctive and fundamentally new psychoanalytic psychology (Kohut, 1977, 1984). The essence of self psychology may well lie in its vision of the human condition. Freud's view of humankind is usually expressed in terms of conflicted desire—an ongoing battle between libidinal or aggressive wishes on the one hand and societal precepts on the other. Within this framework, the individual's capacity to experience guilt, however painful it may prove to be, offers the only certain means for the renunciation of instinct, without which capacity a civilized society is not possible.

Kohut's perspective on the human condition, however, appears to contrast markedly with that of Freud. Kohut was far less interested in primitive desires and the conflicts they engendered than he was in the *loss of meaning* associated with contemporary life—i.e., in those experiences that might lead to a "fractured, enfeebled, discontinuous human existence" (Kohut, 1977, p. 238). In classical theory, man lives within the "pleasure principle," endeavoring "to satisfy his pleasure-seeking drives," whereas self psychology emphasizes human failures, uncompleted projects, and unrequited efforts at work and love (p. 238).

Kohut and his followers, much like the principal figures associated with other psychoanalytic psychologies discussed in chapters 1 and 2, developed not only a framework for clinical interventions but also a model for understanding various aspects of normative human development/developmental deviations, and a theory of psychopathology. However, self psychology has also developed its own lexicon, one sufficiently different from that of other psychoanalytic psychologies to warrant a brief review of several of its key concepts and terms:

Selfobjects

In self psychology, the term *selfobject* is used to represent a particular kind of object relationship in which the object is experienced as being a part of or extension of the subject's self, and in which little or no psychological differentiation occurs. Kohut observed that the control one expects over such selfobjects is roughly equivalent to the sort of control an adult "expects to have over his own body and mind," in contradistinction to the "control which he expects to have over others" (Kohut, 1971, pp. 26–27). He believed that human beings require three distinctly different kinds of selfobject experiences: (1) mirroring, (2) idealizing, and (3) partnering, each of which, assuming optimal conditions for development, is furnished to the child in an attuned, empathically resonant interpersonal milieu. Mirroring selfobjects "respond to and confirm the child's innate sense of vigor, greatness, and perfection," whereas idealized selfobjects offer the child the powerful and reassuring presence of caregivers "to whom the child can look up and with whom he can merge as an image of calmness, infallibility, and omnipotence" (Kohut & Wolf, 1978, p. 414). Finally, partnering objects provide the child with various opportunities through which a sense of belonging and of essential alikeness within a community of others may be acquired.

The Tripolar Self

Kohut's theory identified an intrapsychic structure, the *tripolar self*, that links each selfobject relationship to a corresponding sphere of self experience. Mirroring experiences, which reflect the need for approbation, interest, and affirmation, are associated with the *grandiose exhibitionistic self*; idealizing experiences, which reflect the need for closeness and support from an (omnipotent) idealized other, are linked to the intrapsychic structure known as the *idealized parent imago*; and partnering, associated with the individual's need for contact with others who are experienced as having an essential similarity to oneself, is linked to the *alter ego*. In the course of development, these three poles crystallize as the result of various needs of the evolving self, as well as the responses of significant people in the child's environment who serve as selfobjects (Leider, 1996).

Empathy and Transmuting Internalization

According to the self psychologists, empathic processes originate in early infancy and traverse the entire life span, and breaches or traumatic disruptions in the empathic attunement between self and selfobject are believed to possess special importance. Self psychology defines empathy as "vicarious introspection" or the feeling of oneself into the experience of an other. The capacity of parents or parental surrogates in the child's selfobject milieu to furnish empathically attuned responses is considered a critical sine qua non for the healthy development of the self. However, somewhat paradoxically, self psychological theory also maintains that comparatively minor, nontraumatic lapses in parental empathy are equally important as catalysts for the development of what Kohut termed *transmuting internalizations*—an incremental "taking in" or internalizing of various functions *originally* associated with the selfobjects. These functions and attributes, which include self-soothing and self-calming, pride, wisdom, humor, stoicism in the face of adversity, and indefatigability in the pursuit of personal goals, are absorbed and metabolized through a virtually imperceptible, bit-by-bit process of translocation. Ultimately, they become enduring components of the child's own self-structure, altered by his or her individual imprimatur.

Essential elements contributing to transmuting internalizations are sequenced in the following order: (1) optimal frustration, (2) increased tension, (3) selfobject response, (4) reduced tension, (5) memory trace, (6) development of internal regulating (self) structures.

The Self Types

Self psychologists believe that the self is most usefully understood within the intersecting matrices of developmental level and structural state; they have identified four principal self types: (1) the *virtual self*, an image of the newborn's self that originally exists within the parent's mind, evolving in particular ways as the parental "selfobjects empathically respond to certain potentialities of the child" (Kohut, 1977, p. 100); (2) the *nuclear self*, a core self that emerges in the infant's second year and serves as the basis for the child's "sense of being an independent center of initiative and perception" (Kohut, 1977, p. 177); (3) the *cohesive self*, the basic self structure of a healthily functioning, well-adapted individual, reflecting the harmonious "interplay of ambitions, ideals, and talents with the opportunities of everyday reality" (Leider, 1996, p. 143); and (4) the *grandiose self*, a normal self structure of infancy and early childhood that comes into existence in response to the selfobject's attunement with the child's sense of himself or herself as the center of the universe.

Kohut's ideas about development and psychopathology have been criticized on a number of different grounds. His concept of grandiosity as representing a normal stage of infantile development and his notion of infantile omnipotence have both been challenged, and limited evidence exists to support the child's need for unconditional admiration; furthermore, there is little research evidence confirming the existence of a narcissistic period of development in the child's first two to three years (Fonagy & Target, 2003). However, other self psychological ideas, such as the mother's role in imparting tension-regulation skills to her baby and the relationship of transmuting internalizations to the building up of internal self structures, have received a greater degree of support (Fonagy & Target, 2003).[11]

Although Kohut's discussion of early infantile development focuses on the origin and evolution of the infant's self structure, his ideas regarding development do not appear to be fundamentally incompatible with attachment theory and in fact may possess a certain complementarity with it. While he does not offer a developmental timetable equivalent to others reviewed here, he strongly intimates that specific kinds of selfobject responses prove either facilitative or problematic in the child's quest for the acquisition of stable and enduring self structures and that such experiences are associated with particular developmental epochs. For example, grandiosity is transformed into exhibitionism via maternal mirroring between the second and fourth years, and idealized goals make their appearance sometime between the fourth and sixth years (Fonagy & Target, 2003). Of somewhat greater interest, however, is Kohut's vision of the baby's earliest development, specifically his conception of both *merger* experiences and *idealizing* experiences.

The basic configuration for Kohut's model of idealizing experiences, i.e., self/selfobject encounters with an empathically resonant, calming, reassuring (and from the infant's point of view, omnipotent) selfobject, is that of "uplifting care." Although Kohut employs this phrase in both a literal and a figurative sense, he frequently takes note of the physical dimension of attuned caregiving. At the same time, however, the caregiver's provision of such "uplifting care" is but one aspect of the empathic-responsive human milieu into which each child is born. Kohut acknowledges the importance of the child's physical attachment to her mother when "she is picked up by mother and thereby feels herself part of the omnipotent strength and calmness of the idealized self-object" (Kohut, 1984, p. 186), yet he suggests that such experiences are most usefully understood within the framework of the child's efforts to acquire intrapsychic self structure. Physical attachment, in Kohut's system, represents but one variety of selfobject encounter—granted, a prototypical one; his real focus is on the role of empathic processes or the lack thereof in *shaping* such idealizing experiences. Put somewhat differently, secure attachment, from the perspective of self psychology, is a *result* of optimally functioning maternal empathy rather than a subject of study unto itself. Conversely, the self psychologist's interest in insecure patterns of attachment (anxious, disorganized, and so forth) would likely center on the *traumatic breaches* that gave rise to such patterns and which specific *realm* of selfobject experience was involved. These assumptions may also reveal a more fundamental difference between self psychology and attachment theory: for Kohut, the principal motivating force behind human behavior is that of *self-cohesion*, and the most basic anxiety that of *disintegration*—the individual's experience of "a defect, a lack of cohesiveness and continuity in the sense of self" (Fonagy, 2001, p. 110). By contrast, attachment theory focuses on a biologically predefined pattern of relationship, one in which the attachment figure remains very much at the center of the equation (Fonagy, 2001, p. 110).

Nevertheless, important points of basic convergence between attachment theory and psychoanalytic self psychology remain. Both Bowlby and

Kohut believed that Freud's erogenous zone/libidinal phase model provided an inadequate account of human development, and both attributed importance to the baby's physical attachment to the mother, as well as to the overriding importance of maternal-infant attunement. Moreover, both placed considerable emphasis on the role of maternal regulating functions and on the potentially traumatogenic effects of disruptions in the physical and, later, emotional relationship between infant and caregiver.

This chapter has examined four different contemporary psychoanalytic models of development and their "goodness of fit" with attachment theory. Although important differences exist between Bowlby's ideas and those of Sullivan, Mahler, Erikson, and Kohut, there were, surprisingly, points of theoretical convergence in virtually every case. Margaret Mahler's separation-individuation theory, for example, emphasizes the complementary relationship of exploratory behavior to attachment security, a theme common also to Bowlby's theory. Sullivan's interpersonal conception of development, like Bowlby's ideas about attachment, places considerable emphasis on environmental factors both in shaping the personality and in psychopathology. Kohut's focus on the significance of early merger states and, more generally, on maternal attunement in the formation of healthy self structure also appears compatible with Bowlby's views. And finally, Erikson's epigenetic theory and his conception of basic trust in particular, despite Bowlby's critique of his early adherence to the basic outline of the classical erotogenic zone model and his equation of orality with attachment, demonstrates a meaningful convergence with the Bowlbyan framework.

Research on Attachment FOUR

Since Bowlby's earliest investigations in the 1950s, research interest in the varieties of attachment behavior and their relationships to normal and pathological development has increased exponentially. This chapter focuses on the work done in the area of human attachment, including studies of children, adolescents, and adults. We will review the contributions of prominent empirical researchers in the attachment field and address in greater detail the work of psychoanalytic researchers. Along with current attachment research, we will look at new findings in neuroscience as well, in order to highlight the biological underpinnings of attachment theory. Finally, we will consider attachment and psychopathology, especially trauma and personality disorders, as well as cross-cultural studies of attachment in China, Japan, Africa, and Israel.

A major part of this investigation is the work of Ainsworth's contemporaries and students, including (a) Alan Sroufe, (b) Mary Main and her contributions of the disorganized attachment style and the Adult Attachment Interview, (c) Fonagy and his concept of mentalization, (d) the Sylvan Tomkins theory of affect, (e) attachment studies in diverse populations by Abraham Sagi and others, and (f) infant researchers, especially Daniel Stern. We will conclude with a review of the application of attachment research and theory to clinical practice.

Alan Sroufe and Mary Main

During her lifetime, Mary Ainsworth gathered a group of students around her who have continued to expand attachment research since her death in 1999. Among them were Jude Cassidy, Inge Bretherton, Mary Main, and Robert Marvin. Alan Sroufe, another important researcher in this field, worked at the University of Minnesota. All of these researchers elaborated on Ainsworth's work with the Strange Situation experiment, examining children's behavior in other social contexts and eventually exploring both how early attachment behaviors shape internal development and how they relate to later adult behaviors and parenting styles.

Sroufe was interested in using longitudinal studies to discover whether attachment styles observed during the Strange Situation held constant in other social situations and in everyday life contexts, such as school. In Minnesota, he studied a group of forty-eight children whose attachment styles at twelve and eighteen months had been previously assessed. He wanted to investigate the children's attachment styles across a broader spectrum and longitudinally, including relationships with peers and teachers, how they dealt with stress, and other social and cognitive experiences outside of the Strange Situation. He and his colleagues found that the securely attached children performed better on every social and cognitive task. In play activity, for example, the securely attached children developed more symbolic play, had better impulse control, exhibited better social skills, and displayed more positive emotions (Sroufe, 1988). The children's behavior seems to have been supported by the mother's role; that is, the mothers of the secure children were found to be more supportive and responsive, rather than withdrawing (ambivalent) or impinging (avoidant).

While the Minnesota children were recruited from middle-class homes, in another study, a longitudinal one beginning in 1974, Sroufe and his collaborator, Byron Egeland, recruited 267 pregnant women with low socioeconomic status and followed them and their children for twenty years. Most of these women were young and single: 80 percent were white, 14 percent were black, and 6 percent were Hispanic or Native American (Karen, 1998). The researchers' intriguing finding was that the mother's personality and quality of mothering were far more predictive than the child's own temperament, personality, or genetic makeup were in the development of an attachment style (Sroufe, Egeland, & Kreutzer, 1990). This finding contradicted the theories of developmental psychologists such as Jerome Kagan, who had argued the opposite—that the child's temperament and genetic endowment were much more important for development than attachment bonds with caregivers. In their observations of these children in school, Sroufe and his colleagues found them to be more independent, more empathetic to other children, and more motivated in their academic work. Anxious children, including the avoidant ones, were found to be the most dependent. Avoidant children, however, seemed to mask their dependency needs in oppositional or self-sufficient behavior; consequently they did not elicit help from teachers or other children and were ignored. In this study, Sroufe showed that children's attachment behavior, observed briefly during the earlier Strange Situation, was largely consistent in terms of their broader adaptation to everyday life at four or five years of age.

Main and Disorganized Attachment

One of Ainsworth's most important students was Mary Main, a researcher from Berkeley whose initial interest in linguistics was later channeled into research with adults and, eventually, to development of the Adult Attachment Interview. Main's first study was the Berkeley Study, a longitudinal research project in which she assessed middle-class children's attachment styles toward both parents at twelve to eighteen months of age and then again at six years of age. Main and her assistants, among them Ruth Goldwyn, who became a collaborator, and Jude Cassidy, another of Ainsworth's students, found that attachment styles remained for the most part constant (about 79 percent of the time). They also discovered a fourth attachment style, which they called the *disorganized attachment style*. Children who were so designated seemed fearful and engaged in repetitive or aggressive behaviors. Main noticed that this was a new pattern that did not meet Ainsworth's criteria for insecure attachment, in either the ambivalent or the avoidant style. The children who demonstrated a disorganized style acted in strange or bizarre ways and didn't seem to have a coherent strategy for either approach or avoidance. Main characterized such behavior as disorganized according to the following indicators: display of contradictory behavior patterns, such as attachment followed by avoidance; misdirected or incomplete movement and expression, such as striking parents; crying when a stranger left; stereotypical behavior such as rocking or hair pulling; and freezing, stilling, or otherwise slowed movements that seem disoriented (Main, 1999). She later found out that many of the children who exhibited such behaviors came from abusive or neglectful households, with mothers who were depressed or who had lost their parents early on and carried with them unresolved feelings.

During her close observations of these infants' attachment behaviors, Main became interested in the children's internal experiences and their memories, thoughts, and feelings regarding the experience of separation. In her subsequent research, she made a significant shift from studying the children's behavior to studying their internal experiences of their caregivers—their "mental structure of the imagined, remembered, or observed experience of separation" (Karen, 1998, p. 214). In this way, Main started to bridge the conceptual schism between attachment research and clinical (particularly psychodynamic) practice.

The Adult Attachment Interview (AAI)

Main's second important contribution to attachment research was the development of the Adult Attachment Interview, an instrument that rated the early familial experiences of adults. Rather than focusing on overt behaviors, Main examined her respondents' memories, stories, and quality of demonstrated feeling states regarding their childhood experiences. She reviewed these adults' narratives in relation to their earlier attachment styles as well as their own children's attachment styles and found strong correlations between the variables. While earlier research by Bowlby and Ainsworth had concentrated more on behavioral patterns, Main addressed internal structures such as cognition, perceptions, and emotions, as well as speech patterns. She examined how attachment patterns were internalized and organized into what Bowlby called internal working models. Main's emphasis on internal processes placed attachment research closer to the psychodynamic arena, i.e., developmental considerations and mental processes and their impact on both the inner world and/or relational schemas.

The Adult Attachment Interview (AAI) was developed by Carol George, Nancy Kaplan, and Main, and was later analyzed by Main and Goldwyn (Main & Goldwyn, 1984). It included a series of questions asking participants to describe their parents, aspects of the relationship with them, and perceptions of their own childhoods, especially in connection with experiences of separation, loss, and rejection. The interview focused on the participants' memories as well as on their thoughts and feelings regarding those memories.

Main identified four primary patterns of perceiving past experiences that seemed to correspond to Ainsworth's attachment styles. The first pattern was "secure-autonomous"; adults who exhibited this pattern were able to discuss both the happy and the painful events of their past and to view their parents more objectively, accepting them for who they were—including their problems and limitations. They were also able to demonstrate self-reflective ability and insight that Main called "metacognitive monitoring" (Hesse, 1999). Main found that most of the children of these adults had been categorized as securely attached earlier.

Main's second category, "dismissive," included adults who minimized the value of their earlier relationships, used superficial, stereotypical phrases to describe their parents (such as "they were wonderful" or "they were okay"), did not remember much about their childhoods, and at times described their families as "perfect," despite later evidence to the contrary. They seemed reluctant to engage in self-reflection or to talk about their pasts. This pattern appeared to be similar to the avoidant style of infancy, and in fact three-quarters of the adults in this group had children who were avoidantly attached.

The third pattern, "preoccupied," described adults who were still highly preoccupied with their pasts, expressed a lack of emotional resolution of their childhood experiences, and were filled with hurt and anger. They were also lacking in insight, and there seemed to be little coherence or organization to their narratives. They would lose track or become stuck in describing a particular emotional experience. These participants seemed to have difficulty in separating emotionally from their parents and from their pasts. Not surprisingly, most of their children were found to be ambivalently attached.

A fourth, and less prevalent, attachment category, termed "unresolved-disorganized," was associated with loss or trauma, and corresponded to the disorganized attachment style in children. AAI transcripts of these adults revealed an unresolved and disoriented mental state characterized by irrational beliefs, extreme behaviors, denial of the loss or abuse, and an inability to integrate the loss or trauma.

While studies of the Strange Situation observed actual behaviors, the Adult Attachment Interview reflected the participants' emotional and cognitive childhood memories, interpreted first by the participants themselves and then by the researchers. Because the resulting data are based in part on the interpretation of the researchers, some controversy as to the accuracy of the outcomes has existed ever since the AAI was developed (Karen, 1998).

Attachment Bonds in Adolescent and Adulthood: Romantic Love

A rather interesting direction in attachment research has been investigation of attachment patterns in romantic love, providing. a bridge from attachment patterns in childhood into attachment during adulthood. Cindy Hazan and Phillip Shaver (1987) have argued that romantic love can be viewed as an attachment bonding process and that early attachment experiences shape differences in romantic relational styles. The three major attachment styles, they contend, are replicated in later love relationships (Feeney, 1999). For their study they developed a self-reporting measure that included three paragraphs describing three relationship styles from which their participants were asked to choose. The results showed that participants did demonstrate three distinct attachment styles, which corresponded to the secure, ambivalent, and avoidant styles. While Hazan and Shaver's initial study was limited in that it focused on a single romantic relationship, it nevertheless created a link between attachment styles in infancy and in adulthood. Feeney and Noller (1990) later replicated the study and achieved similar results.

Attachment and Affect Theory

Bowlby was more interested in explaining his attachment theory through the biological, evolutionary, and cognitive theories of the time than in understanding emotional development. Even his theory of internal working models was initially viewed as the internalization of interactive activities rather than as the more complex and abstract notion of memories (Main) and reflection (Fonagy). Bowlby's explanation for attachment behaviors was the child's desire for physical proximity, as well as his or her desire for exploration. Although he referred to attachment as the need for "affectional bonds," Bowlby said very little about the place of affect or its regulation. Sroufe, in a 1996 book, elaborated on the place of affect in attachment theory, following his seminal paper on "felt security," where he argued that attachment needs were based on feelings rather than on physical proximity (Sroufe, 1996).

An important early contribution to the theory of affects came from Sylvan Tomkins, who was more interested in temperament and personality than in developmental considerations. Magai (1999) contrasts Tomkins's work on affects with Bowlby's attachment theory. She notes that Bowlby saw emotion as a response to, or a striving toward, attachment experiences, with emotions as the secondary product. Tomkins, however, developed a theory of affect with emotion as the central event, focusing mainly on facial expressions. For Bowlby, the primary motivators in life were attachment (proximity) and exploration. For Tomkins, they were "to maximize positive affect, to minimize negative affect, to minimize affect inhibition, and to have the power to maximize the other goals" (Magai, 1999, p. 788). While Bowlby viewed attachment as broader and based on the development of internal working models and dyadic interactions between infant and caregiver, Tomkins was interested in individual personality differences and the specific emotions at the core of personality patterns. He was less interested in developmental variables than Bowlby was (Tomkins, 1991).

Some of Tomkins's work was later integrated into attachment research through the concept of *affect regulation,* a notion that has become an important component in contemporary attachment research. Affect regulation includes the parent's regulation of the child's feelings, as well as the individual's mutual affect regulation with others in social and romantic relationships later in life. In this arena affect theory and attachment theory converge, in that individual temperaments and dyadic relationships have both been found to contribute to affect regulation (Cassidy, 1999; Schore, 1997; Thomson, 1999).

Another important contribution to the theory of affect comes from the work of neurobiologists Chris LeDoux and Antonio Damasio. LeDoux, in his work with rats, focused on the significance of fear and made important discoveries on the role of the amygdala and the hippocampus in responding to threats and in storing traumatic memories. He argued that the brain has two emotional response systems. The first is based in the amygdala and the hippocampus and occurs automatically and unconsciously; it is an evolutionary component of all mammalian species. The second involves the neocortex and integrates a more cognitive component, relying on individual experiences, memories, and temperament and allowing more conscious control. LeDoux's work showed how early attachment relationships can affect emotions, as well as their role in later development and adult relationships (LeDoux, 1996).

Damasio, through his work with brain-injured patients, developed a different, more philosophical perspective on the place of emotions in the development of the self. He argued that there is an interconnection between emotion and cognition but that some emotions may be unrelated to cognitive processes. This contrasted with the views of earlier cognitive theorists, who saw cognition as primary to emotional responses. Damasio believed that emotions are rationally based on their own terms, and he maintained that our decision-making process "incorporates gut level responses that are, in fact, automatic signals from the body that protect and help us to limit and choose among possible options" (Fonagy, Gergely, Jurist, & Target, 2002, p. 78). Damasio elaborated on three senses of self: the *proto self*, the *core self*, and the *autobiographical self*. These reflect three levels of the brain, with the *proto self* the most primitive, akin to the reptilian brain or the brain stem; the *core self* "concerned with the experience of the here and now" (Fonagy et al., 2002, p. 79); and the *autobiographical self* reflecting the most highly developed part of the brain, the neocortex, which includes cognitive processes, verbal capacities, and memory storage (Damasio, 1999). Both LeDoux and Damasio have made important contributions to the integration of attachment findings, affect regulation, and brain structure, and their published work has shown how the three may be interrelated and interconnected. Fonagy's work on mentalization, based in part on these neurobiological findings, has further elaborated the developmental and intergenerational aspects of attachment experiences and their impact on the sense of self, as well as on the development of mental disorders and ongoing relational patterns.

Attachment and Mentalization

Peter Fonagy and his collaborator Mary Target continued to elaborate on Main's findings in relation to internal mental processes. They used the term *mentalization* for the capacity to self-reflect, articulate internal states, and accurately perceive the self's emotional states as well as those of others (Fonagy & Target, 1998). The concept of mentalization is similar to Main and Hesse's notion of metacognitive monitoring based on the participants' ability to reflect on their childhood experiences during the Adult Attachment Interview (Hesse, 1999). Fonagy and his colleagues (1999) found that parents' ability to reflect on their inner lives, and on the inner lives of others, was a predictor of their children's ability to self-reflect and to be empathic with others. They also found that the mother's self-reflective ability and her capacity to mirror the child's internal states were better predictors of secure attachment than a consistent physical presence and provision of material goods by mothers who were less successful in handling their children's emotional needs (Fonagy et al., 1999).

Fonagy and Target (2003) found that the child's development of a reflective mind was not a genetic given but was predicated upon a relationship with an adult who was empathetic, attuned, and self-reflective. These authors write: "The baby's experience of himself as having a mind or psychological self is not a genetic given. It is a structure that evolves from infancy through childhood, and its development critically depends upon interaction with more mature minds, which are benign, reflective and sufficiently attuned" (p. 271).

Mentalization, according to Fonagy and Target (2003), is not just a cognitive capacity but also the ability to identify and regulate affect through the empathic process between baby and caregiver. For example, the caregiver may initially help to regulate the baby's emotional states through soothing, holding, talking, and singing, thus modeling self-soothing and self-regulation for the child, who will eventually be able to internalize such functions for him- or herself and, still later, to utilize these skills in social relationships. Sroufe's findings, that secure children showed more empathy toward others than did insecurely attached children, seem to support this idea (Sroufe, 1988). Fonagy and Target state that the capacity to mentalize has an evolutionary purpose, which is "to equip the very young child with an environment within which the understanding of mental states in others and the self can fully and safely develop" (2003, p. 271).

They found that this empathic process is accomplished through the parents' ability to mirror their children's affective states and to understand and regulate themselves, so that children eventually internalize these self-regulatory and empathic functions. The ability of parents to mirror children's feelings without impinging or otherwise burdening the children with their own feelings is deemed critical. Otherwise, the parent's negative emotions can cause an escalation in the child's subjective distress. This mirroring may also help children to develop awareness of parents as separate entities who possess their own thoughts and feelings. Fonagy's research arguably reflects Jessica Benjamin's relational concept of mutual recognition (Benjamin, 1995), wherein she argued that the measure of the child's level of maturation is the ability to view the mother as a separate other with her own needs and feelings, who therefore may not always be available for satisfaction of the child's needs.

Fonagy and his colleagues also asserted that this capacity to mentalize is seriously compromised in children who have experienced a traumatic family history. Such children observe and internalize their parents' own disorganized, frightening, or frightened affects and build their internal models around such affects. They learn to be highly attuned to others' affects but are poorly attuned or unable to reflect on their own feelings and needs (Fonagy et al., 1999).

Attachment and Diversity

Bowlby constructed his attachment theory on the basis of observations of British children during and after World War II, a sample that consisted almost exclusively of white, European-born children. In the early 1950s Mary Ainsworth went to Uganda and initiated her first research project with African children. Thus, almost from the outset, culture, race, and ethnicity played an important part in attachment research, and the question of whether attachment patterns were universal became a central concern of researchers in this area. Other questions came up as well. For example, would the attachment behaviors of Caucasian children, who grew up in a nuclear family and generally with one predominant caretaker (typically the mother), be comparable to the attachment behaviors of children who grew up in an extended-family network, with several caretakers available to them? What would attachment patterns look like for children who grew up in communal situations, such as kibbutz children in Israel? More recently, as the traditional definition of the family has expanded to include gay and lesbian families, questions have arisen about the nature of the attachment styles of children who grow up in same-sex parental households. These questions provide a fascinating and rich arena for investigation that is summarized in the material that follows.

The Ugandan village children of Ainsworth's initial research study grew up in an extended-family context, where they were more likely to be in daily contact with adults other than their mothers. Ainsworth classified these Ugandan infants with three basic patterns of attachment (secure, ambivalent, and avoidant). These same patterns were found in the children of her Baltimore study, who grew up in nuclear-family environments. The Ugandan children's primary attachment was to their mothers, who were their main caretakers. Ainsworth found out that it was the quality of time spent, rather than the quantity, that was central in determining a child's attachment style. Insecure attachment patterns were linked to mothers who were themselves depressed, overwhelmed, or not attuned to their children. It is necessary, however, to understand some of the children's social cues within a context of cultural differences (as in the example given earlier of clapping versus smiling and hugging upon reunion with the mother).

After the Uganda study, several researchers conducted cross-cultural studies in Africa, China, Japan, and Israel. The questions they wanted to answer were whether attachment behaviors are universal and normative, whether attachment security is dependent on sensitive, attuned responses, and whether attachment security leads to differences in children's competence in regulating negative emotions (Van Ijzendoorn & Sagi, 1999, p. 713).

Studies in Africa

While Ainsworth's Uganda study was important, it involved only a small sample in one African country. Several later studies in other African countries and cultures have expanded our knowledge of attachment patterns. One study involved the Gussi of Kenya, a culture in which several caregivers, including older siblings, are available to the child. In this case there was a strict division of tasks among the various caregivers, with the mother responsible for the infant's overall care (Kermoian & Leiderman, 1986). Nevertheless, researchers found similar percentages of secure and insecure infants as in the West, with 61 percent securely attached and the rest insecurely attached. The behaviors, however, varied according to cultural mores; for example, a handshake was a culturally acceptable form of greeting at reunion, rather than a hug (Kermoian & Leiderman, 1986). In another study, of the Hausa in Nigeria (Marvin, VanDevender, Iwanaga, LeVine, & LeVine, 1977), researchers found that because of environmental differences, the children's exploratory behavior was more passive and occurred only in close proximity to their mothers; moreover, they were typically attached to more than one caregiver, which might include the father. Nevertheless, the primary attachment was to the person who spent the most time with the child or held him or her most frequently (which may or may not have been the mother). Consequently, while these infants displayed the universal need for a secure base and a primary attachment figure, they differed in their culturally specific attachment behavior styles. Other studies, by True (1994) with the Dogon in Mali, and by Morelli and Tronick (1991) with the Efe, or Pygmies of the forest in northeastern Zambia, also showed the universal need of infants for a primary attachment figure, regardless of how many caretakers were available. Irrespective of which African culture was studied, it appeared that the majority of infants were securely attached, which paralleled findings with Western infants.

Studies in China

While the paucity of research conducted with Chinese children and their caregivers may raise legitimate concerns about generalizability, three studies suggest the universality of attachment principles to Chinese children, in spite of important cultural differences with the West. Chinese culture emphasizes family interdependence, filial piety, and deference to others. These cultural values contrast with the parental encouragement of independence, autonomy, and exploratory behavior in the West. Despite such cultural differences, however, the investigator of one study found that Chinese mothers had the most positive response to children who behaved in a secure manner, as defined by the Western researcher. For example, these mothers preferred confident, exploratory, and independent behavior over more passive and dependent behavior (Posada et al., 1995). In another study, Chinese parents were found to value independence and individuality in social contexts, such as school and work life, a result that was similar to research with Western parents (Lin & Fu, 1990). In a third study, which replicated the Strange Situation in Beijing, the attachment classification distribution was found to be similar to that in the West, as well as in other international studies, with secure mother-infant dyads constituting 68 percent, avoidant dyads 16 percent, and resistant dyads 16 percent of the sample (Hu & Meng, 1996).[1] Interestingly, secure attachment was found to be equal for boys and girls, despite the strong cultural preference for male children in China. Aside from the problem of generalizability noted above, it is possible that the researcher's Western bias influenced study participants in terms of the social desirability factor, so that the findings were skewed in favor of Western patterns. However, an alternate hypothesis is that Western behaviors and values have infiltrated the world at large through the media and that non-Western cultures such as China have been greatly influenced by the West at every level of society.

Studies in Japan

Similarly to the aforementioned studies in China, research conducted in Japan indicated that the description of a securely attached child there does not differ markedly from that of children in other countries, including Western nations. Despite the fact that in Japan there is a cultural emphasis on *amae*, or dependence on the mother (Doi, 1989), Japanese mothers in the study described a securely attached child in a very different way (Vereijken, 1996).[2] In fact, they did not consider *amae*, or dependent behavior, an ideal style of adaptation. In another study, the mothers' descriptions of a secure child also mirrored that of the Western researchers (Posada et al., 1995). In additional studies, the distribution of specific attachment types (58 percent secure, 24 percent avoidant, 18 percent ambivalent) were similar to the global distribution (van Ijzendoorn & Bakermans-Kranenburg, 1996). Thus in several key areas studies in Japan have reinforced the evidence that attachment needs and attachment styles have a universal pattern that obtains across cultures. As in the Chinese studies, the Japanese studies are few and should therefore not be generalized to Japanese culture as a whole. Social desirability may have been a confounding variable in these studies as well, insofar as the Japanese mothers were subject to the researchers' Western bias.

Studies in Israel

Until the mid-1980s, the Israeli kibbutz was a unique community, inasmuch as children in many kibbutzim lived and slept in communal children's houses, away from their parents. In fact, kibbutz children spent most of their time with peers and with nonrelated caregivers, visiting the parents for only a few hours each day. This arrangement deemphasized the role of family in childrearing, shifting the focus to the peer group as the primary attachment object. Sagi, Lamb, et al. (1985) studied the attachment patterns of kibbutz children through application of the Strange Situation and through comparison of interactions between mothers and infants in the kibbutz and in city day-care centers. They found that 59 percent of the kibbutz children were securely attached, as compared to 75 percent of the children in day care. The ambivalent attachment style was overrepresented in both groups. Another study found an even lower percentage (48 percent) of securely attached children. Even so, the children were primarily attached to their mothers, thus confirming the universality of the attachment hypothesis (Sagi, Van Ijzendoorn, Aviezer, Donnell, & Mayseless, 1994). In a later study (Sagi, Van Ijzendoorn, Scharf, et al., 1997), researchers investigated how strong the intergenerational transmission of attachment between parents and children was in the communal sleeping kibbutz versus those in another sample. They applied the Adult Attachment Interview to a group of mothers and compared their styles with those of their children. The results showed that the overlap between the mother's and child's attachment styles in the communal sleeping situation was significantly lower (40 percent) than those of the other context (75 percent). These results suggested that what the researchers called the "ecological" factors (such as peer relationships and the kibbutz environment as a whole) had a sufficiently strong impact on attachment styles to override the influence of the parents.

These studies and many others suggest that the principal tenets of attachment theory are universal—that is, all infants have attachment needs as well as a primary attachment to one caregiver, although that may be mediated by cultural customs and contexts. In addition, the characteristics of secure attachment, or what the researchers described as an "ideal child," were found to be very similar across cultures, including China, Japan, Colombia, Germany, and the United States (Posada et al., 1995). Experts in these cultures and the mothers studied were in basic agreement on the definition of attachment security. The exact behaviors of a secure child, however, do vary according to the cultural context (Van Ijzendoorn, Schengle, & Bakermanns-Kranenburg, 1999).

Studies of Minority Groups Within the United States

Only a handful of studies have been conducted with African Americans, Latinos, and Asian Americans, and apparently no studies have focused on Native Americans. The few studies that are reported in the literature parallel global findings that attachment behaviors are universal and that children generally develop affectional bonds with a primary caregiver, even in those communities where caregiver networks occur somewhat more commonly, such as the African American and the Latino communities. One study that examined perceptions of attachment behaviors of Anglo and Puerto Rican mothers found that though mothers in both groups considered the accepted secure attachment behavior to be the most desirable, the Anglo mothers showed a greater tendency to emphasize their toddlers' autonomy and exploratory behavior, while the Puerto Rican mothers were more likely to focus on the children's ability to remain calm and develop a "close attachment relationship" (Harwood & Miller, 1991, p. 394). These differences appear to be consistent with cultural values in the Anglo and Puerto Rican communities. Another study, by Harwood (1992), confirms these results, finding that the Anglo mothers focused more on the personal competence of toddlers, thus enabling them to cope with the unfamiliar environment of the Strange Situation, while the Puerto Rican mothers focused on the toddlers' "proper demeanor in public context" (p. 836).

A study of African Americans examining parenting and preschoolers' attachment among black urban families (Barnett, Kidwell, & Leung, 1998) revealed attachment patterns, as well as the intergenerational transmission of insecure attachment, to be similar to the global findings, and the mothers in this study expressed similar approval for securely attached children. Interestingly, there was a much higher percentage of insecure attachment among boys (55 percent) than among girls (26 percent). Finally, the investigators found that the parents of children who were classified as insecurely attached reported that "they were more likely to use corporal punishment and less likely to use verbal reminders when their children misbehaved" (p. 1657).

As did the previous international research, these studies illustrate that general attachment patterns, as well as preferences for a secure attachment behavior as defined by the investigators, are similar across ethnic groups in the United States, while showing cultural preferences for certain behaviors, discipline methods, and gender differences in the Latino, African American, and Caucasian communities.

Two studies undertaken with adolescents reveal an interesting development in parental attachment. One study compared African American, European American, and Mexican American university students. The researchers found that the father played a more important role for this age group than for younger age groups. Additionally, there were no significant differences across the ethnic groups in the quality of attachment to either the mother or the father (Arbona & Power, 2003). These results suggest that attachment needs during adolescence are similar across ethnic groups. Another study, which compared late-adolescent Mexican American women and non-Hispanic white women, underscored the importance of the paternal attachment style for adolescent security in both white and Hispanic college women. In both adolescent groups "no maternal caregiving variables were found to be associated with security, only paternal caregiving variables" (Tacon & Caldera, 2001, p. 82). Collectively, these findings suggest that for all ethnic groups the father's role becomes increasingly more significant at later developmental stages.

These studies strongly suggest that the basic principles of attachment theory possess universality irrespective of ethnic or racial differences in the United States. These principles include (1) a primary attachment to one caregiver, (2) similar percentages of attachment classifications, with the majority of children classified as secure, and (3) a similar need across ethnicities to develop an affectional bond with a primary caretaker.

Studies with Gay and Lesbian Families

In the past few decades, the traditional definition of the nuclear family has evolved so that it now encompasses a variety of other systemic structures, among them gay and lesbian families, and an increasing number of research studies are focusing on lesbian couples who have become co-parents (Chan, Brooks, Raboy, & Patterson, 1998; Patterson, 1992; Sullivan, 1996, as mentioned in Bennett, 2003b). These studies suggest that in many respects lesbian families are not constrained by traditional heterosexual family roles (Bennett, 2003a, 2003b) and that the children in these families develop in positive ways (Patterson, 1992).

While many lesbian families decide to have biological children, a considerable number have sought to adopt children from other countries. However, there is very little research concerning lesbian adoptive families (Bennett, 2003b). The annual number of foreign-born children adopted in the United States increased from about 8,000 in 1989 to more than 19,000 in 2001 (Bennett, 2003a). Bennett (2003b) found that most children in her research (admittedly a small sample—fifteen couples with fifteen children) had a predominant attachment to one parent, as in heterosexual families. Echoing Ainsworth's studies conducted in Uganda and Baltimore a generation before, Bennett's study found that the amount of time spent with the parent proved less important than the quality of interaction, the parent's attachment style, and her personal characteristics, such as nurturing, playfulness, warmth, and patience. The unique minority status of these families, with respect to ethnicity, culture, and sexual orientation does create further complexities for children, who must learn to negotiate intricate social institutions and challenging relationships with peers and others, but lesbian families evince a pattern of attachment bonding that is very similar to that of families in the greater population. This includes the typical attachment to a primary figure as well as the predominance of a secure attachment style.

Contemporary Infant Studies

As noted in chapter 1, D. W. Winnicott, an analyst and pediatrician, was a careful observer of infants and children and their mothers, and developed a whole new lexicon to characterize his observations. Certain of these concepts (e.g., the good-enough mother, the transitional object, and the true and false self) have attained a general usage among nonclinicians paralleled only by Freud's ideas a generation earlier. Although Winnicott did not directly endorse attachment theory and continued to maintain his affiliation with the British Psychoanalytic Association, many of his ideas mirrored findings from attachment theory and research. Since his death, others have continued to observe infant and mother pairs more systematically, recording their observations in videos. Daniel Stern (1985), one of the most important of these infant researchers, decided to slow down his video recordings of these interactions in order to study kinesic, gestural, and other nonverbal aspects of the process microscopically. He discovered subtle nonverbal signals between infants and mothers, revealing interactions that seemed far more reciprocal than previously thought. Even very young infants used signals such as eye contact, turning away, or smiling in order to regulate contact with their caregivers. In effect, they seemed to be learning to self-regulate very early in life. Stern also found that well-attuned caregivers were able to help their infants achieve a greater level of affect and affect regulation through attuned mirroring and modeling.

Stern observed that young infants already demonstrated a distinct sense of self, although his findings led him to further differentiate the sense of self into three discrete developmental stages: the *emergent self*, the *core self*, and the *subjective self*. During the stage of the emergent self, Stern observed, infants as young as two months of age made direct eye contact, began to smile responsively, and chuckled at their mothers. Almost from birth, infants began to turn their heads, suck, and look around. They showed an emergent sense of agency and autonomy. Stern theorized that at the age of two to three months, infants become more social and able to focus more fully on interactions. "It is as if their actions, plans, affects, perceptions and cognitions can now all be brought into play and focused ... on an interpersonal situation" (Stern, 1985, p. 69). These infants seemed to have a more integrated sense of self even at this early stage in their development. Stern found that, in contradistinction to the then-popular separation-individuation model of Margaret Mahler, "the formation of self and other" preceded and made possible a "sense of merger-like experience" (p. 70).

Stern formulated four qualities of a core self, which infants could achieve at this stage: *self-agency,* or the authorship of one's own actions; *self-coherence,* or "having a sense of being a fragment of a physical whole"; *self-affectivity,* or "experiencing patterned inner qualities of feelings"; and *self-history,* or "having a sense of enduring, of continuity with one's own past" (p. 71). Another important aspect of the core self, for Stern, was the developing ability to be with others, which he saw as an important factor in self-integration. Once again, this finding contrasted sharply with the developmental process of differentiation that Mahler had earlier theorized. Stern argued that the caregiver's role in the baby's development was to help in regulating the infant's arousal and affect intensity, a phenomenon examined by other researchers (e.g., Beebe & Stern, 1977; Tronick & Brazelton, 1977). The observations made by Stern and his colleagues reinforced findings from attachment research that emphasized the importance of safety and exploration, both of which are linked to the development of attachment security.

Stern's final sense of self, the *subjective self,* occurs when "the infant discovers that he or she has a mind" distinct from that of others (p. 124). The infant is now able to share his or her own inner subjective experiences, such as the intention to act, a feeling state, or a focus of attention. At this stage, the emphasis of the infant's experience shifts from external actions to internal events. Stern's findings made an important contribution to Bowlby's underdeveloped theory of internal working models, charting this process of development and its gradual integration into a cohesive sense of self. Stern's emphasis on reciprocal attunement, empathy, and sense of self also seemed to corroborate ideas advanced in the 1970s and early 1980s by Heinz Kohut and others who adhered to the theoretical framework of psychoanalytic self psychology. Perhaps more pointedly, Stern's findings may also have offered an early opportunity to bridge the chasm between attachment research and clinical practice.

Beebe, Lachmann, and Lichtenberg made similarly important contributions to clinical practice based on attachment theory. These psychoanalytic clinicians applied findings from infant research to clinical practice with adult clients, which have had the effect of further narrowing the gap between clinical practice and attachment theory and research. In the social work community, however, few publications to date have addressed this topic, and schools of social work have only recently begun to include attachment theory and research in practice courses (see Bennett, 2003b; Ringel, 2003, 2004; Sable, 1992, 1995, 2000).

Attachment and Mental Disorders

Attachment and Trauma

In the past two decades a great deal of attachment research has focused on patterns of disorganized attachment (Lyons-Ruth & Jacobvitz, 1999; Main & Solomon, 1990; Solomon & George, 1999; Van Ijzendoorn, Schengle, & Bakermanns-Kranenburg, 1999). Bowlby, with his deep interest in the phenomenology of attachment disruptions and their impact on children's development, spearheaded this development. He and his colleagues observed children who had been separated from their parents through hospitalization or through death and found that children separated from their parents for prolonged periods exhibited emotional detachment. Nominally, they became avoidantly attached, although they also exhibited increasing disorientation, passivity, disconnection, and dissociation, depending on how long the separation lasted (Solomon & George, 1999). Bowlby's observations laid the groundwork for later researchers who were interested in understanding the relationship between child maltreatment and attachment patterns.

Later studies with children who demonstrated a disorganized attachment style showed the highest proportion of disorganized attachment to occur in children who were maltreated or whose mothers suffered from depression, substance abuse, or other mental illness (Lyons-Ruth, Connell, Grunebaum, & Botein, 1990). According to Main and Hesse (1990), a child's disorganized behavior reflects an experience of the parent as frightened or frightening, which precipitates an approach-withdrawal response from the child and keeps her or him linked to the parent. The authors suggest that if the mother follows up this frightening/frightened behavior with reassurance, the child will not be negatively affected (Solomon & George, 1999). These parental behaviors can be quite subtle and may not be apparent without close attention (Main & Hesse, 1990). The caregiver's empathic attunement and capacity for repairing relational ruptures with the child is reminiscent of self psychology's emphasis on the clinical process of empathic attunement and the repair of subtle empathic breaches between client and therapist. The client's growth and development are predicated upon the therapist's ability to notice and work through these moments of misattunement collaboratively with the client.

Lyons-Ruth, Bronfman, and Atwood (1999) suggested that although many parents have experienced bereavement in their own childhoods, that experience is not necessarily predictive of disorganized attachment in their children. Unresolved losses may, however, contribute to the child's disorganized attachment style. Lyons-Ruth (2003) argued that in talking about children's exposure to their parents' unresolved trauma, "it is apparent that such continuing exposure and/or periodic traumatic eruption must occur in ways that are not monitored and repaired by the caregiver. It is likely that many infants experience frightening events at the hands of their caregivers that do not become disorganizing" (p. 37). However, the parent's failure to respond empathically or to remain attuned to the child's feelings at the time may determine the child's later responses. A parent who has not experienced parental empathy, soothing, and attunement during her or his own childhood may be incapable of offering such responses to the child either because they evoke conflict-laden emotional reactions for the parent or because the child's distress may not be accurately perceived.

Attachment and Personality Disorders

The avoidant attachment style, in particular, has been linked with schizoid and narcissistic personality disorders. Avoidant children seem to respond to their caretakers' dismissive and/or neglectful behavior by overtly hiding their distress and pretending to be autonomous and self-sufficient. However, they continue to experience this rejection internally. This was discovered through the measurement of avoidant children's physiological arousal in response to the mother's apparent abandonment (Spangler & Grossmann, 1993). Interestingly, avoidant children seem to internalize their caregiver's defense of dismissal and rejection, rather than their own emotional experience, a process that leads to the development of what Winnicott would have termed a "false self" (see chapter 1). Such a false self organization, however, ensures the maintenance of the emotional bond with the caregiver (Winnicott, 1960a). Thus, avoidant children learn early in life to shield themselves from their emotional states, an attachment style that would likely compromise, if not derail, development of an authentic sense of autonomy, healthy self-esteem, and other dimensions of selfhood. A dismissive parent does not reflect back the child's feeling states, and it is difficult for the child to move on to the more complex tasks of learning to maintain appropriate boundaries, identifying and expressing complex emotional states, and finally, communicating these feelings to others (Fonagy & Target, 2003).

Lichtenberg, Lachmann, and Fosshage (2002) noted that while avoidant parents may care for children's concrete needs (e.g., food and clothing), they may show little sensitivity to affective signals and distress reactions. These authors suggested that although such children may appear indifferent to their parents, they actually tend to monitor the closeness/distance they need to maintain from others very carefully. Research findings that such children have high cortisol levels may furnish corroborative evidence of their heightened anxiety and hypervigilance. The consequence of such a prolonged pattern of attachment is that the child becomes emotionally constricted and devoid of an authentic inner life.

More recently, researchers have found two distinct avoidant styles: *fearful* and *dismissing*. Fearful attachment is characterized by a "negative view of self and others," while dismissing attachment is "typified by a positive view of self and a negative view of others" (Travis, Binder, Bliwise, & Horne-Moyer, 2001, p. 150). In the clinical situation, dismissive attachments *may* be associated with narcissistic personality disorder. According to Fonagy, the child develops a sense of alienation, when "parental caregiving is highly insensitive and misattuned" (Fonagy & Target, 2003, p. 279). The child then externalizes this alien sense of self by trying to control others in the environment, such as peers and family. During traumatic experiences, Fonagy argues, the child dissociates from pain by using the alien self to identify with the aggressor (p. 279). A child's fearful avoidant style, on the other hand, coincides with schizoid-like behavior. This behavior results from inaccurate parental mirroring of the child; consequently the child's inner experience and external presentation become disconnected, leading to a sense of inner emptiness and a "false" self. These patients become isolated and terrified of intimacy.

A third distorted process of attachment bonding has been described by Fonagy and Target (2003). This pathological adaptation to the parent's distorted mirroring occurs when unresolved parental trauma and emotional lability, or unregulated affects, are projected onto a child who, in turn, is denied the safe space in which to develop an inner self. Thus the child internalizes the parent's negative affects, which are subsequently incorporated into the child's internal working models. Rather than learning affect regulation and self-soothing from the parent, the child becomes a receptacle for the parent's own mood instability. The clinical result may be a borderline personality disorder. Patients who are diagnosed with BPD have trouble self-regulating and suffer from impulsive behaviors and significant mood fluctuations. Moreover, their interpersonal relationships are usually intense and conflictual.

Intergenerational Transmission of Attachment Trauma

Intergenerational transmission of attachment trauma occurs when parents continue to enact their unresolved traumatic bonding patterns with their own children, whether consciously or unconsciously. It was found, for example, that many children who experienced early victim-victimizer relationships become victimizers themselves (Allen, 2001; Lyons-Ruth, 1999). One relational pattern is that of a dominant-submissive enactment, in which "the parent coercively opposes and counters the initiatives of the child" (Lyons-Ruth, Bronfman, & Atwood, 1999, p. 39). Lyons-Ruth suggests that more subtle but equally controlling parental behaviors include helplessness, withdrawal, and unresponsiveness—behaviors that do not allow the child any room for personal agency. In experiments with infant rhesus monkeys raised with peers but without parental figures, researchers found that the monkeys had difficulty managing their aggressive and/or fearful responses. This demonstrated that parental withdrawal, neglect, or absence could be as harmful as abuse, and could lead to a similar result: disorganized attachment behaviors. Lyons-Ruth and Block (1996) located the behaviors of such mothers on a continuum of "hostile" to "helpless," which they linked to a history of unresolved trauma. While mothers who had experienced physical abuse tended to be intrusive and critical, mothers who had experienced sexual abuse were passive and withdrawn.

Psychological/verbal abuse and exposure to violence can also lead to serious physiological and psychological sequelae (Kemp, Rawlings, & Green, 1991). In addition to attachment disturbances, or the reenactment of abusive patterns through the process of traumatic bonding, trauma may exert other profound effects. It affects one's sense of self and feelings of self-worth, and the view of the world as a safe place where a future is possible. Traumatic events, whether experienced, witnessed, or transmitted nonverbally and unconsciously from caregiver to child, were found to have a significant impact, contributing to negative self-image, affective splitting (dissociative episodes), and a fragmented sense of self (Bradley, 2002).

In sum, attachment bonds that stem from the parents' unresolved traumatic history have been shown to have a significant impact on children's physical and psychological development, their ability to form adaptive internal working models, and their ability to engage in social, and later romantic, relationships.

Attachment and Neurobiology

In the past two decades there have been important developments in neuroscience, some of which support the findings of attachment research. Neurobiology and brain imaging techniques (e.g., positron-emission tomography, or PET scans) have shown that early relational patterns between the child and the caregiver can become permanent neurological templates, especially during the child's first few years, during which brain plasticity is greatest. The brain's executive center, the orbitofrontal cortex, is responsible for modulating emotion and behaviors that originate in the more primitive limbic system and in the amygdala, a part of the brain that is responsible for fear responses (LeDoux, 1996). Emotional responsiveness by caregivers was shown to stimulate more rapid firing of neurons in the orbitofrontal neurons, causing greater brain stimulation (Schore, 1997). Because the infant's cognitive capacities are not yet fully developed in terms of language, memory, and perception, experiences are encoded through a variety of nonverbal signals, such as gazing, facial expression, touch, and voice tone, into the limbic system and the amygdala. It is only when language and cognition are more developed that these experiences can be articulated.

In their studies of infants, Fonagy and Target (1998) found a direct link between the more primitive parts of the brain (the limbic system, which stores emotions) and the cortical system, in which the cognitive structure develops. They labeled this connection "mentalization"—the ability to transfer emotional and nonverbal body experiences into a cognitive framework, i.e., verbal memory, self-reflection, and insight. The influence of caregivers may serve to stimulate and sustain the process of creating new and more adaptive internalized patterns for interpersonal relationships. One illustration of the biological basis of internalized mental representations was revealed when PET scans of subjects who had experienced the loss of significant others showed an increased blood flow in the orbitofrontal areas. Researchers believe these findings demonstrate that relational and emotional experiences have a corresponding neurological activity (Schore, 1997). Such evidence lends increasing support to the idea that the caregiver's regulatory functions may help children increase their neuronal activities, develop new neurological structures, and ultimately, internalize appropriate self-regulatory abilities.

Researchers have found that neurobiological structures, such as memory processing, are influenced by the earliest attachment patterns between infants and caregivers (Schore, 1997). Consequently, misattuned interactions between children and caregivers may result in neurological deficits that permanently affect memory, perception, and other cognitive structures. Such evidence strongly reinforces the link between attachment patterns and brain development.

An important recent finding is the existence of *mirror neurons,* neurons that grow in the right orbitofrontal cortex as a result of attuned interactions between mother and infant. Such neuronal structures are later associated with enhanced empathic capability, the ability to pick up accurate cues and to make accurate judgments about another's reactions during interpersonal interactions (Stern, 2003). However, children who have experienced emotional deficits and who have grown up in an environment of abuse or neglect are compromised in their ability to experience empathy or to accurately read the feelings and reactions of others. Therefore, their social skills are poor, and their ability to build stable relationships is limited.

Clinical Applications of Attachment Theory and Research

The majority of publications in the attachment field still come from empirical studies rather than from clinical accounts. More clinicians, however, have started to publish clinical investigations and case studies that aim to provide a connection for attachment research with research on clinical practice with children and adults. For example, Robert Marvin, who was one of Ainsworth's students, designed a study that included clinical interventions with children who have experienced emotional deficits. Marvin and his colleagues coined the term *circle of security,* defining it as both a secure base from which to launch into the world and a safe haven to which children can return after completing their explorations (Marvin, Cooper, Hoffman, & Powell, 2002). The caregiver's functions are to encourage the child's curiosity in exploring the environment, watching over and helping the child in these explorations, and mirroring the child's delight in his or her activities. At the same time, the caregiver should welcome the child's return, to the "secure base," following these explorations. These authors' studies included group-based parent education, as well as therapeutic interventions designed to shift patterns of attachment and caregiving interaction in high-risk caregiver-child dyads. Marvin and his collaborators have had positive results using this intervention with at-risk families in the Washington, D.C., area.

Beebe and Lachmann (2002) and Lichtenberg, Lachmann, and Fosshage (2002), who are psychoanalysts as well as researchers, have written extensively on the application of concepts from attachment theory and infant research to work with adults from an intersubjective, psychodynamic perspective. Intersubjectivity theory, which traces its origins to Kohut's self psychology, emphasizes mirroring and empathy as important therapeutic tools. Self psychology and intersubjectivity theory both emphasize the fundamental importance of the clinician's empathy, regarding empathic breaches or "moments of misattunement" in the treatment process as an opportunity for growth and maturation (Beebe & Lachmann, 2002; Lichtenberg, Lachmann, & Fosshage, 2002). From an intersubjective point of view, the reciprocal interaction between client and therapist can serve as a new relational paradigm in the creation of healthier internal structures, thus helping to build new internal working models and more secure attachment bonds.

On the basis of their observations of caregiver-infant interactions, Stern and colleagues (1998) and Beebe and Lachmann (2002) also examined preverbal, presymbolic interactions in a therapeutic context. This inquiry is especially important with clients who have difficulty verbalizing and elaborating on their affective states, thoughts, and life experiences. Thus gestures, space, eye contact, and tone of voice may become important signifiers in the treatment. Moreover, the mutual affect regulation between client and clinician, and the clinician's close observation of countertransference responses, can provide a key to unverbalized enactments between client and clinician. From a relational point of view, it is important for therapists to be aware not only of their subjective responses to the patient (i.e., countertransference) but also of the patient's perception of their subjectivity toward them (Aron, 1991). Aron observes that even highly disturbed patients who are withdrawn, narcissistic, or psychotic demonstrate some basis of truth in their observations of the therapist; these observations are not simply transference-based fantasies reflecting the client's own distorted reality. Inasmuch as such observations are often communicated nonverbally and indirectly, however, the therapist needs to be attuned to a complex array of signals from the client (Aron, 1991)). Finally, it is vital for therapists to help clients reflect and find their own meanings in emotional and relational experiences, thus assisting them in the development of a capacity for metacognitive monitoring, or mentalization.

In clinical practice with clients who have experienced physical and sexual abuse and neglect, current relational and intersubjective theories are especially consonant with attachment research findings. Children who are highly attuned to their parents' cues may pick up nonverbal and unconscious signals from them and, through this process of intergenerational transmission, internalize parental signals of rejection or violence, as well as their own feelings of being unloved and unsafe. These traumatic experiences can be (re)enacted in the transference-countertransference relationship with the therapist. Davies and Frawley (1994) have elaborated on the client's "internal working models," which manifest in transference-countertransference roles enacted between client and therapist. Their enactment paradigms include the unseeing, uninvolved parent and the unseen, neglected child; the sadistic abuser and the helpless, enraged victim; the idealized omnipotent rescuer and the entitled child; and finally, the seducer and the seduced. Through such role enactments, Allen (2001) suggests, the "traumatized individual influences or coerces the partner into behavior that confirms the disavowed attribution, projection, or role" (p. 69). Important factors in the healing process are the therapist's ability to contain the trauma (i.e., help create safety), to assist clients in modulating and regulating their feelings, to help clients to reconstruct and reflect upon the traumatic event, and, finally, to help them assign new meanings. Davies and Frawley note that therapists "are always shifting between holding from the outside and reworking from the inside; between the background of containment and integration and foreground of active engagement" (p. 203).

Benjamin has elaborated on Stern's concept of a subjective self, developing the concept of mutual recognition between the child and the caregiver (Benjamin, 1995). She sees mutual recognition between child and caregiver as a maturational achievement that makes an enormous contribution to the child's development. In fact, Benjamin states, the child's (or the patient's) ability to recognize mother (or therapist) as a separate being with her own needs and limitations indicates the child's acquisition of a sense of self. In the context of intersubjective treatment, the child's cognitive and affective functions can be enhanced through the relational matrix between client and therapist in a process of self and mutual regulation, and through the resolution of old relational paradigms that may be enacted within the treatment. From a self psychological point of view, the therapist can meet the client's emotional needs, aid in the client's consolidation of a secure sense of self, and finally, through empathically attuned mirroring, assist the client in the creation of more adaptive attachment bonds (Kohut, 1977).

Children | FIVE

Recent years have brought increasing interest in translating the now-con-siderable body of research on human attachment into clinical terms. This chapter will focus specifically on what contributions attachment theory makes to our understanding of child psychopathology and how it may serve as a guide in the clinical assessment and treatment of children. Are existing conceptions of childhood psychopathology enhanced through an understanding of attachment? Does attachment theory offer a unique lens that may be used to understand the process of therapy with children, or does it go even further, furnishing the clinician with a distinctive model for the conduct of therapy that is substantively different from existing dy-namic treatment frameworks? How may knowledge of a child's attachment history influence our conceptions of such phenomena as transference and the child-therapist relationship more generally? Endeavoring to address these as well as other questions, this chapter will also furnish several repre-sentative clinical vignettes and one lengthier clinical case illustration to highlight the potential significance of a clinical child model informed by attachment theory. [1]

Attachment and Pathology in Childhood

Much remains unknown about the relationship between patterns of attachment in infancy and the development of later psychopathology. Although it is tempting to establish an etiological connection, for example, between a latency-age child's school phobia and an infantile pattern of insecure attachment, such associations must be made with caution. To begin with, human development is both complex and dynamic, so that even relatively young children are subject to an array of influences, both endogenous and extrinsic, that shape their course of development. Rarely is it possible to explain the development of an emotional disorder or other form of psychopathology on the basis of a single cause, an idea to which the psychoanalytic principle of *overdetermination* attests. This principle (also referred to as *multideterminism*) stipulates that causation in virtually any aspect of psychic life, including behavior, pathological symptoms, dreams, and so forth, is codetermined by a variable number of intersecting paths. Moreover, the presence of *risk factors* (e.g., poverty, family violence, parental psychopathology) has also been shown to exert a variety of effects on the pathogenesis of childhood disorders.[2]

Without minimizing the importance of such risk factors (and their mitigative counterparts) or the general significance of multideterminism in arriving at a meaningful understanding of the forces that contribute to psychopathology in childhood, it may nevertheless be possible to use attachment theory to clinical advantage both during assessment and in the treatment that follows. Indeed, one prominent attachment researcher has asserted that attachment considerations can serve as an important guide not only in considering the origins of a particular problem but also in subsequent recommendations for treatment (Sroufe, 2003). Relationships have been hypothesized to exist between infantile patterns of attachment insecurity and a number of discrete child psychopathologies. These include but are hardly limited to oppositional defiant disorder (DeKlyen, Speltz, & Greenberg, 1996); gender identity disorder (Birkenfeld-Adams, 1996, cited in Goldberg, 1997); patterns of disruptive behavior (Greenberg et al., 1993); depression (Greenberg, 1999); and anxiety disorders (Greenberg, Speltz, & DeKlyen, 1999). However, such relationships between attachment insecurity and later psychopathology, while perhaps making clinical sense, have remained largely speculative, owing principally to the fact that attachment security can be ascertained directly and reliably only between the ages of twelve and eighteen months (via the Strange Situation procedure); clinical assessments of children who are of preschool age or older become a more challenging and somewhat less certain undertaking.

Clinical Assessment

Various instruments and assessment procedures have been used, albeit with mixed success, in efforts to assess children's quality of attachment in middle and late childhood. One method, a Q-sort technique designed to assess quality of attachment in children up to age five, asks parents to arrange a list of ninety items describing children in relationships according to categories descriptive of their own child (Waters & Deane, 1985). This Attachment Q-Sort, which is designed for use in the home, has not yet been used in clinical studies, although it apparently yields results that are comparable to earlier Strange Situation assessments (Sroufe, 2003). Various projective techniques that rely on children's responses to picture-stimulus cards or stories have also been adapted in research studies to examine attachment themes. One such measure is based on a child's responses to a set of six photographs that portray themes associated with attachment ranging from mild (parent saying good night to a child) to stressful (child watching a parent leave). A classification system developed by Kaplan (1987) assigns one of four attachment categories (*resourceful, inactive, ambivalent,* or *fearful*) to the responses, depending upon the child's emotional openness and ability to conceive of constructive solutions to the feelings evoked by separation (Solomon & George, 1999). In an adaptation of Kaplan's classification system using pictures that portrayed long parental separations, representational classifications of a group of seven-year-old subjects apparently corresponded significantly to Strange Situation classifications for the same children at eighteen months (Jacobsen, Edelstein, & Hoffman, 1994; Solomon & George, 1999). Bretherton and colleagues (Bretherton, 1999) developed a different kind of representational method for measuring attachment security in three-year-olds, involving the use of attachment-specific story themes, which were presented to the children, who were then asked to describe "what happens next" as well as to enact their narratives through doll play. Additional systems and typologies for classifying qualitative dimensions of attachment in children of preschool and kindergarten age include the Main-Cassidy Attachment Classification System (1988), Crittendon's Preschool Assessment of Attachment

(Crittendon, 1992, 1994), and the Cassidy-Marvin System (Cassidy & Marvin, 1987). However, because most of these systems were designed specifically for use in research studies, they are for the most part not easily adapted to clinical settings.

Sroufe (2003) has suggested that the developmental history may yield critical information regarding a child's attachment history, though such data are "embedded" and would likely require follow-up questions. Examples might include parental descriptions of the child as having always been a "troublemaker," or as constitutionally incapable of listening to the parents, or as "always" well behaved and good, without any further elaboration by the parents. Sroufe also notes that clinicians are well advised to ascertain when and in what manner early disruptions in family relationships may have occurred and, more significantly, how coherently the child was able to organize such experience(s) (2003). Analogously, the child's social history may also prove revealing. What is the assessment of the child's current social functioning? What sort of peer relationships has the child had, and are such relationships valued? Does the child demonstrate a capacity for empathy with others?

Clinical assessment also affords the clinician an opportunity to inquire about early separations. Although separation is a ubiquitous theme in human development, its occurrence acquires a particular meaning in the context of early attachment. One wishes to understand not only the timing of such separations but also the way in which they were managed by child and parents. Does a pattern of reaction and response suggesting attachment insecurity or disorganization emerge in the parental descriptions of day-to-day separation events? Are there other events detailed in the family history, such as a parental separation or divorce, or the placement of a maternal grandmother in a nursing facility, that reveal disruptions in the child's relationship system? Some research suggests that in a latency-age child the capacity for stable peer relationships characterized by empathy, loyalty, and relational competence is associated with a secure attachment history (Sroufe, Egeland, & Carlson, 1999).

Although complex and multifactorial, another important source of clinical data is of course the child's relatedness to the therapist during the assessment. It is true that even children with secure attachment histories are ordinarily not enthusiastically receptive to the prospect of therapy. They are not favorably disposed to discussing their wishes or intrapsychic conflicts, and most are brought into therapy, sometimes quite unwillingly, by their parents.

Indeed, treatment may at times be initiated with the child's expression of anger or resentment against parents, teachers, and therapist, although such reactions are typically short-lived. However, therapists might also wish to pay somewhat closer attention to other relational qualities. Sroufe writes: "Aspects of social behavior that may reflect attachment qualities include (1) how the child uses the caregiver as a resource, especially in separating from that person, (2) the quality of cooperation and the regard for emotional honesty in presentation with the therapist, and (3) the quality of emotional regulation that is exhibited" (Sroufe, 2003, p. 213).

The Clinical Diagnostic Interview: The Technique of Autogenic Storytelling

A number of time-honored diagnostic and play techniques with children may serve the purpose of eliciting dynamically significant fantasies and other psychologically meaningful information with particular relevance to the theme of attachment. Aside from those techniques already mentioned, others might include formal projective instruments such as the Roberts Apperception Test or the Children's Apperception Test; semi-structured projective techniques, as for example, kinetic family drawing or house-tree-person drawing; and unstructured play techniques, such as painting and drawing, mud and clay, doll play, or puppetry. In practice, the therapist conducting a clinical child assessment usually makes use of several such techniques in combination.

One relatively simple technique that has proven useful in child assessment is that of *autogenic or stimulus-independent stories*. Although children's stories and storytelling activities are a more or less universal feature of dynamic child treatment, autogenic (make-believe) stories in the context of clinical assessment have not usually been advocated with the same degree of confidence. We know, however, that children's stories constitute an important source of data with respect to intrapsychic structure, characteristic conflicts, and defensive adaptations (Brandell, 2000; Gardner, 1993). They may also furnish us with valuable information about disturbing wishes and fantasies, the development of the self and other aspects of character, and interpersonal relations. Significantly, such stories may also provide a window into the nature of a child's attachments, anxieties that stem from attachment failures or thwarted attachment needs, and overall pattern of attachment.

Assessing Attachment Security via Children's Autogenic Stories

Autogenic stories, in most instances, are elicited midway through the initial diagnostic interview. Children who express curiosity as to the clinician's reasons for requesting a story from them can be told that their made-up stories, like pictures and other play activities, help the clinician to better understand the nature of their problems and ways in which they can be helped to solve them. The self-conscious or shy child may be assisted in starting the story ("Once upon a time, there was a …"), although the clinician is advised to be especially careful not to suggest content to the child. This diagnostic technique is nonreciprocal inasmuch as the therapist offers no story in response to the child's. However, most children will cooperate with the request for one or two such stories, much as they would with a request for a house-tree-person drawing or with other fundamentally (nonreciprocal) diagnostic procedures.

In the following three case vignettes, all drawn from the first or second clinical interview, particular attachment problems subsequently elaborated over the course of treatment are highlighted in the child's autogenic story. Although each story also suggests other, equally significant clinical issues, our focus here is more specific to the information the stories can furnish us about attachment themes and issues.

Clinical Example 1

When Sean was five, his natural parents relinquished custody so that he might be placed in a foster home. It is undoubtedly an understatement to describe his relationships by that time with both of the parents, particularly his mother, as irreparably damaged. Although Sean was completely out of control, destroying furniture and willfully urinating on the carpet and walls, the intensity of his hatred was equaled by theirs; they urgently requested foster placement in the interest of their survival and his.

Sean had been afflicted with a relatively rare neonatal condition known as pyloric stenosis, in which a malformation of the valve connecting the pylorus to the duodenum prevents a baby from digesting milk. Its most common symptom is a rather dramatic one, projectile vomiting. In Sean's case, owing to a combination of professional oversight and maternal denial, this serious condition went undiagnosed for a period of some six weeks, during which time his mother's frustration in feeding him developed into a deep sense of maternal inadequacy and incompetence; both were most certainly mirrored in the disturbed mother-infant relationship that followed. Perhaps it is no exaggeration to speculate that their early, painful experience became a sort of template repeatedly and unconsciously applied to later experiences. Regardless, Sean was a difficult baby whose physical problems and temperament brought little joy to his parents.

Sean was eleven years old by the time I began to work with him. He had spent the last half of his life being shuffled from one placement to another. When our meetings began, he was a co-resident in a privately operated group home staffed by a couple in their sixties who had been hired to serve as "treatment parents" for the eight or nine children in their care. A bright child with a fanciful imagination, Sean already demonstrated a significant degree of emotional disturbance. He had tremendous difficulty in negotiating interpersonal relationships, often losing his temper with other children, teachers, or the adult staff at the group home. He rarely sought out the adult mentors in the treatment home for counsel or comfort, instead evincing a sort of pseudoautonomy. He was quite impulsive; his moods were unpredictable and often vacillated between extremes, further compromising his ability to maintain control over powerful emotions that threatened to overwhelm him. Although a more traditional understanding of Sean's moodiness, impulsiveness, and difficulty in exercising good judgment evokes Freud's metaphor of the id as a "riderless horse" (Freud, 1923)—a bundle of impulses and disturbing wishes and fantasies continually threatening to erupt without the steadying influence of the ego—attachment theory provides us with an alternative view. Attachment theorists would suggest that Sean's difficulty in reining in his powerful emotions stemmed from early attachment insecurity. The more salient developmental derailment is not in the ego per se, but rather in Sean's internal working model of attachment, which sustained an early and massive injury. Because Sean's mother believed herself to be an incompetent mother and her interactions with Sean beginning in early infancy had been fraught with such pain and distress, she became virtually incapable of helping him to regulate and contain his moods, of holding him to calm and soothe him. On the contrary, she began to consider Sean to represent a threat to her own psychological survival as well as that of her family. When his history of marked developmental lags, evident failure to develop a capacity for mentalization, and other deviations and abnormalities was integrated with the emerging clinical picture, the result strongly suggested a nascent borderline personality organization.

During our initial meeting, Sean seemed somewhat intrigued by my request that he "make up" a story, and he produced the first of some sixty stories he was to tell over nine months of twice-weekly treatments. This is what he presented, in dark, almost somber tones:

SEAN'S STORY

Once upon a time there was a cat who lived in a lost alley, and he was all alone. He had no friends. He would catch rats in a trash can and eat them, but he would still feel lonely. One day, he was out on a walk feeling grumpy as usual, and lonely, and kind of low-headed. He walked out and all of a sudden he heard a purr. It was another cat, exactly like him. Same breed, same everything, same eyes, same looks. So they decided to get together and play tricks on people, and they would go and knock on a door. They would scratch on the door to get the people's attention, and then the people would keep them. And then one cat had a favorite sport of clawing people. So, he went scratching on the door, the people kept him and then they sent him to the Humane Society. They thought he was kinda playful, kinda scratchy, but kinda playful. That night the (first) cat snuck out and the other cat came in. The next morning the people were talking about how scratchy he is and that they might have to send him to the Humane Society. [When asked at this juncture to identify the two cats, Sean said Cat Number 1 is the scratchy cat and Cat Number 2 plays with yarn.] So all of a sudden Cat Number 2 snuck in. He looked like he was kinda lonely or something, so the people were thinking that maybe they would send him to someone who might want him. So that morning— the mother knits and she dropped some yarn—the cat started playing with the yarn, so she grabbed the cat and she goes, "The cat doesn't scratch, the cat doesn't scratch!" The cat didn't scratch her. So all was well, you know. They thought, "Oh, wow! Our cat doesn't scratch anymore." So they got their friends over that night, and they (the friends) saw the cat. "Wow, is he nice," they said, and then they got done playing with the cat. That night, while they were asleep the other cat (Cat Number 1) came in. And he started scratching at the covers and everything. Well, they decided that there were two cats, or else he has two personalities. So they went out into the alley, and they caught both of the cats in their little pranks. So they sent them to the Humane Society, and the Humane Society sent them back because they did not want them. And that's what they did. You see, the year right now is 2020. And they took them to a cat place, you know, where cats eat with spoons, and they have meetings, and they play around. So, they kinda adopted the place after a while, and it just gets kinda neat.

Moral: I guess you could probably say the moral is like killing two birds with one stone, 'cause they went out and caught both of the cats. They didn't kill them, but they got them.

Analysis

This story proved to be an exceedingly rich one. The two cats are Sean's personal representatives, his "good" and "bad" parts. There is evidence here of a prominent use of splitting, as well as of concretization. The selection of "cats" as a personal representative seemed at once to reflect Sean's impulsive nature, his pseudoautonomy, and his aggressiveness. The "scratchy" cat at times seems to act in concert with the "playful" cat, although at other times it is held solely responsible for the mischief it creates. We are not surprised to learn that the "scratchy" cat's impulsivity has rather predictably alienated its owners, who finally reject both of the cats. These cats, however, are so undesirable and incorrigible that not even the Humane Society will take them in. In the story's conclusion, there is an attempt at once both magical and desperate to transform multiple experiences of rejection into the assertive adoption of a new home, with a fairly transparent allusion to the group home environment.

Sean's narrative account was especially valuable in that it provided significant psychodiagnostic information about his nuclear conflict and characteristic defensive operations at a very early point in the treatment process. Sean's expectation, like that of many children whose early histories are fraught with traumatic separations and whose attachments are consequently insecure, was that his basic needs for emotional support and stability would remain unmet, not unlike those of the two cats. Given the early history I had obtained, as well as the prominence of the rejection/abandonment theme in this story, I hypothesized that Sean's early attachment pattern was likely of the *avoidant* variety. He had learned, as did the cats in his highly evocative story, that it is dangerous to seek comfort from caregivers, whose behavior is ultimately not only thwarting but rejecting. Once others came to know him, they would recognize him for what he was, history would repeat itself, and he would experience yet another painful rejection. Clinical experience with Sean both confirmed the nuclear significance of this abandonment/rejection motif and supplied regular opportunities to assess clinical improvement.

Clinical Example 2

Robert was a ten-year-old boy whose academic performance had declined steadily despite his high intelligence and the ambitious efforts of both his teachers and his parents. There was also a history of provocative and hostile behavior toward his three siblings and, to a lesser extent, his parents. He frequently violated minor rules at home, at times displaying a striking level of immaturity, was stubborn and noncompliant, and had recently resorted to throwing temper tantrums when he was unable to get his own way. Perhaps on good behavior for my benefit, Robert required little prompting to tell the following story during his initial diagnostic interview:

ROBERT'S STORY

Once upon a time, a long time ago, there was a Prince that was planning on marrying a Princess of a King that lived about a mile away. And the Prince invited the Princess and he had a Grand Ball. They had their wedding session and they didn't know it, but these wicked creatures got invited along with all the other guests. One of the creatures really wanted the Prince and Princess to be bad. This creature appeared in the form of a goose with wings on it, and she said, "The next baby you have will die of thirst and nothing will help it." And so, they had a baby. And a couple of weeks later, it started getting skinnier and skinnier, and you could see its bones popping out. And the Prince and Princess, they took him to the Royal Treatment Center, and the Treatment Center couldn't do anything, so they just let it die. The baby was blind, but it wasn't wicked. Moral: You shouldn't always have to be mean or wicked. You can be nice sometimes and sometimes you can be mean.

Analysis

A sad and tragic tone seemed to pervade Robert's story, in which he revealed some vitally important information about himself and his view of the world. The Prince and Princess can be seen as parent-representatives and the tragically flawed infant as Robert himself, who was undersized for his age and had to wear corrective lenses because of poor vision. In his story, Robert depicts himself as a victim of circumstances, a small and completely vulnerable infant whose inability to derive sustenance and gratification from his environment is the result of an evil spell cast over his parents; he suggests that the Prince and Princess are not responsible for the tragic fate that befalls their infant son, although on the other hand, they do appear to disregard the warning of the wicked goose. This is a child for whom there is no hope, only the inevitability of (psychological) starvation and death.

Robert's mother was a woman in her late thirties who related cordially, if somewhat obsessionally, during the interview. Her focus on her son's behavior showed little recognition of her role in contributing to his emotional reactions, although he often became petulant and oppositional in direct consequence of her inability to allow him psychological distance. What she saw as an appropriate level of maternal concern and involvement not only was excessive but also powerfully communicated both her guilt and the expectation that her son really could not function well enough on his own—an expectation, according to the history the parents were able to provide, that was established before Robert turned two. His father was a warm, emotionally accessible individual who was able to relate to Robert in a more natural, empathic, and less conflicted way, although his influence was largely eclipsed by that of Robert's mother.

Returning to Robert's story, it seems possible to understand the "wicked creatures," and especially the goose, as symbolizing fearful experiences with his mother. Robert's rage had a narcissistic core and was directed at his mother both because he held her responsible for his small size and poor vision and because his mother by her actions confirmed his greatest fear—that without her he will not be able to survive. His mother's historical inability to respond empathically to his needs left him with an unstable and unconsolidated self-identity. Approaching this from a somewhat different vantage point, we could say that her difficulty in modulating the quality of her involvement with him led to significant variations in the kind and degree of maternal caregiving. Her pattern, of which she developed some awareness during her son's treatment, was to compensate for any perceived lapses in caregiving by becoming dramatically overindulgent. This proved an important influence in the development of Robert's attachment pattern, one that was predominantly of the *ambivalent* kind. Like most ambivalently attached children, Robert had adopted a strategy in which the expression of attachment behaviors was maximized, and he remained in a state of hypervigilance vis-à-vis his caregivers, urgently signaling his needs almost as soon as they became palpable (Main & Hesse, 1990). Nevertheless, Robert had little faith that his mother or other caregivers would be able to meet such needs. The fact that in the story the infant's fate is incontrovertible despite the heroic measures performed at the "Royal Treatment Center" (i.e., the mental health agency) may be considered a profound expression of this child's despair.

The moral, which does not at first appear to have direct bearing upon the story, actually contains a statement with a great deal of psychological meaning. In his admonishment that people should be "mean" some of the time and "nice" at other times, Robert is really describing his mother's difficulty in modulating her own affective involvement with him. His subjective experience of her is of a rigid person whose "meanness" (empathic failure) has had far-reaching ramifications for his psychological growth.

Although its full clinical significance could not be grasped immediately, Robert's story provided a point of departure for hypothesis making and later therapeutic investigation. On a purely intuitive level, it served to establish the fragility of Robert's self-esteem and the degree to which his narcissistic integrity had been compromised by repeated injury. Notably, this thematic material was not nearly as distinctly represented in Robert's other productions and activities during the diagnostic phase as it was in this initial autogenic story.

Clinical Example 3

Derek, a rotund and rather shy ten-year-old boy, was referred to a family service agency because of declining academic performance and moderate behavioral difficulties at school and at home. He lived with his maternal aunt, who had recently assumed Derek's legal custody when his mother was hospitalized for inpatient treatment of her alcoholism. By agreement with the Department of Social Services and with Derek's approval, he had remained with his aunt and uncle after his mother's release into a halfway-house program a month later; he stayed there throughout most of the time he was in treatment. I found Derek to be quite cooperative during our early encounters, but even after a couple of diagnostic interviews I still had no sense that I really knew him, that I understood the nature of his behavioral problems or difficulties at school. Although he had attempted to compose a story at my request, he steadfastly maintained that nothing came to mind. Such a response to the interviewer's request is not uncommon in children of this age, and may simply be a function of the newness of the treatment situation, but it may also signal deficiencies in mentalization. Derek's frustration seemed quite genuine, so I suggested that we draw pictures together instead. He immediately agreed to this, at which point we started on squiggles.[3] After each of us had taken a few turns, I asked Derek to compose a story based upon his completed drawing. He did so almost effortlessly, and with no further coaxing from me.

DEREK'S STORY ("THE RIVER")

This is a river that is crazy and never stops emptying, and it has animals in it that never die. It also has food in it that never goes bad. And the most important thing is that the animals never go down the stream. Also, it's super because it's nice, fresh water, and half the cause of the animals never dying. The best and worst thing about "The River" is that if any person gets in it and gets outside it soon enough, then that person will never die. The worst part about it is that if you stay in it long enough, you'll die as soon as you get out of it.

Analysis

Derek's story contained a wellspring of dynamic information and yielded a far more intimate and detailed portrait of this disturbed youngster than I had been able to obtain up to that point. "The River" seemed to be Derek's way of symbolizing his relationship with his mother, a deeply troubling one that had posed nearly insurmountable obstacles for him. In the first place, Derek's river is "crazy," an allusion to her disturbing alcoholic behavior. Of additional significance is the intrauterine imagery here. The river appears to offer protection to the animals that live in it, but there is a catch: they mustn't go downstream. Furthermore, immortality (or perhaps enduring psychological well-being) is ensured for those who venture out of the river as long as they have not remained in the water for too long—but if, on the other hand, one remains immersed for an extended period, physical/psychological separation from the river means certain and swift death. Recast in the language of attachment theory, such a conundrum immediately suggests a pattern of *ambivalent* attachment—in which the prospect of separation poses a risk equal to that of being in sustained contact with the "source."

The precise nature of Derek's template for attachments was somewhat less clear than the story data might have suggested. There had also been a profoundly inconsistent pattern of caregiving in Derek's early childhood, and one might hypothesize that his mother's alcoholism had led to repeated, traumatic lapses in her availability, a developmental threshold that must typically be passed en route to the development of such a pattern, which we would term *disorganized attachment*. Furthermore, research has shown a rather high association between family risk factors such as alcohol and substance abuse and this particular pattern of attachment (Fonagy, 2001). Derek's story and his other early productions portrayed a significant psychological struggle associated with his inability to use his mother as a safe base from which to explore. Derek had been conceived during a very brief relationship that had ended prior to his birth. He had no contact with his birth father and was unable to learn very much about him from his mother. In piecing together what I could from several interviews with Derek's mother and other early history made available to me, it also seemed that even when Derek's mother was physically available, she was nevertheless largely unable to interpret her son's attachment-related cues with any accuracy. By her own admission, this occurred because her own mental state nearly always took precedence over that of her son. Of course, this situation created a rather striking dyssynchrony in exchanges between mother and son, a hallmark of which was the relative absence of mutual regulation (Fonagy, 2001). She confessed that because of her alcoholism, she had often simply been incapable of providing for any but the most basic of his physical needs. The quality and intensity of her connection to Derek was also rather unpredictable; at times she viewed him as perhaps the sole source of meaning in her life, and at other times she experienced him as a great psychological burden.

Since there can be no true attachment security when maternal supplies are both unpredictable and poorly matched to a child's developmental needs, it is not surprising that Derek's internal working model of attachment evolved into one with such disorganized features. Lacking a primary caregiver who could reliably identify, mirror, and respond to his affect states, he had been unable to develop a capacity for either "felt security" or mentalization. He had a correspondingly limited capacity for understanding the feeling states of others, and he was, not unexpectedly, deeply mistrustful of the capacity of anyone—his mother, his teachers, or his aunt—to offer him the attachment security that he craved. Consequently, Derek's relationships with adults as well as peers tended to be characterized by deep suspiciousness.

Returning to Derek's story, there is the strong suggestion that it was the poor judgment or some other fatal flaw of the creatures in the river that led to their demise, rather than the river's misattunement or neglect in failing to assist its inhabitants in determining which "supplies" they required and for how long. Here Derek reveals his unconscious judgment that the ultimate responsibility for his dilemma resides with his own flawed internal working model of attachment. The river could not confer strength or immunity because it possessed neither; ergo, the locus of responsibility must be with the creatures, all of which we can probably assume stand for Derek.

Coming as it did in an early interview, this story offered important insights about Derek, his compromised attachment security, and the psychological traumas to which he had been chronically exposed from infancy onward—insights emerging initially in the form of clinical hypotheses and developing gradually as his therapy evolved. "The River" proved an especially generative narrative account and remained an important referent over the course of treatment.

Incorporating Principles of Attachment Theory Into the Psychotherapeutic Process

The clinician's understanding of a child's attachment history as this is revealed during the clinical assessment may, as the preceding examples indicate, offer valuable opportunities for generating clinical hypotheses that may then be tested as treatment gets under way. However, we would submit that such clinical understanding may also *guide* the therapeutic process. Avoidantly attached children, those with resistant or ambivalent attachments, or those with attachments of the disorganized type offer particular challenges and require different clinical approaches. For example, children whose attachments are of the avoidant type may appear to respond well to therapy but in fact require longer than other children to develop genuine trust, frequently evoking the therapist's pity and remaining ever vigilant for any signs that may be interpreted as the therapist's rejection. Ambivalently attached children might also engage readily in the process of therapy but eventually reveal the ambivalence and emotional instability that have characterized their earlier development (Sroufe, 2003).

The length of treatment, as well as the spacing of sessions, may also be meaningfully associated with the nature of a child's attachment difficulties. For example, a child whose early development has been disrupted by trauma, thus leading to a disorganized attachment experience, may well require a longer period of treatment than children who present with different attachment histories.

Transference

As one might expect, the significance of a child's attachment experience is probably most clearly expressed through the transference relationship. We are defining transference as a reflexive, unconscious repetition or revivification of varying combinations and patterns of ideas, fantasies, affects, attitudes, or behavior originally experienced in relation to a significant figure (generally a parent) and subsequently displaced onto an interpersonal relationship in the present (Brandell, 2004). In the case of children, however, parents continue to exert influence over their daily lives. Accordingly, the sort of "pure" transference displacements we associate with adult treatment, in which the client's parents have been relegated to the timelessness of memory, are generally not possible in the therapy of children. Nevertheless, many psychoanalytic child clinicians (e.g., Abrams, 1993; Chused, 1988, 1992; Fonagy & Sandler, 1996) are in agreement today that children can and do experience transference reactions, that a thorough understanding of transference themes and issues is essential to effective child treatment, and that the systematic analysis of transference is central to effective child analytic work (Yanof, 1996).

In the following detailed clinical illustration, we have attempted to show how principles of attachment theory have been used to advantage not only in enhancing the therapist's overall understanding of the case, in particular the nature of the therapeutic process and important meanings of the client's transference, but also how attachment considerations have actually shaped the conduct of the treatment itself.

Clinical Illustration 1: The Case of Nathan

Nathan was ten at the time of referral and lived with his adoptive mother, his twelve-year-old brother, and his fifteen-year-old half sister.[4] His principal presenting features included disorganized behavior, difficulty in modulating and expressing affects, poor impulse control, rageful outbursts, and marked competitive relations with his siblings. Some six months earlier, Nathan's adoptive parents had separated; his father subsequently announced his intention to seek a divorce, moved nearly two thousand miles away, and abruptly ceased all communication with Nathan, his brother, and his sister. All three children were profoundly affected, and all became symptomatic in the wake of their parents' breakup and their father's abandonment. Such family disintegration would generate considerable upheaval even in the lives of children whose early development was quite healthy. Nathan's infancy and early childhood, however, were not. His natural mother was addicted to alcohol and several other drugs and was episodically involved in prostitution to support her addictions. She had a series of live-in relationships with men; Nathan and his brother were the offspring of one such relationship, which ended shortly after Nathan's birth, and his half sister was the product of an earlier liaison.

When Nathan was still an infant, his mother often left him in the care of the sister, although she was barely six years old herself at the time. At the age of approximately two years, Nathan was forced by his older siblings into a basement room; when they left to play with friends, Nathan remained there for several hours until neighbors responded to his frantic cries for help. On at least one occasion, all three children were left for an extended period without any food, an incident that led to the involvement of child protective services and, in turn, to temporary foster care. The profound maternal neglect that Nathan experienced in this highly pathogenic environment was compounded by his mother's unpredictable and occasionally abusive or even sadistic behavior. (One of Nathan's earliest memories was of being forced by his mother and his older brother to eat his own vomitus.)

Nathan was approximately two and a half when his mother was arrested for driving while intoxicated after a traffic accident. He and his siblings were in the car at the time; they watched their mother being led away in handcuffs, and that, in fact, was the last time they saw her. Nathan was placed in a series of foster homes and separated from his brother and sister during much of the two-year period preceding their adoption—a separation that must have intensified the dislocation and loss he had already experienced.

Whatever caregiving came his way in such a bleak and impoverished interpersonal environment was not attuned to his requirements for physical and emotional sustenance. Indeed, the desolate relational landscape of Nathan's environment captures the essence of the *continuous construction model* of trauma (Zeanah, Anders, Seifer, & Stern, 1989), whereby trauma must be understood relative to the context within which it occurs—and it is more likely to occur when the child is exposed to a chronic and unremitting pattern of insensitive and unattuned caregiving. This is not to deny that single, massive psychological or physical traumas exert profound and enduring effects on psychological behavior (Eth & Pynoos, 1985) but, rather, to affirm the power of traumas involving *prolonged* privation, deprivation, or psychological or physical abuse.

Significantly, Nathan's relationship with his mother was a study in *disorganized attachment*. Although Nathan was naturally inclined to seek physical comfort from her, she had also become a source of fear, in large measure owing to her frank physical abuse. Furthermore, her physical availability was frighteningly unpredictable, and her absences, both during the day and at night, were relatively common. Indeed, even when she was physically available and not behaving abusively, she might be largely incapable of anything resembling attuned care, either because of the acute effects of alcohol and other drugs or, more generally, because of a characterological narcissism that elevated the prominence of her own needs far beyond those of any of her three children. The consequences of the combined effect of these elements were powerful and developmentally disruptive for Nathan. More specifically, owing to this abiding confusion and chaos, he was unable to develop a coherent internal working model of attachment; therefore, even though Nathan's attachment needs might propel him to seek comfort from physical proximity with his mother, she was either not available at times of need or, as described above, incapable of responding maternally. As Sroufe has noted, "Human evolutionary history disposes the child both to run *to* the attachment figure when frightened, and to run *from* the source of the fright" (2003, p. 472). In effect, Nathan's mother represented both of these: though she was Nathan's primary attachment figure, she also was a tremendous source of fear. Faced with the essential paradox of these irreconcilable positions, Nathan developed an attachment pattern best described as *disorganized/disoriented*. As suggested earlier, such a pattern is often associated with risk factors such as parental child maltreatment (Carlson, Cicchetti, Barnett, & Braunwald, 1989; George & Main, 1979; Lyons-Ruth, Repacholi, McLeod, & Silva, 1991) and parental alcoholism (O'Connor, Sigman, & Brill, 1987).

According to his adoptive mother, Nathan at four and a half was incapable of dressing himself, could not use eating utensils properly, and had the personal hygiene skills of a two-and-a-half- or three-year-old. He arrived without any personal possessions aside from a few articles of old clothing. Nathan and his older brother, Hollis, soon began to fight constantly, and Hollis, who reportedly had been sexually abused while in foster care, attempted to reenact this abuse on his younger brother. Fortunately for Nathan and his brother and sister, their adoptive mother was deeply committed to making the adoption work, even when her marriage began to fail.[5]

Slightly above average in intelligence and reasonably verbal, with a good imagination, Nathan seemed to be a good candidate for psychoanalytically oriented individual treatment. Although we used a relatively wide range of play modalities, including therapeutic and conventional board games, dolls, puppets, clay, and sociodrama, he especially enjoyed reciprocal drawing and storytelling games, and these techniques were used with some frequency during the three years we worked together. The following story transcription is a verbatim dialogue derived from an interview that occurred shortly after the initial diagnostic session. Its theme of traumatic separation and abandonment was to become a very common one in the early phase of Nathan's psychotherapy.

The Lost Kids

CHILD: Once upon a time, there was a cat and a dog and all these little children. One time, all these little children got lost. The little girl said, "We're lost! We're lost!" They seen a dog, and the dog said, "Are you lost?" They said, "Yes." Then the cat came along and said, "We'll give you a ride back to where you're supposed to be." Then they took them back where they were supposed to be, and they were happy. That's the end.

THERAPIST: Can you tell me what the story teaches us?

CHILD: It's about people getting lost and helping them, the dog and the cat helped them.

THERAPIST: So, how would you say the lesson? When you get lost, what should you do?

CHILD: Yell.

THERAPIST: Yell?

CHILD: For help.

Analysis

Nathan's story is as important for what it reveals as for what it fails to convey. The readily identifiable theme comes as no great surprise in light of his multiple separation and abandonment traumas. The children in the story, however, express neither fear nor even mild anxiety over being lost; they are simply "happy" when returned to "where they were supposed to be." Like the storyteller, they seem to have difficulty in experiencing, identifying, and, ultimately, giving expression to powerful affects. Such difficulties in affectivity and in the capacity for verbalization, sometimes collectively referred to as *alexithymia*, may be associated with *anhedonia* (the inability to experience pleasure) or impairment in the capacity for self-care, and are in turn often rooted in a lack of maternal responsiveness to a child's earliest attachment behaviors.[6] From a somewhat different perspective, the story, in its magical resolution of the separation situation, furnishes relatively little evidence of anything resembling self-regulatory function of the protagonists (and hence the storyteller). Nowhere do the children console themselves with the idea that they are only temporarily lost or that they will find a way to be reunited with their parents, and so forth.

Indeed, the children in Nathan's story seem unable to resolve their own problems without the use of magical solutions: A dog and a cat appear to assess the situation and then rescue the "lost" children. Nathan's omission of human characters in the "rescue" is of particular interest, for it suggests that the parents of these lost children were not especially reliable or concerned; in fact, they are conspicuously absent from the story. The only characters that seem to have any genuine concern for the welfare of the children are the cat and the dog. In this respect, the story seems to portray a model of attachment that makes attachment figures more or less interchangeable with each other and at the same time diminishes the importance of the primary attachment figures. There has been such profound disappointment in the world of human attachments—one might infer—that the animals offer a far safer alternative. One might also say that the unspoken terror of abandonment, the ensuing state of helplessness, and the paralysis of ego functions are all represented in this brief account. In all likelihood, Nathan's story recapitulates several specific traumatogenic events that occurred before he was three years old; at the same time, it portrays the chronic and enduring aspects of his early caregiving environment and a fairly primitive level of adaptation. The latter is underscored by the noticeable failure of the story protagonists even to *seek* help from adults. Furthermore, there is scant evidence in this story of the storyteller's capacity for mentalization. Indeed, at this early point in treatment, Nathan is largely unable to reflect on his inner experience, and certainly not able to reliably discern the beliefs, attitudes, or feelings of others.

As we approached the end of Nathan's first year of treatment, the relationship had intensified, transferential features were beginning to emerge, and we had started to engage in a very different kind of therapeutic interaction. We continued with storytelling, though somewhat less regularly. Nathan introduced a game in which I was a physician and he was my patient. Usually he would be near death, generally as the result of multiple bullet or knife wounds; he would collapse on the floor, and I would be charged with the difficult task of resuscitating him. Coexisting with his unmistakable portrayal of the world as filled with life-threatening and malevolent forces (paralleling his own early experience) was his ability to entrust his life to another and to derive life-sustaining energy from his interaction with this human partner. This drama alternated with another scenario in which we were two African explorers. Together we would fight wildebeests, alligators, and other dangerous animals. The second play represented the therapeutic alliance itself. The two scenarios revealed Nathan's preliminary efforts to communicate the affective content and environmental context of his early traumatic experiences, his continuing fears and anxieties, and his belief that therapy might help him. I believe that Nathan was also conveying rather important changes in his internal working model of attachment. In fact, he had made a significant attachment, via the transference, that no longer fully conformed to the disorganized/disoriented model he had presented at the beginning of therapy. The patterned interactions of psychotherapy—the scheduling of the hours, the predictable activities and rhythms of treatment, as well as the soothing and containing interpretations of the therapist—offered him the affect regulation that had been so conspicuously absent in his infancy. Now, for the first time, Nathan seemed to be experimenting with a very different kind of relationship, one in which there was no longer an automatic expectation of abandonment and trauma, and in which attachment figures might offer some sense of security and safety.

At the height of this activity, about sixteen months into treatment, Nathan's therapy was disrupted when I left the country for three weeks to attend an international conference. When I returned, Nathan was inconsolably angry with me. I could do nothing right, and I had "wrecked" his therapy beyond repair; my efforts to empathize with the pain and abject distress he had experienced in my absence at first seemed futile. To be certain, the significance of the anger that he was now able to feel, identify, and express toward me was not lost—but the positive valence of the therapeutic climate rapidly deteriorated. For a time, therapy came to resemble the nightmare world of Nathan's early childhood, a place where no one seemed to care, where people disappeared and reappeared without explanation, and where it was simply too dangerous to make *any* kind of meaningful attachment. Though discouraged by this setback in Nathan's treatment, I nevertheless continued as we had before, hoping to reestablish the safe ambience of the treatment, and through my own responsiveness to Nathan's affective cues, the containment and affect regulation that my absence had disrupted.

Some two months after my return, Nathan told a story in connection with a squiggle of mine that he had turned into a picture of a broken heart. The storytelling process with Nathan during this period was framed as a "talk show," a format I had suggested and for which he had shown interest. Such a vehicle can be highly effective with certain children; in addition to appealing to a child's narcissism ("And now, live from New York, it's 'Squiggles,' with our *special* guest, Nathan ..."), it lends a certain excitement to the storytelling process. Nathan decided to play the role of the interviewer rather than the subject—a new experience for him and one that he found particularly gratifying, perhaps because it permitted him to exchange a passive position for a more active one. He had seldom shown interest in listening to the playback at the conclusion of previous session tapings, but he did so eagerly on this occasion.

The Broken Heart

CHILD: This is a TV program—"Squiggles"! We have a guest today. What is your name?

THERAPIST: My name is Jerry.

CHILD: Glad to meet you. You gotta do a squiggle, and I gotta draw a picture.

THERAPIST: Okay. We'll use this paper.

CHILD: Gotta close your eyes, too. It's the rules.

THERAPIST: Gotcha.

CHILD: Now I've gotta draw a picture, folks. [He draws the picture.] I just drew a picture of a heart because it's broken.

THERAPIST: A picture of a broken heart. Okay. And can you now make up a story about the broken heart, Nathan?

CHILD: Okay. Here goes. Once upon a time there was a broken heart. He lived in the land of hearts. There was many, many hearts. He was the only one that was broken. He didn't have any friends or nobody to play with him. He just had a little house, and he just sat there, and when it's dinnertime he would eat, and breakfast... or lunch.... He went outside one day and he seen this girl. He goes, "What is your name?" She goes, "Cathy." He goes, "My name is Gary." She goes, "What happened?" He goes, "I'm shy, and I'm a broken heart. I don't have any friends."

THERAPIST: Can I just interrupt for just a second? This is a made-up story? It's not like from Care Bears or something?...

CHILD: No! [With laughter] I don't watch Care Bears!

THERAPIST: All right. But it is something that's made up?

CHILD: Yes!

THERAPIST: Completely original?

CHILD: Yes!

THERAPIST: Okay. So, you never heard it from anybody?

CHILD: No!

THERAPIST: All right, go ahead.

CHILD: Then he asked her some questions, and he started playing with her and stuff, and they were friends. Pretty soon he was a whole heart! He wasn't broken anymore. Every night after supper he would go over to Cathy's house and would play games with her and stuff. Then all the other hearts would play with him, too. And one day there was this heart who went home crying because *he* was a broken heart. Then Gary went up to him and says, "What is your name?" He goes, "Cary." He goes, "What's the matter?" He goes, "I'm a broken heart now. I don't have any friends anymore." He goes, "Well come with me, I'll make you some friends." So he made him some friends, and … that's end of the story.

THERAPIST: Very good. Is there a lesson to this story?

CHILD: Don't be mean to people…

THERAPIST: Don't be mean—

CHILD: —Or else you'll break their heart. And that is the end of the program. Thank you very much for being here, Dr. J.

THERAPIST: Well, pardon me, but that is the end of the first half of the program—before our commercial break. You did want to do a commercial today, didn't you?

CHILD: Yeah.

THERAPIST: You can do two or three if you want. I'll make my story up while you do that, okay?

CHILD: Uh-huh.

Analysis

Nathan told this story with considerably more feeling than I had grown accustomed to hearing in his earlier story narratives. Although the content and tone were serious, I also detected an emerging playfulness in the telling. The reversal of roles and the repartee near the beginning of his story, which we both experienced as pleasurable, would probably not have been possible at an earlier point in therapy. One might understand such reciprocity as a direct function of Nathan's emerging capacity for self-regulation, and also as a reflection of a significant alteration in his internal working model of attachment. In other words, what had previously been possible only from the side of the therapist was now partially internalized, such that Nathan could begin to draw from internal resources not previously available to him—notably for reflection and mentalization, as well as affect regulation.

Nathan's broken-heart metaphor conveyed the profound pain that multiple abandonments had caused him and, at the same time, captured the enduring desolation and emptiness of his early object world. Although the disruption in his treatment reawakened these older injuries, resulting in a mild degree of retraumatization, the story demonstrated a decidedly more adaptive effort than at any previous time in Nathan's therapy to struggle with the loneliness and despair associated with his early caregiving environment. The first broken heart, Gary, becomes a whole heart when he is able to develop a meaningful affective relationship with Cathy, a representative of the adoptive mother and the therapist. The now-restored heart is then able to establish rapport with another broken heart, Cary, at the story's conclusion. From a somewhat different perspective, we also observe palpable evidence of self-regulatory functioning: Nathan's personal representative, Gary, seems able to rely on internal processes to guide him in a way that was almost inconceivable in the storyteller's life eighteen months earlier; furthermore, there is poignant evidence here of a growing capacity for mentalization in the manner in which story characters are able to empathize with each other's distress.

This story signaled an important development in Nathan's treatment, inasmuch as it reflected considerable evolution of his personal narrative. Still, however, there was evidence of his tendency to employ magical solutions, and Gary's transformation via his relationship with Cathy was not elaborated to any extent. Accordingly, I responded this way:

CHILD: And now, folks, back with Dr. J. and his story.

THERAPIST: Thank you for the kind introduction. Your story was a very good one, so it's going to be a hard one to follow. But I'm going to try. Once upon a time, there was a broken heart—a broken heart who lived in the land of hearts where most of the other hearts were whole hearts. Well, this broken heart was broken for a number of reasons, but especially because of the things he had lost—mostly the people he had lost. He was very sad. He was very depressed and very lonely, and felt very bad inside. Furthermore, there never seemed to be anyone for him to play with. There were hardly any people around near his little house in the little part of town in which he lived.

Well, one day he left his little home in the land of hearts, and he went to live with a family of whole hearts who lived on the other side of the village. It wasn't easy to move in with this family of whole hearts. At times, he still felt really lonely and really depressed and sad. But, little by little, the broken part of him started to mend. But it took a very long time. After a while, though, he began to feel loved. He also began to feel loving toward other hearts—something that he hadn't been able to do for a long time, because he hadn't been able to trust other hearts very much 'cause of how he had been hurt. But everything didn't always go smoothly. Sometimes things were really hard, and sometimes he got into fights, or people yelled at him or he yelled at them. He even felt hatred toward the whole hearts, and felt that they hated him. But those times became fewer and further between, and he felt more and more whole, as he lived with this family of whole hearts. He was even able to give friendship and love toward another broken heart one day when he was called on to do that. And that's the end of the story. It is a story that continues, but that's the end.

There are two morals. The first is: *Becoming a healed heart takes time and hard work.* And the second moral is: *When you feel whole, then you can begin to give to other people, too—or, in this case, to other hearts. And that also takes time, but it's possible.* That is the end of my story.

CHILD: Thank you for being on the show, Dr. J. We'll see you next week.

Analysis

My version of Nathan's story attempted to develop several interrelated themes. One was that a broken heart becomes broken for compelling reasons. Sadness, depression, and loneliness are the sequelae of the painful losses that the broken heart has suffered. A second was that there is, indeed, cause for optimism about the broken heart mending, even though such healing takes a long time and requires hard work; a corollary of this is that there will still be times when the mended heart reexperiences injury, depression, sadness, or even hatred, but because such feelings are part of daily living, they needn't be experienced as jarring or retraumatizing. A third message is the notion that trust and empathic rapport are indeed possible for a mended heart, which was implied in the therapeutic response. However, perhaps the most basic message embedded in my story-response was that a new and substantively different internal working model of attachment is indeed possible, and that the storyteller's newly emerging and fundamentally secure attachment relationships offer this possibility.

As the third year of therapy began, Nathan continued to show improvement generally in the development of stable self-regulatory functions, and more specifically, in his capacity for modulating and expressing affects and in his ability to control his impulses. His interpersonal skills gradually improved and his performance at school remained strong. He also began to address issues at the core of his traumatic past both through play metaphors and in direct verbal discourse.

The last pair of stories comes from a session conducted shortly before we began the termination process, well into the third year of treatment.

The Rabbit

> CHILD: Once upon a time, there was a rabbit. The rabbit was white. One day a girl found this rabbit in the woods. The rabbit was hurt very badly because it got chewed up by some hunting dogs. The dogs chewed some of the rabbit's skin off. So, the little girl took the rabbit home and took care of it until the rabbit got better. Then the girl let the rabbit go. Then it was all better. One year later the girl was going to school. The girl saw the rabbit at her house. When the girl's father saw the rabbit, he started shooting at it. The rabbit ran and ran and ran. Then the girl was really mad because she thought the rabbit was dead. Then one winter, the girl was going to school. She was walking to school, and she saw the rabbit. She didn't think it was the rabbit because it didn't look white. It was very hungry. So the girl gave the rabbit some carrots to eat so it could be healthy again. And they lived on.
>
> The moral of the story is: *Help animals and people, even if you don't know them.*

Analysis

Not only well constructed but also told with a range of powerful affects including anger, sadness, and despair, this story displays the dramatic transformation of Nathan's personal narrative over the course of treatment. Nathan had become far more expressive and was now possessed of a maturity that made him seem much older than the fragile and helpless child I first welcomed to my office some three years earlier. Here we see what can only be described as a transformative shift in his capacity for mentalization. Whereas earlier in therapy he displayed little awareness of either his own emotional states or of the feelings, attitudes, beliefs, etc., of those around him, there is compelling evidence here to suggest a far greater capacity for empathy and for reflective awareness of the inner life of others. The rabbit is, of course, his personal representative, traumatized by a series of vicious attacks and abandonment. The girl represents the adoptive mother and, to a lesser degree, the therapist; the girl's father is the abandoning adoptive father, whom Nathan experienced in real life as inhuman, insensitive, and cruel. The moral of the story is a particularly interesting one, inasmuch as it suggests the process not only of adoption but also of psychotherapy.

The chief source of concern about this story, an otherwise quite adaptive one, was the choice of a rabbit as a personal representative. I tend to view rabbits as exquisitely sensitive but usually mute creatures. Even if they become injured or feel strongly about something, they may be quite limited in their ability to express this. Therefore, I believe Nathan's choice of this animal was not a coincidence but, rather, selected for both its vulnerability and its muteness. In any case, the rabbit's need for time and space in order to come to terms with its past—and, finally, to be capable of accepting help from the girl—isn't developed to any great extent, thus also imparting a somewhat magical and unrealistic quality to the story's resolution. These thoughts influenced the composition of my responding story:

THERAPIST: Once upon a time, a girl found a rabbit in the woods where she had been playing. The rabbit had been very badly hurt; he was seriously injured and very scared. He was also very lonely and was very afraid of people and dogs and just about everything. He couldn't talk and wasn't able to tell the girl everything that had happened to him, although she seemed to know some of the things without his even having to say them. She took the rabbit home and began to care for him. His wounds began to heal and he began to eat again. He gained some weight because he had been awfully skinny when she first found him.

After a while, although the rabbit liked the girl, he wasn't really able to trust her completely, and he decided he wanted to leave. The girl understood this and let him go. For a long time, she never saw him or heard about him, and she missed him very much. The rabbit also missed her, because here was someone who had really been good to him, maybe for the first time ever. The rabbit endured some very bad hardships; some very unpleasant things happened to him during the year he was away, and he began to miss her very much.

One day when the girl was coming home from school she saw the rabbit. He was skinny, so thin you could almost see through him. His eyes were almost popping out from all the weight he had lost, and he was dirty and looked very unhealthy. The girl immediately picked him up and, because she loved him so much, brought him home again to care for him. The rabbit went home and was very happy to be there.

Well, then something *very* unexpected happened. A man who lived next door to the girl, who didn't understand *anything* about this rabbit, one day saw the rabbit, and took out his hunting rifle. He loaded the rifle and was about to shoot it. Suddenly the rabbit lifted up its head and screamed at him, "Don't shoot me"—of course, in a higher voice. The man was startled and didn't know what to do. In amazement he put down his gun and stared at this rabbit that had spoken to him. The rabbit stared back and repeated, "Don't hurt me!" The man was so amazed that, shaking his head, he turned away and walked home. The girl returned from school a bit later that day. The rabbit told her what happened. The girl was less amazed that the rabbit could speak than the man had been, because she had understood a lot about him without his having to speak about it before. But, because he *was* able to speak, he was finally able to tell the girl much more about himself— about all the problems he had had, about the hardships he had suffered, and about many other things that weren't especially bad or frightening, too. So the girl understood him better and better all the time. She continued to care for him. And, because she was able to care for him so well, the rabbit learned how to care for himself better. He learned how to feed himself when he was hungry and to tell people about his feelings when they were important and needed to be expressed. That was a kind of healing, too. It went on for a rather long time, almost until the rabbit was full-grown. And that's the end of the story.

CHILD: (Without missing a beat) What's the moral?

THERAPIST: There are two morals to this one. The first is: *Some wounds never heal completely. They heal pretty much, but they're never completely healed, and they leave scars. But, in time, with love and patience and nurturing and understanding, a rabbit or any creature can begin to feel whole.* And the second moral is: *When somebody does something to you that's painful, that hurts you, or that makes you feel bad, let them know, like the rabbit did. Tell them, "Don't hurt me." And if they won't listen, find someone who will.* That's the end.

Analysis

The responding story expands on the relationship between the girl and the rabbit. The girl, like Nathan's adoptive mother, understands that trust in a relationship must evolve gradually and that there are occasional setbacks. The man whom Nathan designates as the girl's father (representing the adoptive father) is a peripheral character in my version, principally because he was clearly out of the picture by this time. Providing the rabbit with the faculty of speech went a long way toward making him less reliant on others; it also demonstrated the power of self-expression. Despite the fact that my story was somewhat longer than his, Nathan remained intently focused and interested in it from beginning to end. Some sort of synchronicity prevailed between us that made this exchange of stories feel almost as though we had experienced a shared altered state.

Like the rabbit in his story, Nathan had gradually developed a capacity for basic trust and commenced the journey that would culminate in a process of healing. Moving from a disorganized model of attachment, one developed out of internal and environmental chaos, parental abuse, and massive traumas involving separation and loss, a new personal narrative, though incomplete, had emerged. In it is revealed a richness and cohesiveness that stand in marked contrast to earlier versions of his "story" from the first weeks and months of therapy. Significantly, this last story of Nathan's also signals a new internal working model of attachment, yet to be fully elaborated, that portrays both his renewed interest in the human world and a greater capacity to sustain the disappointments and setbacks of everyday living.

Summary of Treatment Principles

It may prove instructive to summarize those principles derived from attachment theory that offer a template from which treatment interventions such as the foregoing may be launched. Basic features of Nathan's or any child's treatment include (a) the incremental development of a safe base from which all treatment interventions proceed, (b) the therapist's assistance—whether via direct interpretation, direct guidance and suggestions, modeling, or interpretation within the metaphor of play—in helping the child in his efforts to regulate and contain affects and impulses, (c) the therapist's assistance in helping the child to develop a capacity for reflective functioning or mentalization, and (d) within the sequence of

> empathic breach or disruption → attuned therapeutic response → subsequent efforts to rerail therapy and repair the relationship

the development of a greater range of adaptive responses that may then be exported and deployed in situations extrinsic to the treatment.

My understanding of Nathan's problematic attachment history, as well as the nature of his particular adaptation to his mother's pathology and the traumagenic and disordered environment that it fostered, was a key element in enabling me to treat him successfully. The basic psychodynamic model used in Nathan's therapy, though clearly informed by attachment theory, is also arguably shaped by several other dynamic theories (e.g., object relations, self psychology, and relational-intersubjective theory). Perhaps it would be fair to say that attachment theory does not necessarily represent a completely unique, substantively different way of approaching this case or that of any other child. Indeed, Fonagy (2001) notes that attachment theory clearly makes use of at least three of the traditional psychoanalytic viewpoints (structural, genetic, and adaptive); therefore, attachment theory may not require a radical revisioning of basic dynamic practice principles. Nevertheless, it also now seems inconceivable to do without a careful assessment of a child's attachment history, its relationship to presenting complaints, and so forth. I have also found that an understanding of transference reactions, as well as the more enduring transference relationship established over the course of a dynamic child treatment, is appreciably enhanced by understanding a child's model of attachment; while this may not require the invention of entirely new varieties of transference experience, it appears to explain more fully certain qualities associated with more traditional transference configurations (e.g., maternal, idealizing, adversarial). And, as this case illustrates so eloquently, a child's internal working model for attachment, even when apparently well entrenched, may not be *truly* immutable; new experiences, including those associated with successful child therapy, may prove compensatory, if not corrective, for early attachment traumas.

Adolescents | SIX

This chapter examines how clinical practice with adolescent clients is informed by attachment concepts. A second, and related, concern is how childhood attachment patterns play out in adolescence and interface with adolescent developmental tasks. Through vignettes[1] that illustrate various clinical issues with adolescents from different practice venues, a clinical perspective that incorporates an understanding of attachment behavior in adolescent clients is presented. The discussion begins with a summary of the basic developmental tasks of adolescence.

Adolescence is a time of biological changes that include the development of secondary sexual characteristics, growing cognitive abilities such as abstract reasoning and logic (Piaget, 1936), and moral development. Because of these profound cognitive and physiological changes, developmental theorists conceive of adolescence as a time of turmoil and emotional lability, or Sturm und Drang. Erikson, whose life stage model we have previously discussed, was the first to systematically explore adolescent development (Erikson, 1950). In his seminal psychosocial epigenetic theory, he suggested that each developmental stage is contingent upon the resolution of a specific developmental crisis. He theorized that adolescence is characterized by the stage of *identity versus identity diffusion* and that during this time the primary developmental task is the development of a cohesive identity.

Other theorists emphasized the environment and family relationships as important factors in the adolescent's struggle for autonomy and a cohesive identity. Peter Blos, for example, noted that adolescents' striving for independence, coupled with continuing dependency on their parents, restimulated the earlier conflicts and anxieties associated with the original infantile matrix of separation—individuation (Blos, 1979). Similarly, others see adolescence as a time for the reconfiguration of familial and social roles (Slavin & Kriegman, 1992). Typical presenting problems for adolescents are familial conflicts and the desire to find a new identity within the peer group and away from the family. Slavin and Kriegman describe the adolescent stage as a "continuously constructed, tested and evaluated fit between oneself and [the] environment" (1992, p. 187), where the process of development continuously evolves within the matrices of self and other, and self and society. Slavin suggests that adolescence is a time to "complete the transition from primary investment in the environment of the family to that of the larger, adult social world" (1996, p. 39). These authors conceptualize adolescence as a time of expanding relational roles and, consequently, tension between old familial attachments and new social responsibilities.

Adolescence, therefore, is a stage in which a transition occurs from the old attachment bonds with parents to new attachments with peers, romantic partners, and the larger social milieu. Though still dependent on their parents for emotional and financial security, adolescents strive for independence and seek new attachments. They are engaged in a competing struggle between autonomy and familial bonds, while new cognitive, emotional, and physiological structures allow them to pursue these developmental goals. This behavior can be understood as an attachment response insofar as it demonstrates the need for both exploration and connection (Allen & Land, 1999). Not surprisingly, research suggests that such autonomous strivings are correlated with the formation of a secure bond between adolescents and their parents (Allen, Hauser, Bell, & O'Connor, 1994). The adolescent's pattern of peer relationships also reflects early attachment patterns (Gavin & Furman, 1989, 1996), which are transferred from parents to peers, from hierarchical relationships to egalitarian and romantic bonds (Allen & Land, 1999). Secure adolescents will likely engage in relationships in which connection and individuation can coexist, while insecure adolescents will tend to develop avoidant or ambivalent patterns of attachment.

The two insecure attachment styles, dismissive (or avoidant) and preoccupied (or ambivalent), illustrate two distinct patterns of coping in adolescence. Adolescents who present with the preoccupied style tend to internalize their problems and to report depression (Allen, Moore, Kuperminc, & Bell, 1998), while those with a dismissive style are more likely to externalize their problems and engage in aggressive behavior, delinquency, and substance abuse (Rosenstein & Horowitz, 1996). While these aggressive behaviors initially seem to be attempts to distance and isolate, they may actually signal a desire to reach out for help and attention and therefore represent an attachment-seeking strategy. Both the internalizing and the externalizing strategies reflect the adolescent's approach to dealing with anxiety and distress (Kobak & Cole, 1994).

Attachment-informed treatment with adolescents involves helping the client to develop a capacity for affect regulation and self-reflection to facilitate the accomplishment of yet-to-be-completed tasks of development. Adolescents are known for extreme mood fluctuations, impulsivity, and difficulty in considering the future consequences of their actions. Typical presenting problems with adolescent clients may involve conflicts with parents, problems in peer relationships, dating, and the search for a unique identity. The clinician's task is to offer a stabilizing and containing presence to help regulate the adolescent's affective states and thereby "permit adolescents to internalize and develop their own capacity for containment " (Brandell, 2004, p. 295) and self-regulation.

It is important for the clinician to encourage the adolescent client's strivings for new attachments while simultaneously recognizing the powerful bonds that continue to influence relationships with parents. Adolescent bravado, which may masquerade as supreme self-confidence, independence, and assertiveness, often conceals underlying dependency needs and a fragile sense of self. Similarly, it is important to facilitate the working through of empathic disruptions between the adolescent client and clinician in order to minimize the likelihood that the adolescent may act out (e.g., by making an impulsive decision to terminate treatment). The clinician can offer the adolescent opportunities to work through old attachment patterns and develop new ones, a treatment objective tied to the therapist's assumption of a co-facilitative and co-constructive role. Finally, clinicians must remain attuned to their own countertransference attitudes and responses, inasmuch as these often incorporate projected contents—emotional reactions, attitudes, and anxieties—that the adolescent client is not yet capable of identifying, articulating, or regulating internally.

Clinical Illustration 1: An African American Adolescent Male in an Urban Environment

The following vignette concerns an African American young man who grew up in a poor urban environment with a single mother. In addition to typical adolescent issues, this case demonstrates how poverty, local cultural values, and a lack of fathering can shape an adolescent boy's attachment patterns. While there is comparatively little research regarding attachment to fathers, one study does indicate that fathers become increasingly important during adolescence (Arbona & Power, 2003). In single-mother households, and in communities where adult males are either only marginally present because of drugs or absent because they are incarcerated, gangs or similar adolescent groups may take the place of a boy's biological family. Despite the lack of traditional family structure, gangs typically offer powerful ties of loyalty and attachment between their members and subsume relationships with adults in the community. Bonds with male peers and with older boys may, in fact, compensate for the absence of fathers. These subcultures develop their own code of ethics and behavioral mores, which are very different from mainstream social values. Violence and aggression, for example, are viewed as ways to prove one's virility and loyalty to the group. The adolescent must adhere to these behavioral codes in order to be respected and accepted, and to fit in with his or her peers. This primary attachment to the group entity, rather than to the parents, may be similar to the pattern found among the Israeli kibbutz children who grew up in communal sleeping arrangements, living together in communal houses from birth, away from their parents. Consequently, they develop a strong attachment to their peer group, and group dynamics play a more important part in their lives than familial bonds, inasmuch as the parents have comparatively little influence on their early lives and daily upbringing (see chapter 4).

Ray was a seventeen-year-old African American young man, living with his mother, in his last year of high school. In addition to going to school full-time, he held a part-time job and paid for his own therapy at a community mental health clinic. He reported that he decided to seek counseling because of difficulties socializing with his peers and dating girls, and because he felt highly "stressed" as a result of his interpersonal conflicts at school, at work, and at home with his mother.

Ray was short and slight, wearing braids, earphones, high-top sneakers, and loose clothing—typical accoutrements in his neighborhood. When I first saw Ray and listened to him speak, I felt certain that our professional relationship would not last long, and that he would not show up for the following session. But Ray surprised me. He came almost every week for a number of months, and proved to be curious, introspective, and insightful. He spoke very softly in street jargon that was difficult for me to understand, he seemed shy, and he displayed excellent manners. He always came to sessions on time, paid his bill, and called in advance if he needed to cancel an appointment.

Ray reported that he did not know his father and had been living with his mother as an only child all his life. His mother was described as hardworking, rarely at home because she held two jobs, and a strict disciplinarian. She expected Ray to earn his own money and pay for his personal expenses, and, according to Ray, she was extremely reluctant to give him financial assistance when he asked for it. He reported that she actually expected him to help her out financially. This made him resentful not only of his mother but also of other women, who, he believed, tried to take advantage of him. Ray described his relationship with his mother as distant. He did not recall receiving any physical affection, encouragement, or interest in his activities and academic performance from her.

Ray described a lonely childhood. He and his mother lived in a dangerous neighborhood, and he was not allowed to go out and play or to invite his friends to his home. He spent much of his time after school alone in his room, daydreaming, talking to himself, and thinking about the future. Though he seemed withdrawn, quiet, and timid, he had created a rich inner world where he was a famous star, rich and popular. In this fantasy world he was not a follower but a leader, a charismatic figure whom people admired and with whom girls fell in love. In truth, Ray was never popular, and aside from two male friends, he felt intimidated by students of both sexes. He was afraid to speak up in class or with his supervisor at work, and he found it difficult to join in conversations among his peers. Ray's avoidant attachment style developed, it seemed to me, because of his early isolation, his cultural environment, and his lack of fathering. He rarely showed any feelings except anger, noting that it was dangerous to show emotional needs or vulnerability in his community, where only the tough and independent seemed able to survive.

Treatment Process

Ray and I frequently found ourselves separated by a cultural divide. Ray grew up and went to school in an inner-city African American neighborhood, where violence, crime, drugs, and a tough street culture prevailed. Most boys his age came from single-parent families, poverty was pervasive, and social survival depended on being tough and resourceful. I, on the other hand, grew up in a small, homogeneous rural community in Israel and lived in a middle-class suburb. I had difficulty understanding Ray's black urban dialect, and Ray in turn had to get used to my foreign accent. It took a while before he lowered his hood and removed his earphones and actually looked me in the eye. In his culture, I learned, it could be dangerous to make direct eye contact. Our cultural notions of respect, self-esteem, and assertiveness were also at odds. I came from a culture that believed in polite verbal interactions, in which "inappropriate anger" would be channeled into productive activities. My culture differentiated between assertiveness and violence. Ray, on the other hand, explained to me that in his culture it was frequently important to respond to insulting or disrespectful behavior with violence and physical and verbal aggression in order to survive. Aggressive behavior, a loud voice, and a readiness to fight were essential in order to maintain one's status and to command respect. Those who responded quietly to a challenge or an insult were considered weak.

Despite our differences, we were able to embark on a mutual examination of Ray's notions of strength and weakness versus my own more middle-class values. We also investigated his assumptions regarding his personality style and his habitual response in social situations. We tried to understand the origins of these notions of self and other. We agreed to examine whether some of his interactive patterns should be modified now that he had become an adolescent and was poised to enter the world of work and to engage in more mature romantic relationships. It became clear that Ray's notions about himself had coalesced during his lonely childhood with a mother who was distant and frequently unavailable, within a social environment where violent behavior was a common response to perceived threats. Our discussions led him to reflect on the nature of his interactions with others and to delay his impulsive actions; he gradually developed a capacity for self-observation, thereby permitting strong impulses and powerful affects to yield to the mitigating influence of reason and understanding. He became aware that he had alternatives and that, with practice, he could alter his relational style of avoidance and withdrawal, as well as his tendency to respond with aggression. He started to report success in peacefully resolving conflicts with his supervisor and a growing ability to socialize with peers at school. He became aware that his difficulty in engaging with others stemmed from a defensive, hyper-alert mode of interaction. He even started a friendship with a female student that was based on greater mutual reciprocity and trust. During our final session, Ray reported that he and his mother had begun to communicate with each other more openly and that he felt she had become more interested in and supportive of him.

Discussion

This vignette demonstrates the impact of poverty, race, and lack of fathering on an African American adolescent's attachment patterns. For Ray, an avoidant style became a relational accommodation that assured protection and safety in a violent, rejecting, and tough environment, but it also left him lonely and socially isolated. Despite emotional and social deprivations, Ray possessed a highly introspective capacity and keen insight, and he started to thrive as our relationship provided him with a validating and safe arena in which to learn affect regulation and new interactive skills. He eventually learned to reflect on his thoughts and reactions, realizing, first, that the "threats" he identified were often misperceived or exaggerated and, second, that far more adaptive alternatives to this "fight or flight" mode of response existed. As he developed greater competence in social interactions and felt more secure, the need for such primitive responses diminished. Our deepening ability to discuss and achieve greater understanding of our differing worldviews and cultures, dialogues that often began as moments of misattunement, allowed me to understand and validate Ray's interactive style and facilitated his trust in me. Finally, a close observation of my initial assumptions regarding Ray's appearance, language, and behavior allowed me to gain insight into others' assumptions about him and the culture from which he came. It also allowed me to notice the schism between his inner gentleness and vulnerability and his hard, defensive, and independent outer shell. Although such "armoring" may have protected him from danger, it also denied him vital intimate bonds with others.

Clinical Illustration 2: The Impact of Chronic Illness

The second case to be discussed concerns a young woman who suffered from epilepsy, a neurological disability that had a profound impact on her development and on her capacity for intimate attachments. Because of this chronic illness, Karla's ability to experience the typical adolescent milestones was seriously impaired. Instead, she faced limited social opportunities and an enduring psychological and material dependence on her parents. Karla's disorder, her inability to maintain a stable medication regimen, and an early neurological surgery combined to make it difficult for her to express her affective states and also compromised her ability to communicate with others and make use of normal cognitive functions. These limitations made peer relationships, romantic partnerships, and academic endeavors extremely challenging.

There has been an increasing recognition among epileptologists that any seizure disorder, particularly one that is poorly controlled, may result in moderately severe psychosocial sequelae. Heightened levels of anxiety, depression, and behavioral maladjustment, as well as low self-esteem and self-dissatisfaction, have been reported in a number of studies of pediatric epilepsy patients (see, for example, MacLeod & Austin, 2003). Many children and adolescents with seizure disorders also tend to view themselves as helpless, powerless, or out of control. These patients typically attribute control to external or unknown sources. A high percentage also experience difficulty in social competencies and in some aspects of school performance. Intractable epilepsy patients, or those whose epilepsy cannot be well managed with standard anticonvulsant therapy, present a particular challenge. Such children and adolescents are increasingly viewed as a psychologically vulnerable population (Vining, 1987).

People with epilepsy encounter powerful social stigmata related to their psychosocial functioning, which in turn, exert a negative effect on their self-concept. During adolescence, ordinarily a time when self-identity is consolidated, epilepsy may present unique psychosocial challenges. While other adolescents experience the strengthening of ties with peers, romantic relationships, and increased independence, adolescents with epilepsy who cannot reach these developmental milestones are likely to experience low self-esteem and depression. Not surprisingly, it was found that these adolescents are likely to keep their epilepsy a secret from their peers, most likely because of fear of stigmatization and rejection (MacLeod & Austin, 2003).

Researchers have also found that people with epilepsy may experience seizures as a result of "emotional conflicts or psychosocial maladaptations" (Miller, 1994, p. 16). Frequently occurring seizures, in particular, may affect the epileptic patient's memory. This, in turn, may make it more difficult for the individual to identify specific emotional triggers that precede the seizures, thus interfering with his or her ability to prevent and/or control future attacks. Certain types of epilepsy have been found to be associated with greater psychopathology, such as bipolar disorder, depression, and dependent personality disorder. Parents may react to an epileptic child with "overprotectiveness, infantilization, scapegoating, embarrassment and guilt" (p. 17), further complicating the development of autonomy and positive self-esteem. Such parental responses to the child are factors in the child's ensuing attachment patterns. Because of their anxiety regarding emotional conflicts that would result in a seizure, adolescents whose epilepsy is not well controlled may tend to avoid social interactions and close peer relationships. Consequently they may become socially isolated and fail to develop age-appropriate social skills.

The cumulative effect is that intimate relationships are avoided, autonomy is further compromised, and their emotional dependence on their parents is heightened. The therapeutic process with such adolescents, predictably, may involve the themes of tension between dependency needs and the desire for autonomy, their frustration regarding academic and social/romantic disappointments, and their inherent feelings of loss and isolation.

Karla was a nineteen-year-old college junior who, at the time I met with her, was making her second attempt to leave home and to live on her own. About a year and a half earlier, she had attended another school for six months, but withdrew because of her isolation, academic difficulties, and chronic health problems. Now, more than a year later, she had decided to try again, but a couple of months into her first semester she came to the counseling center to report difficulties in adjusting to her new surroundings and increasing social isolation.

Rather than stay at the dorms, Karla had decided to get her own apartment this time. She advertised for roommates, and several students responded to her ad, although none called back after a brief interview with her. Karla was finally able to find two somewhat older women from the working-class community around the university. While not revealing the effect of this exasperating search process, Karla did report, with some confusion, that her new roommates avoided her, seemed to talk behind her back, and looked at her in a peculiar way.

It was not surprising to me that Karla had encountered these difficulties. There was something rather eccentric about her clothing and communication style. She was a large young woman, with plain features and a flat and expressionless affect. She frequently wore a Mickey Mouse T-shirt and colorful pants, clothes that seemed designed for a much younger girl and were completely out of step with the fashion styles on campus. Her voice was loud and monotonous, and she seemed oblivious to its volume or to her surroundings. Her thought content was concrete, and there was a sense of emotional disconnectedness and sexual immaturity about her, as if she were still only an eleven- or twelve-year-old girl rather than a young woman of nineteen. Karla's immaturity was reflected in her relationships with her family and friends as well. She had never dated, her only friendships involved relationships from grade school, and the childlike relationship she described with her parents underscored the other characteristics of developmental arrest. Although she reported on her parents' work and activities, Karla had difficulty describing their personalities and articulating her feelings toward them. She seemed resentful of their protectiveness and their constant interference in her life, yet disturbed that they spent less and less time at home; indeed, at times they were quite neglectful, leaving her home alone for extended periods. When she left for college her mother immediately went back to school and her father started a new business, soon becoming extremely busy. Karla, however, was still in the habit of calling them daily to report her experiences and to ask for advice about every aspect of her life.

She reported that she was born without complications and achieved normal developmental milestones, but at the age of six months she began to have severe seizures and was given a diagnosis of six months to live. After undergoing an extremely dangerous neurosurgical procedure, however, she rallied and then experienced a rather dramatic improvement in her epileptic symptoms. Most likely, this was a surgical procedure intended to reduce the incidence of grand mal seizures by severing the neuronal connection between the right and left brain hemispheres, but it may also have contributed to Karla's difficulty in integrating brain functions. During our first meeting she parted her hair, revealing a long scar at the top of her head, which I found dismaying, if not slightly shocking. She seemed, however, proud that she had been able to survive the trauma. Karla's seizures were now mostly controlled by drugs; only occasionally, especially if she was under a great deal of emotional stress, did the attacks return. She had led an extremely protected existence; her parents had not permitted her to drive a car or leave the house without supervision until she left for college. On the other hand, they frequently left her alone to pursue their own interests. Her parents' caretaking pattern of unpredictable contact, overprotectiveness, and neglect was one factor in Karla's ambivalent attachment style. She could be clingy and dependent with them, but at other times she resented their interference and obviously sought to distance herself from their influence by living on her own far away from them.

Unlike Karla, her older sister was attractive, popular with her peers, and now lived with her boyfriend in their own apartment. It was hard to gauge Karla's feelings toward her sister. She described her with some ambivalence, reporting that while she and her sister had been close until her sister left their parents' home, she also thought her sister was irresponsible and selfish. She believed that her sister had caused much grief and concern to their parents because, unlike Karla, she had not pursued her studies. I sensed her underlying envy and resentment and her desire to compete with her sister academically, the one area where Karla still possessed the upper hand.

Karla's ambivalent attachment pattern seemed greatly influenced by her seizure disorder. She was highly dependent on her parents because of it, but at the same time she resented this, trying to break away and start her own life. She longed to develop her own professional career and friendships, perhaps even a romantic relationship. Her parents, on the other hand, seemed concerned only with whether she had taken her medications, found roommates who could help her in case of an emergency, or experienced worrisome symptoms.

Treatment Process

I felt that Karla's parents had infantilized her, treating her as an invalid, though at other times they seemed completely self-involved, showing no interest in her at all and registering relief that she had left home. These reflections became an important clinical tool in my attempt to understand Karla's affective experience, as she herself seemed to lack the appropriate emotional and relational cues to clue me in or give verbal expression to such thoughts and emotions. Perhaps this was in part a result of her early neurosurgery, which had occurred before the full development of cognitive and emotional structures.

Because it was difficult for me to surmise how events and people had affected Karla, I used my imagination to try and reconstruct her emotional struggle and also attempted to identify my own countertransference responses to her, employing these insights to understand her relational experiences with me and with others. Karla's strange appearance, flat affect, and loud voice made it difficult at first to empathize with her. She seemed completely unaware of others' needs and responses (including my own), and her difficulty in discerning emotional and behavioral cues clearly contributed to her poor communication skills. I understood why her new roommates avoided and ignored her and why she couldn't make any friends in school. Her neurological disorder had, in fact, become an integral part of her personality, attachment patterns, and sense of self.

Karla's flat affect and her concrete delivery often made it difficult for me to understand her feelings, thoughts, and inner experience. I had to imagine what it must have been like for her to leave home the second time and to come to school on her own in a last-ditch attempt to create a life away from her parents. If she failed, she would have to return home for good. She may have already surmised her parents' ambivalent feelings, which alternated between expressions of love and concern and resentment toward her. I empathized with both her desperate need for independence and her all-too-obvious inability to sever the umbilical cord.

While she still had difficulty identifying her emotional experience, Karla started to feel safe enough with me to describe her struggle with academic work, her inability to make friends, and even a budding awareness of her own sexuality, in particular the ambivalence she felt regarding her sexual orientation. In turn, I validated her need to remain close to her parents but also encouraged her struggle for independence and self-definition. We tried to examine and gain insight into her ambivalent reactions to her parents and into her confusing "crushes" on female and male peers.

Karla's struggle to keep up went on for some time. She tried hard to be like everybody else, to have crushes on boys, to study all night for exams, and to live independently. But she couldn't maintain it. She found herself falling asleep during classes, being unable to concentrate, and failing her courses. Her roommates excluded her and ignored her when she came in. She was rapidly sinking. One day she felt a seizure coming on, but there was no one around to help and she lost consciousness. She lay on the floor in her apartment for hours, until she regained consciousness. Her roommates didn't care and weren't interested in her medical problems.

She had lost her fight to live on her own. I found this out after a few weeks when Karla did not show up for her regular appointments and did not return my phone calls. A short time later, she came one more time to tell me what had happened, and to say good-bye. Her parents were arriving with a truck any minute to pack up her belongings and to take her back home. She couldn't imagine what would be waiting for her there. I listened with a great deal of sadness as she described her final fantasy, to become a hospitality girl at Disney World, a place she used to visit with her parents as a child and where she had experienced so much fun. She consoled herself with the thought that perhaps it would work out for her there. But as I envisioned the slender, attractive, and smiling girls working at Disney World, I knew that this fantasy would likely never be realized.

Discussion

This case illustrates how a neurological disorder such as epilepsy compounded by early traumatic medical interventions may become an important factor in an adolescent's attachment pattern, influencing her behavior and relational choices, as well as her cognitive and emotional development. The empathic process through which I tried to experience Karla's efforts to struggle with her incapacitating disorder, her losses, and her disappointments was an important clinical tool, inasmuch as accurate emotional and behavioral cues from her were limited. I tried to validate Karla's desire to become more independent, while at the same time helping her to accept her emotional and physical dependence on her parents. When possible, I encouraged Karla to express the ambivalence she felt toward her family members and to permit herself a greater range of feelings. I learned to be attuned to her subtle cues and, sometimes, her miscues, as for example when her affectless appearance and literal descriptions contradicted the pain and anxiety she really felt. I recognized that despite her flat expression and eccentric physical appearance, she longed for loving attachments like everyone else, or perhaps just simply to be noticed and included. By the end of our work together, a few months in all, I had also learned about my own biases and assumptions, and I felt a great deal of respect and admiration for Karla in her losing battle for independence.

My work with Karla demonstrates the utilization of attachment concerns in treatment with adolescents. These include creating a safe base, validating the need for proximity and bonding with parents but also encouraging social explorations with peers and the development of an independent identity. It was difficult to help Karla develop reflective functions because of her cognitive limitations, but I nevertheless tried to help her examine the meaning of the interactions she described in terms of her need for emotional connection and excitement about new explorations. I helped her to examine the conflicting feelings she experienced toward her parents and to identify social cues that would alert her as to whether she should avoid relationships or pursue them further. While no dramatic instances of misattunement occurred between us, I constantly struggled to be affectively connected to Karla by being attuned to my own countertransference process and by learning to interpret her subtle nonverbal cues, such as silence as an indicator of hopelessness and smiling as a sign for confusion or embarrassment. My close observations allowed me to infer Karla' self-states and to check my observations with her.

Clinical Illustration 3: Anatomy of a Treatment Failure— The Sequelae of Parental Suicide

Several years ago I was contacted by a middle-aged woman whom I'll call Jen Daniels.[2] Ms. Daniels was very concerned about her youngest child, Ben, who was at that time twelve years old. Ben, she explained, was very depressed and didn't really seem to care about anything; furthermore, his school performance had plummeted, despite his superior intelligence. And then, in a surprisingly straightforward manner, as though she had told the same story dozens of times before, she told me that Ben's father had committed suicide two years before. The suicide had been a violent one and represented a shocking ending to an intractable depression that had defied virtually every form of treatment attempted. Psychotherapy, marital counseling, pharmacotherapy with a number of different drugs—none of these treatments had appeared to make any real difference. Part of the problem, Ms. Daniels suggested, was undoubtedly her ex-husband's arrogant disdain for therapy and therapists, which he made no effort to conceal as he rapidly engaged and just as rapidly dismissed five psychiatrists in less than two years. Although Mr. Daniels was depressed for a considerably longer period of time, his struggle with depression intensified following a major setback in his professional career and a dislocating family move that occurred in approximately the same time period. Eventually, the marriage began to suffer, and Ms. Daniels in desperation sought a divorce. Shortly before the divorce was finalized, Mr. Daniels moved out of the house and rented his own apartment nearby for about fifteen months. Finally, he disappeared for several weeks, after which he sent a letter to his four children "to say goodbye." Wisely, Ms. Daniels kept the letter, fearing the worst. However, Mr. Daniels subsequently returned, though in an even more agitated state than he had exhibited before leaving. Once again, his wife and others worked very hard to persuade him to seek help, and though he consented to meet with several more psychiatrists, he was equally dismissive of them. Nothing seemed to help. Finally, as a long winter came to an end and the first signs of spring appeared, Marty Daniels took his own life. It is significant that throughout all of this, Ben had been unwilling to give up on his father and religiously walked over to his dad's apartment for daily visits after school, sent him letters, and called him every night. Naturally, Ben and his three siblings were devastated after learning from their mother that their father had committed suicide. Ben, however, seemed even more distraught than his siblings. Ben's pain gradually became worse, so much so that Ms. Daniels grew very concerned and twice sought treatment for her youngest child. In both cases, however, the treatment seemed to fail almost as soon as it began. Ben disliked the two therapists his mother took him to see and, like his father, was openly critical of them. In fact, he was very disinclined to meet with me, although I circumnavigated some of this early resistance to engagement by making independent arrangements with him over the telephone for our first meeting. As it often does with both children and adolescents, this maneuver helped to establish a rudimentary alliance that would not have been as likely to develop had I relied on Ben's mother to make arrangements for her son.

In several meetings and phone conversations with Ben's mother, I was also able to learn a bit about Ben's early development, information that I believe may shed some additional light on the therapeutic process that evolved in Ben's treatment. At the time of Ben's birth, his family resided in Mexico. Ben and his mother were very close, and she nursed him "for that entire first year." However, the burden of managing a household in a foreign country eventually forced her to engage the services of an au pair, when Ben was in the middle of his second year. Ms. Daniels observed that Ben loved the au pair, who has remained a friend ever since, although he also began to display mild separation anxiety at about this time (sixteen to eighteen months). He continued to have some difficulty in separating from his mother and from Rosa (the au pair) as he began kindergarten, although this problem receded over time. Ben also suffered from a facial anomaly that was very noticeable by the time he reached age four; eventually, Ben's doctors recommended surgery, which was performed a few years later. Although Ben's intellectual development was, if anything, precocious, his social development seemed to lag behind. His mother noted that even as early as kindergarten, he didn't seem to get along well with other children, particularly girls, who, his mother observed, tended to "behave aggressively towards him."

One bright spot in Ben's life was his relationship with his father. As the only boy and the youngest of four children, he developed a very close attachment with his father. The two spent a good deal of time with one another, pursuing mutually rewarding activities. Then, as Ben reached latency, his father began to experience work-related problems that eventually led him to resign from his position and move the family back to the States. At this time, pouring himself into a new job for which he was both overqualified and not well compensated, he began to withdraw from contact with his son as well as the other children, growing increasingly resentful and depressed. By the time Ben was ten, his parents had separated, never to reconcile.

Treatment Process

Ben told me straightaway that he hadn't liked his earlier experiences in therapy. He had suffered through six sessions or so of treatment with one therapist not long after his father's death, although the last therapist his mother asked him to see—a well-respected child and adolescent therapist and analyst—he had consented to see for only a single session. He had no worries, Ben told me glibly, and believed that his mother had exaggerated any problems. He was also quite concerned as to the nature of my communications with his mother and wished to ensure that our discussions would remain confidential, a condition to which I agreed with the usual qualifications. At my suggestion, Ben consented to twice-weekly meetings, with no particular time frame. We gradually became more comfortable with each other, and he started to reveal more details about his relationship with his father, how the two used to play chess and checkers together and their mutual interest in science and math. He told me that this experience in therapy actually "didn't seem that bad" compared with his experiences with the other two therapists he had seen, somewhat to his surprise. Spontaneously over the next several sessions, Ben talked about his depressed moods, during which he became very sad and tearful, but which he noted typically lasted only a few days. He quickly added that such moods were infrequent, and during the intervening months, he felt just fine. The discussion shifted, and Ben then spoke excitedly of the television program *Fear Factor*, where people have to do "incredibly gross things like eat maggot-filled cheese." Though I shuddered at the thought, I wondered momentarily if somewhere in his manic excitement was a displacement of the image of his father's body as it might now appear. Later in this session, we played a therapeutic game I have often found useful with latency-aged and preadolescent children, Richard Gardner's Talking, Feeling, and Doing Game. Ben drew a "feeling" card that asked, "What do you think of a boy who curses at his father?" His response was immediate and angry. "Any kid who does that is a spoiled brat." "Might it be," I wondered aloud, "that this kid at that moment was very angry at his father, but still loved him?" Ben was adamant. "*No*, he's a *stupid*, spoiled brat." At session's end, he asked whether he might take something home with him. We explored the meaning of this briefly, since it was my supposition that he wished to preserve some aspect of the now-good experience with me during the time between appointments. Could he take a game piece with him? Maybe a book? He persisted, asking for any small token he might "borrow just for the next few days." Finally he asked if he might take a little rubber band. Sensing that such an item might help him bridge the transitional space between appointments, I consented. On his way out, he also told me with almost gleeful anticipation that during the next meeting, he wanted to play Candy Land with me, a family game that had been a favorite when he was much younger.

Over the next several sessions, some important dynamic themes emerged. Ben suggested that we play Hangman, which I believed to be his way of introducing the theme of his father's suicide without actually discussing it openly. During one memorable round, Ben managed to stump me by using a word I'd not heard before—*yegg*. "A yegg," he announced triumphantly, "is a safecracker, a burglar." This seemed to lead to another important theme, one that was repeated in some manner in virtually every subsequent session—that of *protecting one's treasures from thieves and burglars*. Ben described an elaborate device he and a friend had designed to defeat even the most ingenious efforts of such criminals. In another session, Ben designed a board game, which he simply called Evil, the whole point of which was to wear down the player with innumerable twists and turns that return him to an earlier position on the board, ensnare him in traps, or prevent him from making progress by dispensing almost unending penalties. It was a game that was virtually impossible to complete, so that the question of who "won" became a moot point. After a number of experiences with this frustrating game, I observed to Ben that the player seemed to receive more punishment than satisfaction. Ben seemed slightly hurt by this quasi-interpretative comment and claimed that it was simply supposed to be "fun." Over the next few sessions, the positive transference remained strong. At the very end of the eighth session, again in connection with the Hangman game, Ben began to talk about Judas Iscariot, suggesting that "Judas had to kill himself because he had betrayed Jesus…and he didn't have any other solution open to him." At that moment I knew that Ben was saying something very important to me and that it had to do with both his father and himself. Initially, I commented that perhaps Judas might have confessed to God, or sought forgiveness from Jesus, and that there were wise and compassionate souls to whom he might also have turned. Early in the next session, when Ben didn't reintroduce this theme, I brought it up, suggesting that perhaps when Ben had spoken of Judas "running out of options" he was, in a way, also talking about his dad. Perhaps, too, his dad's actions felt like a betrayal to Ben. He denied this, although he agreed that his father had just kept going "downhill" and that nothing had seemed to make much of a difference—neither the drugs he tried, nor the treatments he received (and rejected), nor even, finally, the feelings of his wife and his children. There was a kind of inexorable progression in his long decline, and it did not yield to anything. But Ben was not able to tolerate any additional frank discussion, and so we moved on to other topics. Later in this session, however, Ben seemed to gravitate back to the theme of suicide, excitedly mentioning a story he had heard about a recipient of the so-called "Darwin Awards," who had intentionally driven a knife into his brain, severing the hemispheres in the process. Although it hadn't occurred to me at the time, I believe that with this comment Ben may have been making an oblique reference to his experience of treatment—telling me that in effect, I, too, was trying to "get into" his brain and that he felt not only anxious but attacked.

In the next session, just a few days later, Ben told me that he believed he wasn't getting anywhere in his treatment, and furthermore, that he could not trust me because "You're not really a friend—you're a therapist." And

neither Ben nor the one sibling he was closest to, his oldest sister, Annie, really believed that therapists could do much (after all, look at how miserably
they had failed Ben's father). It occurred to me almost immediately that we
had reached a very perilous stage of his therapy. I believe that this strong
resistance signified precisely the opposite of what he was consciously articulating: now that he had begun to experience some pleasure in his visits with
me, and actually looked forward to his sessions, he had become painfully
aware that I might betray him just as his father had. Were he to become close
to me, depend on me in some way, history might repeat itself. I presented
this idea in a few different ways to Ben over the next couple of sessions. I
also told him that I believed there was a parallel between his description
of his dad's experience in treatment and the way he was now describing his
own. He claimed that I was the "last person" he'd ever trust and denied the
existence of any meaningful parallel. However, I somehow managed to con-
vince him that it was too soon to give up, and he reluctantly agreed to continue with me on a trial basis. Interestingly, it was my strong conviction that
he seemed very angry at several junctures during this particular session, although when I pointed this out to him, he responded dismissively, admitting
only to feeling bored or maybe a little irritated. In the very next session, he
was able to speak somewhat more openly about his father's death, partly in
response to my having suggested (though not for the first time) that anyone
whose parent dies suddenly is likely to have a range of very strong and often
contradictory feelings, regrets, and anxieties—especially when the death is a
suicide. Ben seemed to relax a bit and told me that what I had said had got-
ten him thinking. He then produced some rather poignant early memories,
one of which had to do with his father. This memory, which Ben told me was
the earliest experience he was able to recall, was of his father pushing him
in his tricycle in the rain; he even remembered playing with the wet handle.
This led to memories of how soothing the rain was for him in later years; in
fact, he sometimes had fallen asleep sitting in a chair inside the garage, with
the door open. What is most clear in these memories is what a soothing and
reassuring presence his father had been early on, though this later had been
painfully interrupted by his father's depressive illness and then traumatically
altered by the suicide. As we ended the session, Ben, perhaps again feeling
that he had exposed himself in some way, suddenly eyed me with suspicion
and told me that he felt I was "trying to get at something."

In the next session, Ben told me how stupid one of his teachers was,
essentially for not noticing that Ben had been out of the room for twenty

minutes on an extended (and illicit) bathroom break. He spoke again of the Darwin Awards, sharing several evidently true stories involving individuals who died or were severely injured doing foolish things. Each account seemed to minimize the importance of what had occurred, seeming mockeries of the tragedy of death, which Ben portrayed as a trivial or unreal event. In my view, these accounts were of course thinly veiled allusions to his father's death and represented an effort to minimize or dismiss its profound meaning in his own life. Nevertheless, Ben's vehement denials of any relationship between this topic and the suicide had the effect of making me tread more lightly than usual. In the fifteenth session, which in fact turned out to be Ben's final meeting with me, I returned to the Darwin Awards and the teacher who didn't notice his absence. I told him once again that although I understood that he focused on the Darwin Awards because he found the stories amusing, I wondered whether other reasons might account for his returning to this theme repeatedly over time. Was he perhaps also talking about his father, and the feelings he had about what his father did? I then suggested to Ben that perhaps he was wondering once again how much trust he could place in me; would I be fully attentive to him, notice him, or would he begin to feel disconnected from me, as with his teacher at school. He then gradually became very angry, telling me that he hated coming in to see me and that I could "never know" him, that therapy is pointless, and so forth. Glowering at me, he told me how mad he was that I was trying to find out things about him, things that were happening inside of him. I was surprised by the ferocity of his anger and offered an apology if I had offended him. However, he would have none of this. Although he stayed until the end of the hour, he told me that he would not be back. He held to this promise, and though I made several efforts to contact him, he refused any further treatment and we did not meet again.

I don't think I was very helpful to Ben. In some measure, this was a result of his unconscious identification with his father, particularly his father's experience in treatment. In this regard, it seemed as though Ben was intent on proving his father's case against therapy and therapists and that I had been assigned a scripted role in a scenario over which the playwright, Ben, exercised complete artistic control. Indeed, Ben had very compelling reasons to feel anger toward the therapists who had failed his father, a theme about which I had tried (though without success) to communicate my understanding to Ben. Put differently, his relationship with me—and I assume it to have been equally true of my two predecessors—offered a convenient venue in which such feelings might be expressed. Of course, I assume that Ben was also furious with his father and to a lesser degree his mother, although he was mightily defended against any awareness of this; in a sense, I and all therapists became a convenient object for such redirected or displaced rage. There was, moreover, a sort of sadomasochistic enactment or what the psychoanalyst Heinrich Racker might have termed complementary countertransference in Ben's therapy. In effect, Ben induced in me his own feelings of helplessness, bewilderment, and guilt, treating me as he undoubtedly felt his father had treated him during the former's long and painful illness. Ben's traumatic loss and the conflicted feelings and disturbing wishes it had evoked within him, however, were treated as deep secrets whose disclosure would prove ultimately to be an insurmountable obstacle. Although he understood that a part of my role as his therapist would be to work with him to gradually bring to the surface those issues that he found most troubling, he was also ever-vigilant to guard against this possibility. Like the "yegg," I was perceived to be untrustworthy and interested only in getting at or into things—in this specific instance, the highly personal contents of his psyche. I suppose that finally, like Ben in his efforts to reanimate an already psychologically deceased father before the suicide, I had tried virtually every technique and way of approaching this case, yet remained incapable of reversing or even forestalling its inexorable decline.

A substantial component in my treatment of Ben was to offer assistance to him in the forging of a new and more adaptive internal working model of attachment. He possessed a keen intellect, and unlike many adolescents seen in therapy, he was neither impulse-ridden nor compromised in his ability to reason or use good judgment. Nevertheless, he was unable to understand the dynamic link between his profound anger and the deep injury his father's emotional withdrawal and subsequent suicide had inflicted upon him. Ben longed for the father of his earlier childhood. Marty Daniels had been Ben's close companion and, significantly, had offered him something he was unable to obtain in the same way or to the same extent from either his mother or Rosa, the au pair—the ability to regulate affect through the use of reason and cognition. Although this represented an important early internal relational pattern for Ben, it had been derailed by his father's emotional withdrawal. My tasks in Ben's treatment were several: (a) to offer him the opportunity to mourn both the loss of the early relationship with his beloved father and the subsequent actual loss through his father's suicide; (b) via the inevitable sequence of therapeutic attunement and misattunement, to furnish Ben with opportunities to identify, articulate, and ultimately reflect on my emotional availability and/or unavailability, as both a real person and a transference object; (c) to offer Ben greater understanding of his distress, as well as emotional catharsis and insight, leading to a basis for a new and more adaptive internal structure for relationships; and (d) to work toward an expansion of his repertoire of adaptive strategies and solutions for mitigating distress and resolving conflict. Our various play activities, dialogues per metaphor, and more direct discussion of Ben's day-to-day experiences, his occasional dreams, and waking fantasies furnished the therapeutic vehicles through which I had hoped to accomplish such goals.

Ben did appear to derive a modicum of relief from treatment, at least in the beginning. However, the very prospect of change seemed to signify a loosening of the memories and affective connections that he had worked so hard to preserve, poignant memories of an adult companion whom he had loved dearly. Ben's solution, as formidable as it was desperate, was to keep these memories alive by identifying completely with his father—even to the point of developing an untreatable, angry depression that closely paralleled his father's illness. It may be argued that our work had offered him a limited opportunity to reflect on the meanings of certain early, emotionally charged memories of his father. However, therapeutic progress represented an intolerable threat to the integrity of these tenuous ties and eventually proved an insurmountable challenge.

Attachment, Loss, and Mourning in Ben's Therapy: Afterthoughts

It is possible that Ben's early attachment history, which involved the substitution of an au pair for his mother at a time of heightened sensitivity to attachment security issues, was a major factor in his early social difficulties. Indeed, such compromised attachment security may also have contributed to his inability to recover psychological equanimity after his father's admittedly shocking suicide. However, the evidence here is incomplete at best. Ben may well have been ambivalently or anxiously attached, although his mother also described him as being able to seek her out for comfort when he was unhappy or upset; even now, he sometimes seemed responsive to his mother's efforts to console him. It is also useful to consider the distinct possibility that Ben possessed more than one internal working model, representing different experiences of attachment with his two parents; indeed, my experience of Ben in treatment strongly suggested this. Yet, whatever the nature of Ben's internal models of attachment, there were now serious social and emotional problems, difficulties that none of the other children in the family had experienced to nearly the same extent after the father's suicide.

Suicide represents a special subset of childhood bereavement. Children whose parents commit suicide, we are told, are many times more likely to develop subsequent psychological problems, even when the suicide is handled with great sensitivity and the surviving parent is able to convey empathic attunement and psychological availability. Arguably, Ben's mother was for the most part able to remain psychologically accessible in the weeks and months following her ex-husband's suicide, largely because she had in a sense already mourned the loss of this relationship. Ben's vulnerability was, however, far greater, both because this was his parent and because of the psychological loss that had silently and insidiously cumulated ever since he had first felt forsaken by his father more than four years earlier. It was, in effect, the *ambivalence* associated with his attachment to his father that contributed so heavily to his experience of loss and to his relative inability to achieve anything resembling a satisfactory resolution. At the same time, I do not believe that this explanation is fundamentally incompatible with the clinical summary given above. The course of Ben's present disturbance is unclear: perhaps he will continue, as his father did, in a sort of relentlessly downward spiral of depression; on the other hand, the substantial emotional support his mother and siblings have provided may over time prove reparative. I can only hope that one day this sensitive and deeply hurt child will be able to derive some relief from the unremitting pain he carries within.

In this chapter we discussed the implications of attachment theory for clinical practice with adolescents. Typical developmental tasks illustrated by the three clinical cases presented here include peer relationships, familial conflicts, and the search for identity. The cases also considered the contextualizing factors of race and class, neurological disability, and the traumatic loss of a parent, spotlighting diverse adolescent clients who had a range of problems relevant to social work practitioners. We examined how adolescent attachment is mediated by single-parenting, by neurological illness, and finally by a parent's suicide. Ecological factors such as the social and cultural contexts are also shown to shape the adolescent's attachment patterns.

Attention to attachment concerns in treatment with adolescents includes the therapist's active efforts to create a safe base, encouraging the adolescent client to experiment with new attachments in peer and romantic relationships, exploring his or her identity apart from the family of origin, and validating his or her continuing bond with the parents. Furthermore, it is important to help adolescents regulate their often intense and volatile affectivity and to help them develop self-reflective functions that permit more successful negotiation of the inevitable anxieties, conflicts, and disappointments of this period of development. In addition, clinicians should reflect on their own countertransference reactions to adolescent clients in order to avoid mutual enactments and empathic disruptions with this volatile population. Finally, working with adolescent clients involves the understanding of and sensitivity to a host of complex ecological, cultural, and developmental factors that affect the client's still-fluid and evolving relational patterns. An attachment-informed clinical practice with adolescents is also an opportunity to help these clients revise old internal working models and practice new patterns of attachment.

This chapter will examine adult disorders of attachment and how these may correspond to discrete forms of psychopathology or to particular character disturbances. Other topics for investigation are the role of an adult client's particular attachment style within the treatment relationship or in the transference-countertransference dynamics; general practice principles that attachment-oriented clinicians follow; and the effect of diversity considerations such as race and disability on patterns of attachment and transference-countertransference dynamics.

Each case illustration, selected from a broad spectrum, will include historical antecedents, characteristic behaviors, cognition and feeling states, the impact of attachment styles on the therapeutic relationship, and a treatment process informed by attachment concerns. Treatment with such an orientation will address the following core issues: (a) development of a secure base that permits the client to experiment with attachment (proximity, intimacy) and exploratory behaviors (i.e., practicing new modes of behavior and cognition); (b) development of reflective functioning, or what is referred to by attachment researchers as mentalization or "metacognitive monitoring" (Hesse, 1999), and clients' capacity to reflect upon their state of mind and cognitive processes; (c) affect regulation, including distress, anger, and pleasure (Slade, 1999), since adults who have grown up with emotionally attuned and responsive caregivers learn to self-regulate through their parents' mirroring and accurate attunement, whereas those raised in neglectful, abusive, or chaotic families often demonstrate deficits in self-regulation and self-soothing; (d) development of a flexible response repertoire unique to each situation; (e) the therapist's own reflective ability, which includes recognizing the client's attachment patterns, understanding early disruptions with caregivers, and identifying dissociated emotional experience; and (f) the therapist's awareness and utilization of the moments of misattunement with clients, a key to helping clients transform old, distorted affects and cognitions into new internal structures and more adaptive patterns of interaction.

An Adult with Developmental Disabilities

This vignette demonstrates an avoidant attachment pattern. Through the Adult Attachment Interview (AAI) and the work of several researchers such as Blatt and Levy (2003), Lyons-Ruth (2003), and Fonagy, Gergely, Jurist, and Target (2002), the major classification categories have been further refined. Consequently two subcategories have been identified within the avoidant pattern: the avoidant-fearful attachment style, which entails more schizoid-like characteristics, and the avoidant-dismissive attachment style, which presents with narcissistic features. The case illustration and analysis involves a client whose attachment style was avoidant-fearful and follows a brief discussion of the developmental and clinical issues associated with this style of attachment.

Avoidant children appear to be self-sufficient and independent, hiding their distress from caregivers despite the fact that they continue to experience it internally. This response is frequently associated with particular kinds of misattuned behavior on the part of care providers—either emotional neglect or intrusiveness, or both. Avoidant-dismissive children seem to internalize their caregivers' attitude, which is dismissive of emotional needs, rather than adopting their own authentic emotional experience. By internalizing their caregivers' attitudes of dismissiveness and avoidance, they manage to maintain some semblance of a bond with their parents. Through this process, however, they develop a "false self" (in this instance an external self that serves as protection from adults who are rejecting, dismissive, or over-intrusive). Although these children soon learn to detach themselves from their own emotional states (which their parents had tolerated with such difficulty), such an adaptation impinges on their development of a sense of autonomy and self-esteem. Because a dismissive parent does not mirror back the child's affective state, it is difficult for the child to move on to the more challenging interpersonal tasks of learning to maintain appropriate boundaries with others, identifying and expressing complex emotional states, and communicating these to others (Fonagy & Target, 1998).

Of the two distinct avoidant styles (fearful and dismissive), fearful attachment is characterized by a "negative view of self and others," while "dismissing attachment is typified by a positive view of self and a negative view of others" (Travis, Binder, Bliwise, & Horne-Moyer, 2001, p. 150). With avoidant-fearful clients, it is important to carefully construct a "secure base" and then to track subtle nonverbal cues such as gestures, space, eye contact, and tone of voice from these highly withdrawn, frequently inarticulate clients. The clinician may then help the client identify, articulate, reflect, and assign meaning to his or her core feelings and experiences.

Intersubjective and relational theories emphasize the techniques of mirroring and empathy as important therapeutic tools, and together with the use of moments of misattunement between client and therapist, these techniques can offer the client opportunities for growth and maturation (Beebe & Lachmann, 2002; Lichtenberg, Lachmann, & Fosshage, 2002). Reciprocal interactions between client and therapist can serve to revise old internal working models and thus help the client achieve better relational skills, improved self-esteem, and a coherent sense of self (Blatt & Levy, 2003).

Clinical Illustration 1

Howie was a forty-seven-year-old bicycle messenger.[1] His job changed, however, when phone, fax, and e-mail cut down on his assignments. He lived alone in a seedy downtown hotel and attended a local community college. A talented draftsman, he had also been taking regular life-drawing classes at a well-known art school. His previous therapist, whom he saw for about two years, referred Howie to me. Howie reported that he simply needed someone to talk to.

During our first meeting Howie appeared messy and bedraggled; his clothes were old and wrinkled, and his gray hair was wild and unruly. His appearance, behavior, and name struck me as more fitting for a child than for a mature man. Howie glanced at me shyly and furtively and spoke in monosyllables. He seemed to have a limited and extremely concrete vocabulary. When asked about his previous therapy, he described his therapist as "nice" but somewhat formal. He reported, however, that he felt sad when she left for professional reasons and was surprised to find himself crying during their last session. I later found out that she was the only person with whom he regularly spoke until he met me.

I learned that Howie had lived an almost completely isolated life. His parents had died a number of years before, and since that time his contacts with his younger brother, who lived in a nearby state, had been infrequent. Howie had never had a romantic relationship or even a friendship. After his parents died, their house was sold and he moved to a tiny room in the run-down hotel where he had lived ever since. He seemed to present an extreme case of a fearful-avoidant attachment style. He was fearful of interacting with others and had poor social skills. Although he appeared to be self-sufficient, living his life completely alone with minimal interactions with others, this impression was misleading. He had great difficulty in understanding and expressing his feelings, and his verbal skills were limited to single words and short sentences.

I eventually found out from Howie that his father had been extremely critical and disappointed in him, showing preference to his brother, whom he took on camping trips and invited to his carpentry workshop. Howie's mother had provided for his physical needs, such as food and clothing but, according to Howie's laconic descriptions, had been either critical or uninterested in him. I later speculated that she might have been depressed, and thus emotionally detached from Howie, a common phenomenon among children with an insecure attachment style. As long as he could remember, Howie felt different from everybody else. He didn't fit in at school, and his poor social skills and immature behavior had led to his being bullied by the local boys.

Despite these problems, which were compounded by Howie's compromised communication skills, I believed that he was talented and possessed a considerable intelligence. I could sense his deep loneliness and longing for human contact, buried under his seeming nonchalance and hard-earned self-sufficiency, as well as his fear and overwhelming social anxiety. Howie had never developed the skill to use words in communicating his wants and feelings, in part because meaningful human interactions with others had been so limited, but also because he had never felt that others were especially interested in listening. I inferred that no one had ever mirrored or reflected his thoughts and feeling states, or responded accurately to his distress and helped him to learn how to regulate it. Consequently he could become overwhelmed very quickly, and he soon learned to hide his feelings from others.

Treatment Process

Our first task was to build a safe, consistent therapeutic relationship. When I sensed that Howie had started to feel at ease with me, I began to help him identify his emotional reactions and to model words and phrases to help him communicate both internal states and experiences in the real world to me. His thwarted attempts at closeness with his parents, and perhaps others, had resulted in his withdrawal into a shell of deep and fearful isolation, but the fact that he invariably showed up on time and didn't miss a session was a strong indication to me that despite his fears he longed for friendship and connection. While initially I found myself playing the role of Howie's advisor on day-to-day concerns, I gradually began to encourage him to examine his deeply buried feelings of anger, grief, and loss.

Although Howie did not often refer to his mother, it was clear that his memory of her had a deep effect on his internal life. Initially, he was unable to speak of her beyond the most mundane details, such as her preparing and cooking his meals. Whenever I asked him to talk about their relationship in greater depth, he would become overwhelmed and start to cry uncontrollably. He would then threaten to leave if we continued to pursue the subject. Her loss, it seemed, had been profoundly traumatic and disorganizing for him. Indeed, regulation or integration of these powerful, affect-laden memories seemed so completely beyond his capacity, that he had simply been unable to fully mourn his mother's death. I recognized that he needed to feel more secure with me in order to express these feelings and that I had to help him learn to regulate and manage them.

About a year later, as we were again discussing the loss of his therapist and his unexpected, intense grief reaction, I wondered aloud if this loss had reminded him of his mother's death. Again, he wept uncontrollably, but this time he was able to stay with his emotional experience and to express his grief. He told me that he still missed his mother deeply and that he felt especially sad because he had never told her how much he appreciated her. This was the first time that Howie allowed himself to reveal his feelings of grief and loss to another, and to reflect upon the meaning his mother's death held for him. In addition, through our shared experience, mine as a listener and his as a narrator, he started to process and integrate this painful experience.

After this session, Howie seemed to change. He became more expressive and, with my encouragement, better able to identify and articulate his emotional needs. As we continued to examine his relationship with his mother, he also started to express feelings of ambivalence, a more advanced stage of maturation; he expressed affection mixed with resentment over his mother's lack of understanding and her lack of interest, her characteristic impatience, and her generally gruff attitude toward him. He was also able to identify both anger and sadness toward his father, who always preferred his younger brother's company to his. Howie's growing ability to experience, regulate, and articulate an increasingly complex and subtle array of feelings toward his family gradually seemed to characterize our relationship, as well.

As he gained inner security and confidence, Howie was eventually able to trust our relationship enough to express thoughts and reactions to my own behavior. He started to perceive me as a person with needs and limitations and to risk my rejection and potential retaliation by expressing his observations. For example, he accurately commented once that at times I seemed impatient and inattentive to him, and he added that sometimes he wondered whether I wanted to "get rid of him" and to end our sessions early.

While I would like to present myself here as consistently patient, empathic, and caring, I occasionally did feel impatient, irritated, and resentful during our sessions, particularly at the beginning. Howie would frequently sit passively throughout the session, waiting to be asked questions and dutifully reporting the minute details of his daily life. He would describe what he had eaten and how well he had slept the previous night. I began to feel as I imagined a mother of a young child might—in effect, that I was a source of nourishment and protection but not a person in my own right. I started to resign myself to the idea that Howie was one of those clients who would be coming to see me for a long, long time for support and maintenance, without demonstrating much progress or change. To add to my irritation, he was never late and he never missed a session. This negative countertransference was mixed, of course, with my deep feelings of empathy for his pain, loss, and abiding loneliness. I was the only person with whom he spoke on a consistent basis. I later hypothesized that my impatience and irritation, and Howie's subsequent emotional retreats, were complementary elements in a (re)enactment of his early interactions with his mother.

Howie's courageous observation of me, however, effected a more open and spontaneous dialogue between us, with the result that I started to feel invigorated and more fully engaged in our therapeutic process. I admitted to Howie that although I liked him a great deal and often enjoyed our sessions, I frequently found myself wanting him to take the initiative and to become bolder and more expressive. He seemed both surprised and pleased that I expected more of him. He soon became more active, introducing new material and demanding greater engagement, not only from me but also from others in his life. He recalled, for example, that he had often felt infantilized by his younger brother, who rarely spent any significant time with him and was condescending and impatient, often cutting their conversations short. This sibling had also waited for Howie to beg before doling out his inheritance money. Howie subsequently decided to ask his brother for a meeting and requested a more equitable financial arrangement and regular communication between them. I felt that along with his growing skills in interpersonal communication, his self-confidence was growing as well.

Howie's aspirations for this life developed along with his psychological and interpersonal gains. With his excellent grades at school, he applied for and was accepted to a good university outside the city. At the age of fifty-one, he finally left his old life behind and started anew. For several years, I received occasional cards from him. One day I received a phone call. A male voice introduced himself as "*Howard's* new therapist" (my emphasis). With Howard's permission, his therapist proceeded to ask me a number of questions about him. For me, the transformation of *Howie* to *Howard* aptly captured the process of his growth and maturation and was emblematic of his shift toward a more secure attachment style.

Discussion

Howie's personality and behavior demonstrate how the roots of an avoidant attachment style develop and take hold. With parents who did not supply him with the attention, emotional mirroring, and recognition that he desperately sought as a child, Howie shut himself off and withdrew from all contact with others, fearful of criticism and rejection and easily overwhelmed by his feelings. Though he appeared to be entirely self-sufficient, his defensive style disguised a fragile sense of self and a deep desire for an affective connection with others. His childlike need to be cared for emotionally emerged only in the safety of the therapeutic milieu. My work with Howie therefore entailed (a) building a secure bond between us, (b) helping him to examine and reflect upon his history and identify his needs, (c) teaching him to regulate his emotions and process them, and (d) encouraging him to take interpersonal risks and to utilize his new experiences with me in his interactions with others (with his brother, for example). During this time, it was important that I, too, reflect on our work together and on my own responses to him. Howie learned that an interpersonal bond may endure despite differences and through times of conflict, and that he had become resilient enough to weather such storms.

It is important to include here a discussion of transference-counter-transference dynamics with regard to the two subcategories of the avoidant style, the fearful and the dismissive. Clients who display more schizoid-like (fearful) characteristics tend to take responsibility for everything that happens to them and may appear to idealize the therapist and/or be withdrawn and difficult to engage. A typical countertransference reaction on the part of the therapist may include frustration, boredom, or a tendency to take on a protective parental role. With the more narcissistic-like (dismissive) characteristics, the client's typical defense is to blame others in order to protect the fragile self. In the therapeutic situation, the avoidant-dismissive client is likely to put the therapist down, criticize him or her, or ignore him or her. The client may alternately idealize and devalue the therapist. Typical countertransference reactions on the part of the therapist may be rage, a desire for retaliation, or feelings of incompetence and powerlessness. In both cases it is important to recognize these reactions and to utilize them in skillful ways rather than retaliating or internalizing self-blame. Such countertransference responses can be employed to help identify clients' personality structures and, further, to assist the client in understanding the impact of these behaviors on others. With such difficult clients, ongoing supervision is necessary to help the therapist both understand and contain the complex array of transference-countertransference dynamics that may occur.

The Impact of Early Sexual Abuse

Disorganized attachment is usually preceded by a serious relational disruption, perhaps abuse, neglect, or other early traumatic events that impinge on the child's emotional and relational development. In the Adult Attachment Interview (AAI), these adults appear to be intensely preoccupied with their family's past and to exhibit incomplete resolution of early issues in family relationships. They are, moreover, overwhelmed by feelings of anger or helplessness stemming from these early events and at times may appear to be dissociated from certain memories and experiences. They may present as needy and dependent, desperately seeking care and connection, or as compulsive caregivers (Blatt & Levy, 2003).

Mothers of disorganized infants were found to demonstrate two distinct personality styles. The mothers of disorganized-avoidant infants presented with role confusion and negative intrusive behaviors and seemed hostile and self-involved. On the other hand, mothers of disorganized-approach infants seemed more withdrawn, fearful, and inhibited; they sometimes appeared fragile, and they failed to initiate contact with their infants, at times appearing helpless and fearful of contact with their children (Lyons-Ruth, 2003). As suggested previously, one consequence of early sexual abuse is that a child's attachment style will become more disturbed and disorganized. According to Fonagy et al. (2002), children will defend themselves against acknowledgment of betrayal by a parental figure, who is expected to offer safety and intimacy, by learning to ignore or misinterpret their own mental states and those of others. Fonagy and his colleagues state that such individuals become extremely vulnerable in intimate relationships, as they distort, exaggerate, or misperceive interpersonal cues and fail to communicate their own affect states to others. Main (1999) observes that these clients seem to lack insight and are unable to separate emotionally from their early experiences with their parents. Furthermore, they seem unable to integrate these early experiences into their personality structure or into their current lives as adults. While one group of disorganized clients, including the client presented here, may seem passive, vague, and inarticulate, the other group may appear preoccupied with anger and rage at others.

Clinical Illustration 2

Jean was a twenty-five-year-old middle-class woman who came to therapy both because of social difficulties and out of a desire to be a better mother to her two-year-old daughter. Jean was a tall, robust young woman who seemed to slouch, as if trying to hide herself. She reported that she experienced herself as "too much" for others. She felt too emotional and too needy—and sensed that people saw her as strange. Indeed, according to Jean, many of her friendships had ended because friends felt that she was too "intense." In response, she became afraid of reaching out and engaging in new relationships. Although she described her marriage as good, she reported that her husband was emotionally constricted and overrational. Often she found it difficult to communicate her inner turmoil to him. She was extremely close to her young daughter and did not want to repeat the inadequate parenting that she had received from her mother.

Initially Jean seemed passive, vague, and inarticulate. She had difficulty finding words to describe her emotional experience, and she seemed to wait for me to ask her questions and to point a direction. She described herself as fluctuating between extreme emotional states such as fear, anger, and depression. She was extremely sensitive to the slightest criticism and to what she perceived as failures on her part. With time, she became more expressive, even eloquent. She described a dual reality. Until her adolescence she remembered a happy family, with a mother who was cheerful and a socially engaging father. She remembered family friends coming over and frequent family outings. From adolescence on, however, this happy experience seemed to change abruptly. Jean's mother withdrew into an unexplained depression, and her father started to drink heavily and became emotionally inaccessible. The family grew increasingly isolated, and Jean and her older sister felt frightened and unhappy, without really understanding what had happened. Jean clung to her sister for closeness and support.

Jean reported that as an adolescent, she also began to feel disgusted by her father and became distrustful of him. She avoided being in the same room with him and would not talk to him. She felt lonely and lost, and no one in the family paid any attention to her. Her sister, on the other hand, was the "good child"; she received top grades and enjoyed compliments and praise from their parents. Jean decided to excel in school as well, so that she too would be praised and recognized for her accomplishments. However, she reported, no matter how well she did, her parents never praised her, and her accomplishments did not seem to matter to them. She gradually became rebellious and outspoken, feeling that no one else in the family was willing to confront their dysfunctional family dynamics or to call her father to account on his drinking problem, which the family had colluded to ignore for so many years. At the end of high school, in front of the entire family, she finally confronted her father over his drinking. The result was unexpected and dramatic. Surprisingly, her father became sober after many years of alcohol abuse. Jean reported that she then began to get closer to her father. He even walked her down the aisle at her wedding. Soon after, however, he became seriously ill and died, leaving her the main emotional support for her mother, since by then her older sister had moved three thousand miles away.

I sensed that there was more to Jean's story. It became evident that she felt intensely conflicted toward her father. She had desperately wanted his approval as a child and as an adolescent, and yet she had also said she couldn't stand to be in the same room with him and didn't trust him. Her relationship with her mother seemed alternately close and distant. They never discussed any family history and didn't mention Jean's father. Their roles seemed reversed, with Jean taking a protective role, as if to guard her mother's fragility. Eventually, Jean reported that she remembered an incident of sexual abuse perpetrated by her father and that there might have been more that she was unable to remember. Jean strongly suspected that her sister had been abused as well, though the two never discussed this. She vaguely remembered her father entering her room one night, at age "ten or twelve" (she wasn't sure). Suddenly he was lying on top of her and asking her to touch him inappropriately. She didn't think that her father was drunk at the time, but it was soon thereafter that he began to drink heavily and their family life changed drastically.

Jean admitted that she still had trouble sleeping at night, and suffered intrusive memories and nightmares in relation to the abuse incident. Like the split experience of her family, she felt herself to be split, as well: one persona was that of a competent, bright, happy, and outgoing individual who had never had the chance to blossom and emerge; the other persona was that of a childlike, isolated, scared, and vulnerable person, who experienced herself as damaged, soiled, and unworthy. The entire course of Jean's childhood and adolescence had been foreshortened by her father's actions, the memory of which continued to cast a giant shadow over her life. She was forced to reexperience this abuse again and again. Jean reported that after the incident, she remembered her father sending her notes stating that he loved her and asking her forgiveness, but she couldn't forgive or trust him. From then on, she would no longer trust words, only actions. How could someone who wrote such loving notes also abuse and betray her? Because there had been no reconciliation between Jean and her father over this chapter from their past, Jean saw their rapprochement as an opportunity. Finally, the two of them might be able to discuss it, for her father to explain to her what had happened and why. It was at this time, however, that her father became ill and died. She was angry with him not only for hurting her but also for abandoning her and for leaving this painful issue unresolved.

Jean never discussed the incident with her mother, although she kept wondering what had happened to her family and how it was possible that her mother neither knew nor even suspected. She believed her mother to be too fragile and vulnerable to handle her disclosure and felt that it was her duty to protect her. Jean and her mother had never been able to speak intimately, as her mother seemed to withdraw into a depressed isolation around the time of the abuse. Jean's older sister, with whom she was close, was very much like her mother. Although she was loving and supportive, she never confided in Jean and refused to talk about the past. Thus, Jean alone carried the burden of memory and pain.

Treatment Process

In therapy, Jean started to recognize how desperately she craved praise and validation. She was sensitive to criticism and to others' responses to her, and she always experienced herself as being too intense and too open. She sensed when others disapproved of her, thought she was "strange," or withdrew from her as if something were wrong with her. She was deeply wounded when friends' promises weren't kept, and she experienced these disappointments as personal betrayals. Her need for acceptance and for a deeper connection and intimacy with others alternated with a need for autonomous identity and self-integrity. She realized that she was always looking for others to validate her sense of self-worth, because internally she felt confused, terrified, and lost.

In the beginning of our work together, Jean seemed unsure of her ability to articulate her inner experience or make a worthwhile contribution to our sessions. She was vague about many details, seemed confused at times, and had trouble identifying or expressing her conflicting feelings toward her parents and her sister. With time, however, she became surer of herself, and sometimes even disputed my interpretations. For example, when I once interpreted her lack of self-confidence as stemming from a mother who failed to mirror and validate her, she corrected me. Her predominant experience, she noted, was that of feeling physically and emotionally damaged and of experiencing inadequacy and shame because of her father's abuse. After this interaction we both realized that it was time to deal with the abuse and with the unresolved feelings it had mobilized. Jean discovered that along with pity and longing, she felt a deep sense of fear and anger toward her father. He was both the scary, drunken monster and the beloved, pitiful father who begged for her forgiveness. He abandoned her by dying before they were able to process the abuse and thus left her feeling ashamed, damaged, and unreal. As our work progressed, she also started to express her anger toward her mother, who wasn't there to protect her from her father and to provide respite. Jean's mother refused to hear and acknowledge her daughter's pain and the family trauma, and, through her withdrawal and emotional absence, she forced Jean to fend for herself and to become her mother's caretaker. Jean felt conflict between her need for recognition and validation from her mother and her anger at her mother's withdrawal and passivity.

A dream that Jean reported around this time conveyed her inner experience. In the dream she was standing by a fishbowl, holding a fish that was cut in half and trying to sew it together. To her the dream reflected her experience of being trapped and confined yet also transparent and vulnerable, and it showed that she was trying to heal her broken self. I thought that the fishbowl referred to the therapy situation, in which Jean and I observed and tried to understand her anguish and pain. Her identification with a fish, which is cold, slippery, and smelly, may have reflected her sense of being unlovable and damaged beyond repair.

Discussion

Jean's disorganized attachment style stemmed from her history of paternal sexual abuse and a distant, depressed, and emotionally absent mother who did not provide her with consistent emotional responsiveness, mirroring, and protection. Jean's excessive need for external validation and recognition, her hypervigilance, and her emotional lability are typical characteristics of this attachment pattern.

During the treatment process, Jean's experience of relative safety, security, and validation with me enabled her to share her abuse history and to reflect on the meaning it had for her. She gained insight into the origins of her father's behavior and her mother's depression, and the consequences of both for her own sense of self, her intimate relationships, and, especially, the bond she had formed with her daughter. She would describe to me how she would try hard to respond to and acknowledge her daughter's joy and distress, and how at times her daughter seemed to offer her comfort and responsiveness as well, as if she empathized with her mother's pain. She was able to identify and express difficult and conflicting feelings. Furthermore, through my willingness to listen and contain the rage, ambivalence, and pain to which she gave expression, she gradually learned to tolerate and regulate these feelings. In the past, such feelings had triggered three habitual responses: self-blame, depression, and overeating. She gradually learned to reflect on her experiences and to extrapolate and construct meanings, and she arrived at a better understanding of the relationship between the disparate roles she had filled as daughter, wife, mother, and woman. Finally, her eventual integration of dissociated experiences and feelings offered both new understandings and a more flexible range of responses, rather than the reflexive use of old defensive strategies. For example, she became more spontaneous in her social interactions and more adaptable to life changes (such as her husband's new job in another city).

Through our work together, Jean was able to process the abuse and its impact upon her life and relationships. She could now face a frightening inner world and conflicted feelings and put into words previously unarticulated affect states. Jean has started to take significant emotional risks, discussing the abuse with her sister and fully confronting her feelings toward both parents. Through her own process of growth, she is also becoming more emotionally responsive to her daughter, thus creating a safe base that can allow her to explore and experience on her own, away from Jean.

During the treatment process, I was careful not to intrude on or violate Jean's personal space. I respected her silences and her need to reflect and take time to articulate her thoughts and feelings, even though at times she seemed lost and confused. I tried to be attuned to her feelings, holding her gaze, acknowledging and mirroring her insights and affect states. I knew that such responses were important for a client who had alternately suffered neglect and lack of attunement from her mother and severe boundary violations by her father. She needed to be recognized and validated, with great respect to her own needs and personal boundaries. I encouraged her to take the initiative, to decide how deep to go and when to stop, an option that early on was taken away by her father. I encouraged the "dark part" of her to speak up and express itself and supported what she called "the real Jean" in her efforts to develop strength and confidence. My long-term goal is to help Jean accept and integrate more fully these split-off parts into a more consolidated and cohesive sense of personal identity, where the past has its place and no longer impinges on her present experience.

The Impact of Immigration

The following case describes the treatment process with a client who presents with a somewhat different style of disorganized attachment. In this case, rage and hostility are more evident than helplessness. Unlike the previous client, who demonstrated traits of vagueness and passivity, this client seems preoccupied with anger and also possesses paranoid- fearful traits. According to attachment researchers such as Main, Hesse, and Fonagy, this attachment style may emerge from specific parental behaviors, which may include unresolved childhood traumas (such as the experience of loss and abuse) and the parent's frightening or frightened behavior. Typically, mothers of such individuals were found to engage in "negative intrusive" behavior and to be both "rejecting and attention seeking" (Lyons-Ruth, 2001).

Several complementary styles of relating in the parent-child dyad are possible in the disorganized schema. These styles eventually become the child's internal working models. One schema may depict the attachment figure, typically a parent, as frightening, and the child as frightened (victim and perpetrator). A second schema is a representation of the self (the child) as disoriented or dissociated. A third schema may represent the attachment figure (the parent) as frightened, a situation that leads to role reversal, with the child taking care of, or controlling, the parent (Liotti, 1995). These internal schemata form the patterns of the adult's interpersonal relationships and his or her view of self. Insecure and even disorganized attachment styles, however, may continue to change throughout life, especially when as an adult one is able to confront and work through early traumatic experiences. Such resolution obviates the need to engage in traumatic bonding with significant others or to transmit these unprocessed experiences to one's own children.

Clinical Illustration 3

Nicole was a deeply anxious and depressed middle-aged Haitian immigrant who was described by the intake worker at the community mental health clinic as paranoid and incoherent.[2] Her appearance was bizarre, as she had coal black hair and was wearing garish makeup, with thick black eyeliner and bright red lipstick, making her face look like a mask. She always came in wearing her nursing uniform or tight, revealing outfits. Despite her seductive appearance, she possessed a tiny, childlike voice and spoke very quickly, with a pronounced French accent that made her hard to understand. I sensed that underneath her strange appearance Nicole felt frightened, desperate, and lost. From the start, she stared at me throughout the session and talked nonstop. Her stories invariably centered on persecutory themes, describing the behavior of boyfriends, employers, and peers. Everyone was out to get her, conspiring to "gang up on her," and trying to frighten her in a variety of ways. She rapidly developed an intense and positive alliance with me, likely because of the appeal my own immigrant background held for her.

Nicole was either angry or frightened of everyone in her life. This included her domineering, verbally abusive mother, her alienated older sister, and her immature, untrustworthy "boyfriend" with whom she had had no sexual relationship for a long time and whom she suspected of cheating on her. Soon after we started treatment, she lost her job as a nurse's aide and then proceeded to get fired from a succession of low-level jobs, all of which she hated. Her understanding of these events was that her coworkers conspired to make her life miserable and to upset her, and she didn't know what her bosses expected of her; further, they treated her badly and humiliated her, and she was terrified of them. Nicole's moods were constantly shifting between rage and despair. She would frequently come in or call me between sessions, crying, threatening suicide because of her lonely and miserable life, or expressing her rage at people, including friends and boyfriends, who had disappointed her, let her down, or manipulated her, as she saw it. She felt that the whole world had "ganged up" on her, a metaphor for her inner experience of deprivation, isolation, and dread. She seemed to present the disorganized internal paradigm of a victim who is frightened of an abusive other. Indeed, her childhood confirmed this model of self and other representation, with a mother who was verbally and psychologically abusive, a series of male "babysitters" who sexually abused her, and relatives who treated her poorly.

Nicole was born in Haiti to an impoverished family. Her father was a Caucasian of French descent, and her black Haitian mother made her living cleaning wealthy people's homes. Nicole's father, described as a gentle, quiet man who was bossed around by his domineering wife, left for the United States when Nicole was still very young, in an effort to help the family financially. She didn't see him again until she came to the States with the rest of her family as a late adolescent. Rich and childless relatives adopted her older sister, whom Nicole described as "the lucky one," and soon thereafter Nicole lost contact with her. Nicole's mother was frequently absent because of her work schedule, and Nicole remembered her as critical, manipulative, and verbally abusive. She often humiliated Nicole by calling her "stupid" and "useless." Initially, she left Nicole with a succession of male "babysitters," some of whom, according to Nicole, abused her. Eventually, she was sent to live with her mother's well-to-do sisters. There, Nicole believed, her darker-skinned cousins were envious of her and hated her for her looks and her light complexion. She reported that her aunts forbade her to attend school for fear she would become too popular, and she was hidden at home, only occasionally receiving tutoring. Consequently, she never received a standard education and could barely read or write. She would describe to me how she used to sit alone looking through the window, yearning to go to school and learn. Her greatest wish was to be able to go back to school, complete her education, and become a professional.

When she was sixteen, Nicole, her mother, and her younger brother came to join her father in the United States. Although Nicole loved her father and identified with him as a "victim," she also despised his passivity and his inability to stand up for himself or to protect her from her mother's wrath. He died a few years later. Nicole's brother, who seems to have suffered from schizophrenia, often frightened her with his violent and unpredictable behavior. She described how he would open her bedroom door in the middle of the night and stand there, glaring at her and, at times, threatening violence. He later became involved with drugs and eventually committed suicide. During her childhood, Nicole suffered from obvious abuse and neglect. She described being constantly frightened of her mother, brother, and aunts. In her representational world, she saw herself as a victim and others as perpetrators, and she continued to re-create these schemata in current relationships and in the workplace.

Nicole's adult relationship with her mother illustrated this victim-perpetrator dynamic that ruled her inner and outer worlds. Nicole's mother was by now an elderly woman, but for Nicole she was an all-powerful, evil woman. She reported how her mother forced her to serve her meals, clean her house, and run errands for her. She still criticized and humiliated Nicole often and promised her financial rewards if she did her bidding. Nicole felt beholden to her, powerless, and unable to resist or escape. She reverted again to being a small, helpless child.

Treatment Process

Nicole's internal working models were chronically and unconsciously repeated with other people in her life. Though she described her errant boyfriend as unfaithful and unreliable, she was completely obsessed with him, calling him at all times of the day and night, spying on him, and unable to stop thinking of him. I wondered if he felt pursued and intruded upon. This pattern continued with her intense transference to me, which gradually shifted from a positive to a negatively valenced one in which Nicole became my pursuer and I felt victimized and trapped. This began with Nicole identifying with me as a fellow immigrant. She fantasized and constructed narratives about my difficulties in adjusting to the United States and my struggle to get an education and to become successful. My "life story," as Nicole imagined it, gave her great hope and inspiration. When she eventually found out that I had a teenage daughter, she visualized her, too, as a pretty, ambitious young woman who took after her mother and had become a great success. This fantasy seemed to deepen Nicole's transference to me as an idealized maternal and inspirational figure. She hoped that someday she herself would have a daughter whom she could love and nurture.

Nicole's idealization of me, however, didn't stop there. She started to project onto me her own yearnings and unrequited desires. She soon started to comment on my clothes, jewelry, and makeup, and proceeded to give me advice on hairstyles, shopping, and current fashion sales. Eventually, she moved on to counsel me on my career as well. She demanded that I go on the Sally Jesse Raphael and Oprah shows and then suggested that I start my own television show so that I could become one of "the rich and famous," which is how she saw me. She envisioned me as living in Los Angeles in a big mansion with a swimming pool and a Jacuzzi, and seemed distressed by the fact that I worked in a somewhat dilapidated mental health center. To my great discomfort, our roles seemed to have reversed, with Nicole becoming my mentor and consultant. I frequently felt impinged upon, trapped, and even concerned for my safety at times (more on that later). I certainly experienced Nicole's behavior as intrusive and aggressive. As her focus on me intensified, I became increasingly uneasy. I felt violated, imprisoned in her idealization of me, a play object rather than a real person in our interactions. Nicole reported that she had started to talk about me to people she had just met on the street or on the bus, to her rejecting coworkers, and to her abusive employers. While I seemed to have become the shield she used to protect herself from harm, I started to feel somewhat concerned for my own privacy and safety. I reflected, however, that although I didn't know where this was going, our relationship seemed to have a markedly beneficial effect on Nicole. She clearly needed to use me in this way and was not yet ready to recognize me as a real, multidimensional person with my own privacy needs and an existence independent of hers. This was strangely confirmed when once, as I walked home from work, I saw her coming toward me. I wanted to say hello, but she passed right by me without seeing me, as if I, the real person, did not exist.

This interactive pattern repeated itself in my office, where Nicole seemed unable to "hear" anything that deviated from her beliefs and fantasies. When I asked her to consider other potential perspectives on her experience besides the victim/perpetrator scenario, or to reflect on the consequences of certain actions before taking them, she wouldn't hear of it. Instead, she chose to use me in her own unique way. She reported that she would tell employers, coworkers, boyfriends, and strangers that they couldn't hurt or insult her, because she had me, her exotic Israeli therapist. She acted on my imagined "advice" and "took me" along with her wherever she went. This helped her, she reported, to maintain her "self-respect" and to feel protected. While I experienced myself as Nicole's hostage, I also felt flattered by her intense idealization of me. I found her attempts to nurture me and give me advice endearing and somewhat entertaining. Nicole, it seemed, enjoyed taking the initiative in our relationship, and she was developing a new sense of mastery and adventure.

Our transference-countertransference relationship also had an important cultural aspect. Race and ethnicity are described as the "third" presence in the therapeutic encounter, in addition to the client and the therapist (Mattei, 1999). For Mattei, the notion of the ethnic third contains dimensions of mutuality and difference, exclusion and inclusion between clinician and client. While we did not explicitly discuss these dimensions of our therapeutic relationship, they were clearly present from the very beginning, and it is therefore important to examine them here. Nicole's transference to me was twofold: She felt that as an immigrant myself, I shared some of her own struggles and determination in a new country. As an Israeli, I embodied for her strength, independence, and resilience, qualities that she also associated with Haitian women, including her mother and her aunts. As a Caucasian woman, I was in her eyes a refuge from the frightening black women of her past, her mother and her aunts, of whom she experienced an almost primordial terror. This terror was projected onto any African American woman that Nicole encountered in her present life. She was sure that black women wanted to persecute and harm her. My ethnicity therefore initially served to shelter her, to help her feel safe and protected. With time, of course, as she started to internalize a sense of resilience and security, she was able to develop positive relationships with black women in her life and to see them for who they actually were.

Nicole gradually made me an integral part of her "family." She informed me that she had told all her friends about me, how smart and successful I was, and then conveyed to me their holiday greetings and well wishes. She started to bring me small presents on the holidays. While initially I was reluctant to accept them, I realized that for Nicole, being able to give something back and, symbolically, to nurture me represented a small token of appreciation for my presence in her life. Later I found out that in Haitian culture it is considered rude to return gifts. Once, when I went on vacation, Nicole asked me to give her a photograph of myself so she would feel less alone while I was away. Thereafter, she reported, my photograph became a prominent fixture in her spartan and tiny studio apartment, strategically placed and in full view to all her friends.

With time, Nicole's intensive, idealizing transference to me seemed to bring about significant changes in her. She reported that she had started to experience herself as more feminine (like me), rather than as an androgynous, sexless figure, and that for the first time she had started to enjoy looking at herself in the mirror. She took a new interest in her makeup and clothing and started to see herself as a lovable and desirable woman. She began to envision a different life for herself, one with "normal" relationships, a good education, and even a career.

Our transference-countertransference dance continued to evolve and eventually became a form of mutual, interactive play. With time, I became a more active participant in Nicole's creations. She had started, she reported, to adopt my voice, my walk, and the way I moved and held myself. She would come in and show me her version of how she would walk like me, proud, with her head held high, her voice deeper and more confident. She reported that as she "took on" my personal characteristics, she noticed that people started to treat her with more consideration and respect. It took me some time to adapt to this new and playful rhythm in our interaction. Eventually, however, I, too, "loosened up" and started to enjoy Nicole's truly hilarious impressions of me. We developed a certain ritual, a mutually interactive pattern of playfulness around her impersonations and my appreciative responses to them. Instead of feeling a sense of trepidation before our sessions, I began to look forward to them. While Nicole initially "took me" along with her, she eventually started to internalize and transmute into more enduring structures the qualities of self-esteem, confidence, and emotional stability that she saw in me. I, on the other hand, mirrored her newfound confidence and sense of humor, and began to enjoy every new nuance that she added to her repertoire. Our sessions had been transformed into reciprocal play and mutual pleasure.

My willingness to tolerate Nicole's fantasies and demands, and my ability to join in her play served slowly to bring about a shift in both her sense of self and in her interpersonal relationships. In Winnicott's terms, she used me as a "transitional object," dressing me up and playing with me as if I were her doll, as if she were practicing and preparing herself through these symbolic activities to move out and become an adult in the real world. When she first consulted me, Nicole was filled with fear and distrust. Her experience was of a world in which "everyone was ganging up on her" and trying to persecute her, over which she felt a sense of rage, isolation, and despair. Gradually, she became more trusting, playful, and open to new experiences. With a new sense of herself as lovable and competent, she started to initiate new friendships in which she was an equal partner rather than a powerless victim. She learned to have more fun in her life, including swimming and Rollerblading. With time, her relationship with her boyfriend improved considerably; as she became able to trust him more and to allow him some space, he started to treat her with more consideration and respect. She was finally able to sever her untenable relationship with her mother, who seemed to have lost her power over Nicole. In sessions, however, she was able to think of her mother in a more integrated way, as someone who, despite her faults, was financially successful in a new country, without formal education or a profession. Nicole started to see that she had inherited her mother's own determination and resilience.

Nicole went back to school and eventually obtained her General Education Development certificate, a bachelor's degree, and finally, a graduate degree. Her lifelong dream was fulfilled: she finally became a professional. This change was clearly apparent in her behavior and in her appearance. She seemed more confident, self-possessed, and at ease with herself. She spoke with more measured tones and was able to listen. She had become her own person and was now better able to experience me as *my* own person as well. By the time we decided to conclude the treatment, Nicole had created a new life for herself. She had started a professional career, and she and her boyfriend were discussing the adoption of a little girl.

Discussion

My work with Nicole reflects a gradual process during which both of us influenced and shaped each other. I provided Nicole with a protective space in which to practice playfulness and creativity by idealizing, using, shaping, and finally playing with me. Nicole's idealization of me and my function as a stabilizing, organizing, and containing presence for her eventually shifted as she started to develop and solidify her own sense of self and to internalize our positive interactive experiences with each other. Over time her personality and relational style shifted from a disorganized, paranoid, and sometimes delusional internal working model to a more stable, secure, and integrated personality structure, with correspondingly healthier self-other interactions. She learned to regulate her emotional experience, to respond in less reactive ways, and to reflect on her feelings and interpersonal experiences that in the past had caused her emotional disintegration. During our work together, she developed a growing capacity for interactive play. She changed from a child-woman whose relationships with others were driven by primal needs for bonding and survival to a mature woman who started to experience a new sense of competence and whose relationships reflected mutuality, growth, and intimacy. This change was clearly apparent in her style of play, which had become increasingly more humorous, imaginative, and relationally complex.

Nicole's creative process was of course contingent upon my own capacity to provide a consistent, safe space in which she could "try on" and experiment with different behaviors and identifications. Eventually, I, too, learned to adapt my own personal style in order to become a more responsive and interactive partner in our intersubjective play. Lichtenberg and Meares (1996) note that as attachments develop, affectionate reciprocity and communication provide the foundation for, among other functions, the capacity for symbolic play, or the ability for substitution and pretense. In the process, they suggest, gestures or words become alternative substitutes for actions. This capacity is akin to Fonagy's concept of "mentalization," which we have previously defined as the ability to create a space for reflective thinking rather than taking an impulsive action. Through her use of the potential space between us for practicing and play, Nicole learned and internalized new responses and relational patterns that she could then use in her everyday world.

In summary, intersubjective play and playfulness contribute to cognitive, affective, and even physiological developmental processes in children. As reflected in the vignette presented here, play and creativity in the context of adult treatment may also help transform old internal working models and relational blueprints in later adult development. Play fosters socialization, creativity, and adaptation, and ultimately, as noted by Lichtenberg and Meares (1996), enhances the experience of intimacy between people, as well as the experience of knowing and accepting oneself authentically.

The three case vignettes presented in this chapter demonstrated clinical practice with adults from an attachment-informed perspective, with attachment disruptions as the major focus of the treatment. We tried to select clients who were well suited to social work practice because of diversity issues (immigrants and disabled clients) and early abuse and neglect.

In each of the case examples, we have explained how a treatment informed by attachment concepts builds on the development of a safe base between client and therapist and focuses on helping clients regulate affect through the therapist's modeling as well as through mutual regulation between therapist and client. The therapist helps the client develop a greater capacity for reflective functioning, as well as for more flexible responses to situations, culled from an expanding repertoire of adaptive strategies. Finally, through their own self-reflection and sensitivity to moments of misattunement with clients, therapists help clients repair old attachment disruptions and begin experimenting with new, healthier ones.

Close observation of the client's behavior, language, affect states, interpersonal relationships, and transference-countertransference paradigms reveals that attachment styles in childhood have significant impact on adult development and that the therapist's careful observation of verbal and nonverbal signals, the ability to help process therapeutic interactions, and the mutual regulation of affect between client and therapist are all crucial to the treatment process. Significantly, the therapist's ability to identify and understand his or her own countertransference reactions to a particular client may enhance understanding of the historical origin of specific behaviors and assist the client in efforts to develop a more adaptive relational accommodation as well as a more secure sense of self.

Levels of communications are the focal point of a treatment in which attachment and relationship issues are examined. Intersubjective and relational theories offer a perspective in which the mutual influence of client and therapist is central to the treatment process. Rather than focusing more or less exclusively on insight, as classical psychoanalytic theory has advocated, the "communicative exchange from a systems perspective becomes far more complex" (Lichtenberg, Lachmann, & Fosshage, 2002, p. 76). The therapeutic action in these models begins with an enhancement of self-knowledge through reflection, insight, and observation of both self and other; it leads later to new experiences based on the therapist's facilitation of affect regulation and the repair of disruptions in attunement; and finally, it results in full engagement in a relationship defined by the mutual regulation of affect and the contribution of both to the resolution of relational impasses. When sensitively timed to coincide with the client's newly emerging capacities, such a model offers a solid foundation for psychodynamic treatment in which attachment concerns are central.

Notes

1. Beginnings: Early Conceptions of the Mother-Infant Relationship

1. The Oedipus complex actually consists of both positive oedipal and negative oedipal strivings. The "positive" Oedipus complex is associated with the wish for a sexual union with the parent of the opposite sex and a coterminous wish for the same-sex parent's demise. However, in consequence of the fact that such wishes are inherently conflict-laden, giving rise to both ambivalence and vulnerability, "negative" oedipal strivings—consisting of the desire for a sexual union with the same-sex parent and feelings of rivalry with the opposite-sex parent—coexist with the positive ones. According to classical theory, the positive Oedipus complex supersedes the negative Oedipus complex, and this is considered a prerequisite for the emergence of a heterosexual orientation and cohesive identity in adulthood.

2. Fonagy and Target note that following the publication of Bowlby's highly controversial 1960 paper, in which he took the position that mourning was indeed possible for infants and young children, his attachment theory became the target of a number of other criticisms by mainstream psychoanalysts. He was seen as "having renounced drives, the Oedipus complex, unconscious processes, particularly unconscious fantasy, complex internalized motivational and conflict-resolving systems ... [for] having discarded the richness of human emotions, be these affects experienced by the ego and involving socialization or sources of pleasure rooted in the baby's body ... [for] ignoring biological vulnerabilities other than those rooted in the caregiver's behavior and ... blaming all pathology on physical separation ... [for] ignoring negative attachment related to fear of the mother and trauma

other than physical separation ... and for being reductionist[ic] in his emphasis on evolution at the expense of recognition of complex symbolic functioning" (2003, pp. 236–237).

3. The "environment" had not always been relegated to the ancillary status it came to have in Freud's libido theory, however. Interestingly, in his earliest publications, works such as the *Studies on Hysteria* (1893–1895), Freud had imputed a good deal of importance to "actual" experience in the formation of psychopathology. A prime example is his *seduction theory*, later abandoned in favor of a more purely psychological explanation, which made an explicit link between actual experiences of sexual abuse or incest and the psychogenesis of hysterical symptoms.

4. In contrast, Bowlby differed pointedly with Freud over what have come to be known as the "metapsychological perspectives." The metapsychological perspectives, or simply metapsychology, was a collection of six axiomatic principles (*topographical, structural, dynamic, economic, genetic*, and *adaptive*) that served as the explanatory basis for Freud's most important formulations about human behavior and psychopathology. Although untroubled by Freud's emphasis on the *structural* (conflict-mediating structures), *genetic* (past persists into the present), and *adaptive* (the organism's commerce with reality) viewpoints, he took exception to Freud's *topographical* (layering of consciousness), *economic* (i.e., existence of psychological energy) and *dynamic* (existence of psychological forces) hypotheses.

5. While Freud relinquished his "seduction theory" in favor of a more purely psychological explanation for the psychogenesis of various neurotic disorders, he continued to believe that actual "seduction has retained a certain significance for etiology," observing that in at least two cases with which he was familiar, those of Katharina and Fräulein Rosalia H, the patients had been sexually victimized by their fathers (Gay, 1988).

6. Klein's fundamental premise was that the play of young children was equivalent to the free associations of adult clients; so long as the meaning of their play was interpreted to them, children, like adults, were suitable subjects for psychoanalytic treatment. Anna Freud's position, however, was that small children could not be analyzed, since they had an inherently weak and rudimentary ego that would be incapable of managing deep interpretations of instinctual conflict (Mitchell & Black, 1995).

7. An excerpt from an interview with Bowlby conducted by Robert Karen on January 14–15, 1989.

8. These ideas were especially troubling to Bowlby, who was critical of Klein's notion that the significance of infantile anxiety could be fully understood only within the context of infantile aggression and, moreover, that aggression constituted the sole source of anxiety (Bowlby, 1973). Further distancing himself from Klein and her theoretical framework, Bowlby noted that Klein's followers "have been slow to recognize that, significant though depressive and persecutory anxieties may sometimes be, the origin of separation anxiety cannot be understood in such terms, and, more important, that disturbances of the mother-child relationship that arise during the second and many subsequent years can have a far-reaching potential for pathological development" (Bowlby, 1973, p. 387).

9. In the early 1950s, Winnicott had written of the "well-known observation that the earliest anxiety is related to being insecurely held" and, further, that "it is normal for the infant to feel anxiety if there is a failure of infant care technique" (Winnicott, 1952).

10. Mahler's separation-individuation theory is discussed in far greater detail in chapter 3.

11. Self psychological ideas about development will also be explored more systematically in chapter 3.

12. Evidently, Bowlby found this Winnicottian concept of the true/false self to be a serviceable one, making several references to it in his multivolume work on attachment, separation, and loss.

13. Although acknowledging that Winnicott's conception of relationship always seemed "far less dominated by food and orality than" that of Klein (Bowlby, 1969, p. 372), Bowlby was nonetheless critical of the Winnicottian notion of the transitional object. He wrote that a "much more parsimonious way of looking at the role of these inanimate objects is to regard them simply as objects towards which certain components of attachment behavior come to be directed or redirected because the 'natural' object [defined as "an object towards which the behavior is directed in an animal's environment of evolutionary adaptiveness"] is unavailable" (Bowlby, 1969, p. 312).

14. Freud was actually the first to employ this term, though his use differs somewhat from that of Fairbairn. Freud conceived of *primary identification* as a primitive form of internalization characterized by its directness, immediacy, and the fact that it was unrelated to object loss (Moore & Fine, 1990).

15. Bowlby had also noted that "a principal point of difference" between his work and Fairbairn's resided in the latter's tendency "to identify attachment with feeding and orality and so to attribute a proportionately greater significance to a child's first year or two" than he (Bowlby) did (1973, p. 256).

16. Balint based this claim on research reported in 1937 by Peto. Although relatively unsophisticated by contemporary standards, Peto's observations are at striking variance with those of Mahler and, at the same time, appear to adumbrate the well-documented research of psychoanalytic researchers, such as Dan Stern, who have challenged the evidence upon which Mahler's assumptions about the objectlessness of early infancy rests.

17. Nevertheless, Bowlby did acknowledge the importance of both Suttie's and Hermann's conception that frustrated attachment might explain the relationship of psychopathology to the "central role of separation anxiety" (1973, p. 397).

2. Bowlby's Theory of Attachment

1. In a more general way, ego psychology became the predominant paradigm in the American psychoanalytic community and remained so for the next thirty years.

3. Contemporary Psychoanalytic Perspectives on Attachment

1. The close parallel between Sullivan's use of this term and the social work paradigm of *person-in-environment* seems unmistakable here, although Sullivan has not often been cited by social work historians as having exerted significant influence on the evolution of social work theory.

2. This "need," however, is put forward far more tentatively than many of Sullivan's other ideas about early development, a fact that did not escape the notice of John Bowlby (1969, pp. 374–375).

3. Researchers in the field of infant development have challenged such ideas, as the upcoming discussion of Margaret Mahler's separation-individuation theory will highlight.

4. This was particularly true with respect to the timing and characteristics of the phases (Greenberg & Mitchell, 1983).

5. Masterson and Rinsley (Masterson, 1976, 1985; Masterson & Rinsley, 1975; Rinsley, 1977, 1978) are perhaps best known for their distillation of separation-individuation theory and their application of it to the understanding and treatment of borderline, schizoid, and other character-disordered clients.

6. Such *libidinal* object constancy is, however, not the equivalent of the Piagetian *object permanence*; the latter represents a milestone in cognitive development held to occur at eighteen to twenty months and concerned primarily with the child's relationships to the world of *inanimate* objects.

7. Bowlby had earlier (1973) taken exception to Mahler's (1968) assertion that *separation anxiety* was possible only after completion of separation-individuation and the attainment of object constancy. However, Mahler's use of this term gradually expanded to include infants in not only the rapprochement but also the practicing subphase (1978), which would appear to address Bowlby's objections.

8. Dr. Martin Loeb (deceased), a cultural anthropologist and social worker, shared an office with Erikson in the 1950s. He once recalled that one of Erikson's greatest pleasures was simply to watch the children at play in the schoolyard across the street from their office building, a pursuit in which he spent countless hours (personal communication to J. Brandell).

9. Erikson's detailed description and comparative analysis of child-rearing practices of the North American Sioux and Yurok tribes in *Childhood and Society* is one such example.

10. The first portion of this section was adapted in part from Brandell & Perlman (1997) and Brandell (2002).

11. The reader is referred to Fonagy & Target (2003) for additional discussion of the scientific status of self psychology.

4. Research on Attachment

1. These studies were quoted in Van Ijzendoorn & Sagi, 1999.

2. As quoted in Van Ijzendoorn & Sagi, 1999.

5. Children

1. All clinical examples used in this chapter are derived from the first author's clinical practice.

2. Somewhat analogously, protective or mitigative factors (e.g., temperament, intelligence, quality of the child's social relationships, superior schools, safe neighborhoods) that may reduce the risk of childhood psychopathology have also been identified (Greenberg, 1999; Luthar & Zigler, 1992). Perhaps not surprisingly, secure attachment appears to confer at least some protection from potentially pathogenic influences and maladaptive outcomes (Greenberg, 1999).

3. A simple but time-honored technique of child psychotherapy originally introduced by D. W. Winnicott (1971), which calls for the clinician and child to take turns drawing "squiggly" lines and completing each other's squiggle drawings. The squiggle is made with one's eyes closed, although the other subject always completes the drawing with his or her eyes open. Winnicott characteristically used the squiggle content as a springboard for analytic investigation, although I have found it has considerable value as a "lead-in" to the story-making process with children such as Derek.

4. An earlier rendering of this case appeared as, "Psychotherapy of a Traumatized 10-Year-Old Boy: Theoretical Issues and Clinical Considerations," *Smith College Studies in Social Work*, 62, 123–138 (March, 1992).

5. In an interesting parallel that may partially explain the strength of Nathan's adoptive mother's commitment to these three children, I later learned that she had been abandoned by her own mother in mid-latency. Although she had been deeply hurt at the time by her mother's abandonment of the family, her description of their early relationship suggested a relatively stable and secure attachment. She was subsequently raised by her father and stepmother, and was only many years later successful in her determined efforts to locate her mother and reestablish a relationship with her.

6. This symptom constellation appears often in post-traumatic conditions, according to H. Krystal (1993). J. McDougall (1984, 1985, 1989), expressing a similar viewpoint, prefers the term *disaffectation* to *alexithymia* to underscore her application of dynamic rather than neurobiological principles to explain the mechanism whereby a sort of psychological foreclosure of potential affects and affect representations occurs. The result is that "certain people are psychologically separated from their emotions and may indeed have 'lost' the capacity to be in touch with their psychic realities" (McDougall, 1989, p. 103).

6. Adolescents

1. The first two clinical illustrations, the cases of Ray and Karla, were contributed by the second author; the third vignette, Ben, was written by the first author.

2. Adapted from a case presentation originally presented by the first author at a mini-conference, "Challenging Moments in Clinical Practice," sponsored by the

Ruth Koehler Trust and the Michigan State University School of Social Work, East Lansing, Michigan, in March 2004.

7. Adults

1. An earlier version of this case appeared in *Psychoanalytic Social Work 11* (2), 71–82 (Ringel, 2004).

2. An earlier version of this case appeared in *Clinical Social Work Journal 31* (4), 371–381 (Ringel, 2003).

References

Abrams, S. (1993). The developmental dimensions of play during treatment: A conceptual overview. In A. Solnit, D. Cohen, & P. Neubauer (Eds.), *The many meanings of play* (pp. 221–238). New Haven: Yale University Press.

Ainsworth, M. (1963). The development of infant-mother interaction among the Ganda. In B. M. Foss (Ed.), *Determinants of infant behavior* (pp. 67–104). New York: Wiley.

——. (1967). *Infancy in Uganda.* Baltimore: Johns Hopkins University Press.

——. (1983). A sketch of a career. In A. N. O'Connoll & N. Russo (Eds.), *Models of achievement: Reflections of eminent women in psychology* (pp. 200–219). New York: Columbia University Press.

——. (1989). Attachments beyond infancy. *American Psychologist, 44,* 709–716.

Ainsworth, M., & Bell, S. (1970). Attachment, exploration, and separation: Illustrated by the behavior of one-year-olds in a strange situation. *Child Development, 41,* 49–67.

Ainsworth, M., Blehar, M. C., Waters, E., & Wall, S. (1978). *Patterns of attachment.* Hillsdale, N.J.: Lawrence Erlbaum Associates.

Allen, J. (2001). *Traumatic relationships and serious mental disorders.* New York: Wiley.

Allen, J., Hauser, S., Bell, K., & O'Connor, T. (1994). Longitudinal assessment of autonomy and relatedness in adolescent-family interactions as predictors of adolescent ego development and self esteem. *Child Development, 65,* 179–194.

Allen, J., & Land, D. (1999). Attachment in adolescence. In J. Cassidy and P. Shaver (Eds.), *Handbook of attachment: Theory, research, and clinical applications* (pp. 319–335). New York: Guilford.

Allen, J., Moore, C., Kuperminc, G., & Bell, K. (1998). Attachment and adolescent psychosocial functioning. *Child Development, 69*, 1406–1419.

Arbona, C., & Power, T. (2003). Parental attachment, self-esteem, and antisocial behaviors among African American, European American, and Mexican American adolescents. *Journal of Counseling Psychology, 50*(1), 40–51.

Aron, L. (1991). The patient's experience of the analyst's subjectivity. *Psychoanalytic Dialogues, 1*(1), 29–51.

Bacciagaluppi, M. (1993). Ferenczi's influence on Fromm. In L. Aron & A. Harris (Eds.), *The legacy of Sandor Ferenczi* (pp. 185–198). Hillsdale, N.J.: Analytic Press.

Bahrick, L., & Watson, J. (1985). Detection of intermodal proprioceptive-visual contingency as a potential basis of self-perception in infancy. *Developmental Psychology, 21*, 963–973.

Balint, A. (1949). Love for the mother and mother-love. *International Journal of Psychoanalysis, 30*, 251–259.

Balint, M. (1949). Early developmental states of the ego: Primary object love. *International Journal of Psychoanalysis, 30*, 265–273.

——. (1952a). Early developmental states of the ego: Primary object love. In M. Balint (Ed.), *Primary love and psychoanalytic technique* (pp. 90–108). New York: Liveright Publishing.

——. (1952b). New beginning and the paranoid and depressive syndromes. *International Journal of Psychoanalysis, 33*, 214–224.

——. (1959). *Thrills and regressions.* London: Hogarth.

——. (1968). *The basic fault: Therapeutic aspects of regression.* London: Tavistock.

Bandura, A. (1971). *Social learning theory.* Englewood Cliffs, N.J.: Prentice Hall.

Barnett, D., Kidwell, S., & Leung, K. (1998). Parenting and preschooler attachment among low-income urban African American families. *Child Development, 69*(6), 1657–1671.

Beebe, B., & Lachmann, F. (2002). *Infant research and adult treatment: Co-constructing interactions.* Hillsdale, N.J.: Analytic Press.

Beebe, B., Lachmann, F., & Jaffe, J. (1997). Mother-infant interaction structures and presymbolic self and object representations. *Psychoanalytic Dialogues, 7*, 133–182.

Beebe, B., & Stern, D. (1977). Engagement-disengagement and early object experiences. In M. Freedman & S. Grand (Eds.), *Communicative structures and psychic structure* (pp. 35–55). New York: Plenum.

Bell, R., & Ainsworth, M. (1972). Infant crying and maternal responsiveness. *Child Development, 433*, 1171–1190.

Benjamin, J. (1995). Recognition and destruction: An outline of intersubjectivity. In *Like subjects, love objects* (pp. 27–48). New Haven, Conn.: Yale University Press.

Bennett, S. (2003a). International adoptive lesbian families: Parental perceptions of the influence of diversity on family relationships in early childhood. *Smith Studies in Social Work, 74*(1), 73–91.

——. (2003b). Is there a primary mom? Parental perceptions of attachment bond hierarchies within lesbian adoptive families. *Child and Adolescent Social Work Journal, 20*(3), 159–173.

Blatt, S., & Levy, K. (2003). Attachment theory, psychoanalysis, personality development, and psychopathology. *Psychoanalytic Inquiry, 23*(1), 102–150.

Blos, P. (1979). *The adolescent passage.* New York: International Universities Press.

Bowlby, J. (1940). The influence of early environment in the development of neurosis and neurotic character. *International Journal of Psychoanalysis, 21,* 1–25.

——. (1944). Forty-four juvenile thieves: Their characters and home-life. *International Journal of Psychoanalysis, 25,* 107-128.

——. (1949). The study and reduction of group tensions in the family. *Human Relations, 2,* 123–128.

——. (1951). *Maternal care and mental health.* World Health Organization Monograph, series 2. Geneva: World Health Organization.

——. (1958). The nature of the child's tie to his mother. *International Journal of Psychoanalysis, 39,* 350–373.

——. (1959). Separation anxiety. *International Journal of Psychoanalysis, 41,* 1–25.

——. (1960). Grief and mourning in infancy and early childhood. *Psychoanalytic Study of the Child, 15,* 3–39.

——. (1963). Pathological mourning and childhood mourning. *Journal of the American Psychoanalytic Association, 11,* 500–541.

——. (1969). *Attachment and loss.* Vol. 1. *Attachment.* New York: Basic Books.

——. (1970). *Child care and the growth of love.* Harmondsworth, England: Pelican Books.

——. (1973). *Attachment and loss.* Vol. 2. *Separation.* New York: Basic Books.

——. (1980). *Attachment and loss.* Vol. 3. *Loss.* London: Hogarth.

——. (1981). Psychoanalysis as natural science. *International Review of Psycho-Analysis, 8,* 243–255.

——. (1988). *A secure base.* New York: Basic Books.

Bradley, R. (2002). The impact of sexual abuse on self and identity in adolescents and adults. International Conference on Traumatic Stress, Baltimore.

Brandell. J. (1992). Countertransference phenomena in the psychotherapy of children and adolescents. In J. Brandell (Ed.), *Countertransference in psychotherapy with children and adolescents* (pp. 1–44). Northvale, N.J.: Jason Aronson.

——. (2000). *Of mice and metaphors: Therapeutic storytelling with children.* New York: Basic Books.

——. (2002). Using self psychology in clinical social work. In A. R. Roberts & G. J. Greene (Eds.), *Social workers' desk reference* (pp. 158–162). Oxford: Oxford University Press.

——. (2004). *Psychodynamic social work.* New York: Columbia University Press.

Brandell, J., & Perlman, F. (1997). Psychoanalytic theory. In J. Brandell (Ed.), *Theory and Practice in clinical social work* (pp. 101–131). New York: Simon and Schuster/Free Press.

Brandell, J., & Ringel, S. (2004). Psychodynamic perspectives on relationship: Implications for social work education of new findings from human attachment and the neurosciences. *Families in Society, 85*(4), 549–565.

Bretherton, I. (1999). The origins of attachment theory: John Bowlby and Mary Ainsworth. In J. Cassidy & P. Shaver (Eds.), *Handbook of attachment: Theory, research, and clinical applications.* New York: Guilford.

Breuer, J., & Freud, S. (1893–1895). *Studies on hysteria.* Vol. 2. (J. Strachey, trans.). London: Hogarth.

Cabral, R., & Scott, D. F. (1976). Effects of two desensitization techniques, biofeedback and relaxation, on intractable epilepsy: Follow-up study. *Journal of Neurology, Neurosurgery, and Psychiatry, 39,* 504–507.

Carlson, V., Cicchetti, D., Barnett, D., & Braunwald, K. (1989). Disorganized/disoriented attachment relationships in maltreated infants. *Developmental Psychology, 25,* 525–531.

Cassidy, J. (1999). The nature of the child's ties. In J. Cassidy & P. Shaver (Eds.), *Handbook of attachment: Theory, research, and clinical applications* (pp. 3–20). New York: Guilford.

Cassidy, J., & Marvin, R. (1987). *Attachment organization in pre-school children: Coding guidelines.* Unpublished manuscript. MacArthur Working Group on Attachment, Seattle.

Chan, R., Brooks, R., Raboy, B., & Patterson, C. (1998). Division of labor among lesbian and heterosexual parents: Associations with children's adjustment. *Journal of Family Psychology, 12*(3), 402–419.

Chapman, A. H. (1976). *Harry Stack Sullivan: The man and his work.* New York: Putnam.

Chused, J. (1988). The transference neurosis in child analysis. *Psychoanalytic Study of the Child, 43,* 51–81.

——. (1992). The transference neurosis in child analysis. In A. G. Schmukler (Ed.), *Saying goodbye: A casebook of termination in child and adolescent analysis and therapy* (pp. 233–264). Hillsdale, N.J.: Analytic Press.

Craik, K. (1943). *The nature of explanation.* Cambridge: Cambridge University Press.

Crittendon, P. (1992). *Preschool assessment of attachment.* Unpublished manuscript. Family Relations Institute, Miami.

——. (1994). *Preschool assessment of attachment.* 2nd ed. Unpublished manuscript. Family Relations Institute, Miami.

Damasio, A. (1999). *The feeling of what happens: Body and emotion in the making of consciousness.* New York: Harcourt Brace.

Darwin, C. (1872). *The expression of emotions in man and animals.* New York: Philosophical Library.

Davies, J., & Frawley, M. (1994). *Treating the adult survivor of childhood sexual abuse: A psychoanalytic perspective.* New York: Basic Books.

DeKlyen, M., Speltz, M., & Greenberg, M. (1996). *Predicting early starting behavior disorders: A clinical sample of preschool oppositional defiant boys.* Paper presented at the International Society for Research in Child and Adolescent Psychopathology, Santa Monica, California.

Doi, T. (1989). The concept of amae and its psychoanalytic implications. *International Review of Psychoanalysis, 16,* 349–354.

Dupont, J. (Ed.). (1988). *The clinical diary of Sandor Ferenczi.* Cambridge, Mass.: Harvard University Press.

Durett, M., Otaki, M., & Richards, P. (1984). Attachment and the mother's perception of support from the father. *International Journal of Behavioral Development, 7,* 167–176.

Erikson, E. (1950). *Childhood and society.* New York: Norton.

——. (1959). *Identity and the life cycle.* Vol. 1. *Selected papers, psychological issues.* New York: International Universities Press.

——. (1968). *Identity: Youth and crisis.* New York: Norton.

——. (1997). *The life cycle completed.* New York: Norton.

Eth, S., & Pynoos, R. (1985). *Posttraumatic stress disorder in children.* Washington, D.C.: American Psychiatric Press.

Fairbairn, W. (1941). A revised psychopathology of the psychoses and the psychoneuroses. In *An object relations theory of the personality.* New York: Basic Books.

——. (1952). *An object relations theory of the personality.* New York: Basic Books.

Farber, S. (2000). *When the body is the target.* Northvale, N.J.: Jason Aronson.

Feeney, J. (1999). Adult romantic attachment and couple relationships. In J. Cassidy & P. R. Shaver (Eds.), *Handbook of attachment: Theory, research, and clinical applications* (pp. 355–377). New York: Guilford.

Feeney, J., & Noller, P. (1990). Attachment style as a predictor of adult romantic relationships. *Journal of Personality and Social Psychology, 58,* 281–291.

Fenichel, O. (1945). *The psychoanalytic theory of neurosis.* New York: Norton.

Ferenczi, S. (1924). *Versuch einer Genitaltheorie.* Leipzig and Vienna: International Psychoanalytisher. [Translated into English and published in 1933-34 under the title *Thalassa: A theory of genitality* in 3 parts by *The Psychoanalytic Quarterly, 2,* 361-403; 3, 1-29, 200-222].

Ferenczi, S. (1949). Confusion of tongues between adult and child. *International Journal of Psychoanalysis, 30,* 225–230.

Fonagy, P. (2001). *Attachment theory and psychoanalysis.* New York: Other Press.

Fonagy, P., Gergely, G., Jurist, E., & Target, M. (2002). *Affect regulation, mentalization, and the development of the self.* New York: Other Press.

Fonagy, P., & Sandler, A. M. (1996). Il transfert e la sua interpretazione (On transference and its interpretation). *Richard e Piggle, 4,* 255–273.

Fonagy, P., Steele, M., Teele, H., Leigh, T., Kennedy, R., Mattoon, G., & Target, M. (1999). Attachment, the reflective self, and borderline states: The predictive specificity of the adult attachment interview and pathological emotional development. In S. Goldberg, R. Muir, & J. Kerr (Eds.), *Attachment theory: Social, developmental, and clinical perspectives* (pp. 233–278). Hillsdale, N.J.: Analytic Press.

Fonagy, P., & Target, M. (1998). Mentalization and the changing aims of child psychoanalysis. *Psychoanalytic Dialogues, 8*(1), 87–114.

——. (2003). *Psychoanalytic theories: Perspectives from developmental psychopathology.* New York: Brunner-Routledge.

Freud, A. (1981). *A psychoanalytic view of developmental psychopathology.* New York: International Universities Press.

Freud, S. (1905). Three essays on the theory of sexuality. In J. Strachey (Ed.), *Standard Edition of the Complete Psychological Works of Sigmund Freud* (hereafter cited as *SE*), *7*, 125–245. London: Hogarth Press.

——. (1911). Formulations on the two principles of mental functioning. In J. Strachey (Ed.), *SE, 12*, 213–226.

——. (1917 [1915]). Mourning and melancholia. In J. Strachey (Ed.), *SE, 14*, 1–64.

——. (1923). The ego and the id. In J. Strachey (Ed.), *SE, 19*, 12–66.

——. (1924). Neurosis and psychosis. In J. Strachey (Ed.), *SE, 19*, 1, 149–153.

——. (1926). Inhibitions, symptoms, and anxiety. In J. Strachey (Ed.), *SE, 20*, 75–175.

Frogget, L. (2002). *Love, hate, and welfare.* Bristol, England: Policy Press.

Gardner, R. (1993). *Storytelling in psychotherapy with children.* Northvale, N.J.: Jason Aronson.

Gavin, L., & Furman, W. (1989). Age differences in adolescents' perceptions of their peer groups. *Developmental Psychology, 25*, 827–834.

——. (1996). Adolescent girls' relationships with mothers and best friends. *Child Development, 67*, 375–386.

Gay, P. (1988). *Freud: A life for our time.* New York: Norton.

George, C., & Main, M. (1979). Social interaction of young abused children: Approach, avoidance, and aggression. *Child Development, 50*, 306–318.

Goldberg, S. (1997). Attachment and childhood behavior problems in normal, at-risk, and clinical samples. In L. Atkinson & K. Zucker (Eds.), *Attachment and psychopathology* (pp. 171–195). New York: Guilford.

Goldberg, S., Muir, R., & Kerr, J. (Eds.). (1995). *Attachment theory: Social, developmental, and clinical perspectives.* Hillsdale, N.J.: Analytic Press.

Goldfarb, W. (1943). Infant rearing and problem behavior. *American Journal of Orthopsychiatry, 13*, 249–265.

Goldstein, E. (1995). *Ego psychology and social work practice.* New York: Free Press.

Greenberg, J., & Mitchell, S. (1983). *Object relations in psychoanalytic theory.* Cambndge: Harvard University Press.

Greenberg, M. (1999). Attachment and psychopathology in childhood. In J. Cassidy & P. Shaver (Eds.), *Handbook of attachment: Theory, research, and clinical applications* (pp. 469–496). New York: Guilford.

Greenberg, M., Speltz, M., & DeKlyen, M. (1993). The role of attachment in the early development of disruptive behavior problems. *Development and Psychopathology, 5*, 191–213.

Grosskourth, P. (1986). *Melanie Klein.* Boston, Mass.: Harvard University Press.

Grotstein, J. (1996). Object relations theory. In E. Nersessian & R. Kopff (Eds.), *Textbook of psychoanalysis* (pp. 89–125). Washington, D.C.: American Psychiatric Press.

Grotstein, J., & Rinsley, D. (Eds.). (1994). *Fairbairn and the origins of object relations.* New York: Guilford.

Harlow, H. (1958). The nature of love. *American Psychologist, 3*, 673–685.

Hartmann, H. (1956). *Notes on the reality principle.* In *Essays on ego psychology* (pp. 268–296). New York: International Universities Press.

Harwood, R. (1992). The influence of culturally derived values on Anglo and Puerto Rican mothers' perceptions of attachment behavior. *Child Development, 63,* 822–839.

Harwood, R., & Miller, J. (1991). Perceptions of attachment behavior: A comparison of Anglo and Puerto Rican mothers. *Merrill-Palmer Quarterly, 37(4),* 583–599.

Hazan, C., & Shaver, P. (1987). Romantic love conceptualized as an attachment process. *Journal of Personality and Social Psychology, 52,* 511–524.

Herzog, J. (2001). *Father hunger: Explorations with adults and children.* Hillsdale, N.J.: Analytic Press.

Hesse, E. (1999). The Adult Attachment Interview: Historical and current perspectives. In J. Cassidy & P. Shaver (Eds.), *Handbook of attachment: Theory, research, and clinical applications.* New York: Guilford.

Holzman, P. (1998). *Psychoanalysis and psychopathology.* New York: McGraw-Hill.

Hu, P., & Meng, Z. (1996). *An examination of infant mother attachment in China.* Poster presented at the meeting of the International Society for the Study of Behavioral Development, Quebec City, Quebec, Canada.

Isabella, R. A., & Belsky, J. (1991). Interactional synchrony and the origins of infant-mother attachment: A replication study. *Child Development, 62,* 373–384.

Jacobsen, T., Edelstein, W., & Hoffman, V. (1994). A longitudinal study of the relation between representations of attachment in childhood and cognitive functioning in childhood and adolescence. *Developmental Psychology, 30,* 112–124.

Kaplan, N. (1987). *Internal representations of attachment in six-year-olds.* Paper presented at the biennial meetings of the Society for Research in Child Development, Baltimore.

Karen, R. (1998). *Becoming attached.* New York: Oxford University Press.

Kemp, A., Rawlings, E. I., & Green, B. (1991). Post-traumatic stress disorder (PTSD) in battered women: A shelter sample. *Journal of Traumatic Stress, 4,* 137–148.

Kermoian, R., & Leiderman, P. (1986). Infant attachment to mother and child caretaker in an East African community. *International Journal of Behavioral Development, 9,* 455–469.

Kernberg, O. (1980). *Internal word and external reality.* Northvale, N.J.: Jason Aronson.

Klein, M. (1952). Some theoretical conclusions regarding the emotional life of the infant. In *Envy and gratitude and other works, 1946–1963.* New York: Delacorte, 1975.

——. (1964). *Contributions to psychoanalysis, 1921–1945.* New York: McGraw-Hill.

——. (1975). *The psychoanalysis of children.* New York: Free Press.

Kobak, R., & Cole, C. (1994). Attachment and metamonitoring: Implications for adolescent autonomy and psychopathology. In D. Cicchetti (Ed.), *Rochester symposium on development and psychopathology: Vol. 5. Disorders of the self* (pp. 267–297). Rochester, N.Y.: University of Rochester Press.

Kohut, H. (1966). Forms and transformations of narcissism. *Journal of the American Psychoanalytic Association, 14,* 243–272.

——. (1971). *The analysis of the self.* New York: International Universities Press.

——. (1977). *The restoration of the self.* New York: International Universities Press.

——. (1984). *How does analysis cure?* Chicago: University of Chicago Press.

Kohut, H., & Wolf, E. (1978). The disorders of the self and their treatment: An outline. *International Journal of Psychoanalysis, 59,* 413–425.

Krystal, H. (1993). *Integration and self-healing: Affect, trauma, alexithymia.* Hillsdale, N.J.: Analytic Press.

LeDoux, J. E. (1996). *The emotional brain: The mysterious underpinnings of emotional life.* New York: Simon and Schuster.

Leider, R. (1996). The psychology of the self. In E. Nersessian & R. Kopff (Eds.), *Textbook of psychoanalysis* (pp. 127–164). Washington, D.C.: American Psychiatric Press.

Lichtenberg, J. (1987). Infant studies and clinical work with adults. *Psychoanalytic Inquiry, 7,* 311–330.

Lichtenberg, J., Lachmann, F., & Fosshage, F. (2002). *A spirit of inquiry: Communication in psychoanalysis.* Hillsdale, N.J.: Analytic Press.

Lichtenberg, J., & Meares, R. (1996). The role of play in things human. *Psychoanalysis and Psychotherapy, 13*(1), 5–18.

Lin, C., & Fu, V. (1990). A comparison of child-rearing practices among Chinese, immigrant Chinese, and Caucasian American parents. *Child Development, 61,* 429–433.

Liotti, G. (1995). Disorganized/disoriented attachment in the psychotherapy of the dissociative disorders. In S. Goldberg, R. Muir, & J. Kerr (Eds.), *Attachment theory: Social, developmental, and clinical perspectives* (pp. 343–363). Hillsdale, N.J.: Analytic Press.

Luthar, S., & Zigler, E. (1992). Intelligence and social competence among high-risk adolescents. *Development and Psychopathology, 4,* 287–299.

Lyons-Ruth, K. (1999). Two-person unconscious: Intersubjective dialogue, enactive relational representations, and the emergency of new forms of relational organization. *Psychoanalytic Inquiry, 19*(4), 576–617.

——. (2001). The two-person construction of defenses: Disorganized attachment strategies, unintegrated mental states, and hostile/helpless relational processes. *Division 39 Newsletter,* Winter 2001, 1–12.

——. (2003). *Psychoanalysis and developmental psychology: Adult dissociative symptoms and the early parent-child relationship.* Paper presented at the 92nd annual meeting of the American Psychological Association, Boston.

Lyons-Ruth, K., & Block, D. (1996). The disturbed caregiving system: Relations among childhood trauma, maternal caregiving, and infant affect and attachment. *Infant Mental Health Journal, 17,* 257–275.

Lyons-Ruth, K., Bronfman, E., & Atwood, G. (1999). A relational diathesis model of hostile-helpless states of mind: Expressions in mother-infant interaction. In J. Solomon & C. George (Eds.), *Attachment disorganization* (pp. 33-70). New York: Guilford.

Lyons-Ruth, K., Connell, D., Grunebaum, H., & Botein, S. (1990). Infants at social risk: Maternal depression and family support services as mediators of infant development and security of attachment. *Child Development, 61,* 85–98.

Lyons-Ruth, K., & Jacobvitz, D. (1999). Attachment disorganization: Unresolved loss, relational violence, and lapses in behavioral and attentional strategies. In

J. Cassidy & P. Shaver (Eds.), *Handbook of attachment: Theory, research, and clinical applications* (pp. 520–554). New York: Guilford.

Lyons-Ruth, K., Repacholi, B., McLeod, S., & Silva, E. (1991). Disorganized attachment behavior in infancy: Short-term stability, maternal and infant correlates, and risk-related subtypes. *Development and Psychopathology, 3,* 377–396.

MacLeod, J., & Austin, J. (2003). Stigma in the lives of adolescents with epilepsy. *Epilepsy and Behavior, 4*(2), 112–117.

Magai, C. (1999). Affect, imagery, and attachment: Working models of interpersonal affect and the socialization of emotion. In J. Cassidy and P. Shaver, (Eds.), *Handbook of attachment: Theory, research, and clinical applications* (pp. 787–802). New York: Guilford.

Mahler, M. (1954). Contribution to problems of infantile neurosis: A discussion. *Psychoanalytic Study of the Child, 9,* 65–66.

——. (1968). *On human symbiosis and the vicissitudes of individuation.* New York: International Universities Press.

——. (1979a). *The selected papers of Margaret Mahler: Vol. 1. Infantile psychosis and early contributions.* New York: Jason Aronson.

——. (1979b). *The selected papers of Margaret Mahler: Vol. 2. Separation-individuation.* New York: Jason Aronson.

Mahler, M., & Furer, M. (1968). *On human symbiosis and the vicissitudes of individuation: Vol. 1. Infantile psychosis.* New York: International Universities Press.

Mahler, M., & Gosliner, B. (1955). On symbiotic child psychosis: Genetic, dynamic, and restitutive aspects. *Psychoanalytic Study of the Child, 10,* 195–212.

Mahler, M., Pine, F., & Bergman, A. (1975). *The psychological birth of the human infant.* New York: Basic Books.

Main, M. (1999). Recent studies in attachment: Overview, with selected implications for clinical work. In S. Goldberg, R. Muir, & J. Kerr (Eds), *Attachment theory: Social, developmental, and clinical perspectives* (pp. 407–474). Hillsdale, N.J.: Analytic Press.

Main, M., & Goldwyn, R. (1984). Predicting rejection of her infant from mother's representation of her own experience: Implications for the abused-abusing intergenerational cycle. *Child Abuse and Neglect, 8,* 203–217.

——. (1991). *Adult attachment classification system, Version 5.* Berkeley: University of California Press.

Main, M., & Hesse, E. (1990). Parents' unresolved traumatic experiences are related to infant disorganized attachment status: Is frightened and/or frightening parental behavior the linking mechanism? In M. T. Greenberg, D. Cicchetti, & M. Cummings (Eds.), *Attachment in the preschool years* (pp. 161–182). Chicago: University of Chicago Press.

Main, M., & Solomon, J. (1990). Procedures for identifying infants as disorganized/disoriented during the Strange Situation. In M. Greenberg, D. Cicchetti, & E. M. Cummings (Eds.), *Attachment in the preschool years: Theory, research, and intervention* (pp. 121–160). Chicago: University of Chicago Press.

Marvin, R., Cooper, G., Hoffman, K., & Powell, B. (2002). The circle of security project: Attachment-based intervention with caregiver–pre-school child dyads. *Attachment and Human Development, 4*(1), 107–124.

Marvin, R., VanDevender, T., Iwanaga, M., LeVine, S., & LeVine, R. (1977). Infant caregiver attachment among the Hausa of Nigeria. In H. McGurk (Ed.), *Ecological factors in human development* (pp. 247–259). Amsterdam: North Holland.

Masterson, J. (1976). *Psychotherapy of the borderline adult: A developmental approach.* New York: Wiley Interscience.

——. (1985). *The real self: A developmental, self, and object relations approach.* New York: Brunner/Mazel.

Masterson, J., & Rinsley, D. (1975). The borderline syndrome: The role of the mother in the genesis and psychic structure of the borderline personality. *International Journal of Psychoanalysis, 56,* 163–177.

Mattei, L. (1999). A Latina space: Ethnicity as an intersubjective third. *Smith College Studies in Social Work, 69*(2), 255–267.

McDougall, J. (1984). The "dis-affected" patient: Reflections on affect pathology. *Psychoanalytic Quarterly, 53,* 386–409.

——. (1985). *Theaters of the mind.* New York: Basic Books.

——. (1989). *Theaters of the body.* New York: Basic Books.

Meissner, W. (2000). *Freud and psychoanalysis.* Notre Dame, Ind.: University of Notre Dame Press.

Meltzoff, A., & Moore, M. (1989). Imitation in newborn infants: Exploring the range of gestures imitated and the underlying mechanisms. *Developmental Psychology, 25,* 954–962.

Meyer, R. G. (1974). Phased biofeedback approach to epileptic seizure control. *Journal of Behavior Therapy and Experimental Psychiatry, 5,* 185–187.

Miller, L. (1994). Psychotherapy of epilepsy. *Journal of Cognitive Rehabilitation, 12*(1), 14–30.

Mishne, J. (1993). *The evolution and application of clinical theory.* New York: Free Press.

Mitchell, S. (1993). *Hope and dread in psychoanalysis.* New York: Basic Books.

——. (1994). The origin and nature of the "object" in the theories of Klein and Fairbairn. In J. Grotstein & D. Rinsley (Eds.), *Fairbairn and the origins of object relations.* New York: Guilford.

——. (2000). *Relationality from attachment to intersubjectivity.* Hillsdale, N.J.: Analytic Press.

Mitchell, S., & Aron, L. (1999). *Relational psychoanalysis: The emergence of a tradition.* Hillsdale, N.J.: Analytic Press.

Mitchell, S., & Black, M. (1995). *Freud and beyond: A history of modern psychoanalytic thought.* New York: Basic Books.

Moore, B., & Fine, B. (1990). *Psychoanalytic terms and concepts.* New Haven, Conn.: Yale University Press.

Morelli, G., & Tronick, E. (1991). Efe multiple caretaking and attachment. In J. L. Gewirtz & W. M. Kurtines (Eds.), *Intersections with attachment* (pp. 41–52). Hillsdale, N.J.: Erbaum.

Mullahy, P. (1970). *Psychoanalysis and interpersonal psychiatry*. New York: Science House.

O'Connor, M., Sigman, M., & Brill, N. (1987). Disorganization of attachment in relation to maternal alcohol consumption. *Journal of Consulting and Clinical Psychology, 55*, 831–836.

Patterson, C. (1992). Children of lesbian and gay parents. *Child Development, 63*, 1025–1042.

Perry, H. (1964). Introduction to H. Sullivan, *The fusion of psychiatry and social science*. New York: Norton.

——. (1982). *Psychiatrist of America: The life of Harry Stack Sullivan*. Cambridge, Mass.: Harvard University Press.

Peto, E. (1937). Saugling und Mutter. Translated in *International Journal of Psycho-Analysis, 11*, 260 (1949).

Piaget, J. (1936). *The origins of intelligence in children*. New York: International Universities Press.

Posada, G., Gao, Y., Wu, F., Posado, R., Tascon, M., & Synnevaag, B. (1995). The secure base phenomenon across cultures: Children's behavior, mothers' preferences, and experts' concepts. In E. Waters, B. Vaughn, G. Posada, & K. Kondo-Ikemura (Eds.), *Caregiving, cultural, and cognitive perspectives on secure base behavior theory and research. Monographs of the Society for Research in Child Development, 60*(2–3), 27–48.

Rachman, A. (2000). Ferenczi's "confusion of tongues" theory and the analysis of the incest trauma. *Psychoanalytic Social Work, 7*, 27–53.

Ringel, S. (2003). Play and impersonation: Finding the right intersubjective rhythm. *Clinical Social Work Journal, 31*(4), 371–381.

——. (2004). The man without words: Attachment style as an evolving dynamic process. *Psychoanalytic Social Work, 11*(2), 71–82.

Rinsley, D. (1977). An object relations view of borderline personality. In P. Hartocollis (Ed.), *Borderline personality disorders: The concept, the syndrome, the patient* (pp. 47–70). New York: International Universities Press.

——. (1978). Borderline psychopathology: A review of etiology, dynamics, and treatment. *International Review of Psycho-Analysis, 5*, 45–54.

Robbins, M. (1994). A Fairbairnian object relations perspective on self psychology. In J. Grotstein & D. Rinsley (Eds.), *Fairbairn and the origins of object relations* (pp. 302–317). New York: Guilford.

Robertson, J. (1953). *A two-year-old goes to hospital*. (Film). University Park: Pennsylvania State Audio Visual Services.

Rosenstein, D., & Horowitz, H. (1996). Adolescent attachment and psychopathology. *Journal of Consulting and Clinical Psychology, 64*, 244–253.

Rovee-Collier, C. (1987). Learning and memory in infancy. In J. Osofsky (Ed.), *Handbook of infant development*. 2nd ed. New York: Wiley.

Sable, P. (1992). Attachment theory: Application to clinical practice with adults. *Clinical Social Work Journal, 20*(3), 271–283.

——. (1995). Attachment theory and social work education. *Journal of Teaching in Social Work, 12*(1–2), 19–38.

——. (2000). *Attachment and adult psychotherapy.* Northvale, N.J.: Jason Aronson.

Sagi, A., Lamb, M., Lewkowicz, M., Shoham, K., Dvir, R., & Estes, D. (1985). Security of infant-mother-father and metapelet attachments among kibbutz-reared Israeli children. In I. Bretherton & E. Waters (Eds.), *Growing points of attachment theory and research. Monographs of the Society of Research in Child Development, 50*(1–2), 257–275.

Sagi, A., Van Ijzendoorn, M., Aviezer, O., Donnell, F., & Mayseless, O. (1994). Sleeping out of home in a kibbutz communal arrangement: It makes a difference for infant-mother attachment. *Child Development, 65,* 992–1004.

Sagi, A., Van Ijzendoorn, M., Scharf, M., Joels, T., Koren-Karie, N., Mayseless, O., & Aviezer, O. (1997). Ecological constraints for intergenerational transmission of attachment. *International Journal of Behavioral Development, 20,* 287–299.

Schore, A. (1997). Interdisciplinary developmental research and a source of clinical models. In M. Moskowitz, C. Monk, & S. Ellman (Eds.), *The clinical significance of early development: Implications for psychoanalytic interventions* (pp. 1–72). Northvale, N.J.: Aronson.

——. (2002). Clinical implications of psychoneurobiological model of projective identification. In S. Alhanati (Ed.), *Primitive mental states: Vol. 2. Psychobiological and psychoanalytic perspectives on early trauma and personality development* (pp. 2–65). New York: Karnac.

Singer, E. (1998). The interpersonal approach to psychoanalysis. In R. Langs (Ed.), *Current theories of psychoanalysis* (pp. 73–101). Madison, Conn.: International Universities Press.

Slade, A. (1999). Attachment theory and research: Implications for the theory and practice of individual psychotherapy with adults. In J. Cassidy & P. Shaver (Eds.), *Handbook of attachment: Theory, research, and clinical applications* (pp. 575–594). New York: Guilford.

Slavin, J. (1996). Readiness for psychoanalytic treatment in late adolescence: Developmental and adaptive considerations. *Psychoanalytic psychology, 13*(1), 35–51.

Slavin, M., & Kriegman, D. (1992). *The adaptive design of the human psyche: Psychoanalysis, evolutionary biology, and the therapeutic process.* New York: Guilford.

Solomon, J., & George, C. (1999). The place of disorganization in attachment theory: Linking classic observations with contemporary findings. In J. Solomon & C. George (Eds.), *Attachment disorganization* (pp. 3–32). New York: Guilford.

Spangler, G., & Grossmann, K. (1993). Biobehavioral organization in securely and insecurely attached infants. *Child Development, 64,* 1439–1450.

Spitz, R. (1945). Hospitalism: An inquiry into the genesis of psychiatric conditions in early childhood. *Psychoanalytic Study of the Child, 1,* 53–74.

Sroufe, A. (1988). A developmental perspective on day care. *Early Childhood Research Quarterly, 3,* 283–291.

——. (1996). *Emotional development: The organization of emotional life in the early years.* New York: Cambridge University Press.

——. (2003). Applications of attachment theory to the treatment of latency age children. In M. Cortina & M. Marrone (Eds.), *Attachment theory and the psychoanalytic process* (pp. 204–226). London: Whurr.

Sroufe, A., Egeland, B., & Carlson, E. (1999). One social world: The integrated development of parent-child and peer relationships. In W. Collins & B. Laursen (Eds.), *Relationships as developmental context: The 30th Minnesota Symposium on Child Psychology* (pp. 241–262). Hillsdale, N.J.: Erlbaum.

Sroufe, A., Egeland, B., & Kreutzer, T. (1990). The fate of early experience following developmental change: Longitudinal approaches to individual adaptation in childhood. *Child Development, 61*, 1363–1373.

Stern, D. (1985). *The interpersonal world of the infant.* New York: Basic Books.

——. (2003). *The present moment in psychotherapy and everyday life.* New York: Norton.

Stern, D., Bruschweiler-Stern, N., Harrison, A., Lyons-Ruth, K., Morgan, A., Nahum, J., Sander, L., & Tronick, E. (1998). The process of therapeutic change involving implicit knowledge: Some implications of developmental observations for adult psychotherapy. *Infant Mental Health Journal, 19*(3), 300–308.

Sullivan, H. (1930). Socio-psychiatric research. In *Schizophrenia as a human process.* New York: Norton, 1962.

——. (1940). *Conceptions of modern psychiatry.* New York: Norton.

——. (1953). *The interpersonal theory of psychiatry.* New York: Norton.

Sullivan, M. (1996). Rozzie and Harriet? Gender and family patterns of lesbian coparents. *Gender and Society, 19*(6), 747–767.

Suttie, I. (1935). *The origins of love and hate.* New York: Matrix House, 1952.

Tacon, A., & Caldera, Y. (2001). Attachment and parental correlates in late adolescent Mexican American women. *Hispanic Journal of Behavioral Sciences, 23*(1), 71–87.

Thomson, R. (1999). Early attachment and later development. In J. Cassidy & P. Shaver (Eds.), *Handbook of attachment: Theory, research, and clinical applications* (pp. 265–286). New York: Guilford.

Tomkins, S. (1991). *Affect, imagery, consciousness: Vol. 3. Anger and fear.* New York: Springer.

Tosone, C. (1997). Sandor Ferenczi: Father of modern short-term psychotherapy. *Journal of Analytic Social Work, 4*, 23–41.

Travis, L., Binder, J., Bliwise, N., & Horne-Moyer, L. (2001). Changes in clients' attachment styles over the course of time-limited psychotherapy. *Psychotherapy, 38*(2), 149–159.

Tronick, E., & Brazelton, T. (1977). The infants' capacity to regulate mutuality in face to face interaction. *Journal of Communication, 27*, 74–80.

True, M. (1994). *Mother-infant attachment and communication among the Dogon of Mali.* Unpublished doctoral dissertation. University of California at Berkeley.

Tyson, P., & Tyson, R. (1990). *Psychoanalytic theories of development.* New Haven, Conn.: Yale University Press.

Van IJzendoorn, M., & Bakermans-Kranenberg, M. (1996). Attachment representations in mothers, father, adolescents, and clinical groups: A meta-analytic search for normative data. *Journal of Consulting and Clinical Psychology, 64*(1), 8-21.

Van IJzendoorn, M., & Sagi, A. (1999). Cross-cultural patterns of attachment: Universal and contextual dimensions. In J. Cassidy & P. Shaver (Eds.), *Handbook of*

attachment: Theory, research, and clinical applications (pp. 713–734). New York: Guilford.

Van IJzendoorn, M., Schengle, C., & Bakermanns-Kranenburg, M. (1999). Disorganized attachment in early childhood: Meta analysis of precursors, concomitants, and sequelae. *Development and Psychopathology, 22*, 225–249.

Vereijken, C. (1996). *The mother-infant relationship in Japan: Attachment dependency and amae.* Unpublished doctoral dissertation. Catholic University of Nijmegen, The Netherlands.

Vining, E. (1987). Psychosocial issues for children with epilepsy. *Cleveland Clinic Journal of Medicine, 56*(supplement to part 2), 214–220.

Waters, E., & Deane, K. (1985). Defining and assessing individual differences in attachment relationships: Q-methodology and the organization of behavior in infancy and early childhood. In I. Bretherton & E. Waters (Eds.), *Growing points of attachment theory and research. Monographs of the Society for Research in Child Development, 50*(1–2), 41–65.

Weininger, O., & Whyte-Earnshaw, C. (1998). The work of Melanie Klein. In R. Langs (Ed.), *Current theories of psychoanalysis* (pp. 197–225). Madison, Conn.: International Universities Press.

Winnicott, D. W. (1951). Transitional objects and transitional phenomena. In *Through paediatrics to psychoanalysis.* London: Hogarth.

——. (1952). Anxiety associated with insecurity. In D. W. Winnicott, *Through paediatrics to psychoanalysis.* London: Hogarth.

——. (1958a). The capacity to be alone. In D. W. Winnicott (Ed.), *The maturational process and the facilitating environment* (pp. 29–36). New York: International Universities Press, 1965.

——. (1958b). *Through paediatrics to psychoanalysis.* London: Hogarth.

——. (1960a). Ego distortion in terms of true and false self. In D. W. Winnicott (Ed.), *The maturational processes and the facilitating environment* (pp. 142–152). New York: International Universities Press, 1965.

——. (1960b). The theory of the parent-infant relationship. In D. W. Winnicott (Ed.), *The maturational process and the facilitating environment* (pp. 37–55). New York: International Universities Press, 1965.

Winnicott, D. W. (Ed.). (1965). *The maturational process and the facilitating environment.* New York: International Universities Press.

——. (1971). *Therapeutic consultations in child psychiatry.* New York: Basic Books.

Yanof, J. (1996). Language, communication, and transference in child analysis. *Journal of the American Psychoanalytic Association, 44*, 79–116.

Zeanah, C., Anders, T., Seifer, R., & Stern, D. (1989). Implications of research in infant development for psychodynamic theory and practice. *Journal of the American Academy of Child and Adolescent Psychiatry, 28*, 657–688.

Ziegler, R. (1982). The child with epilepsy: Psychotherapy and counseling. In H. Sands (Ed.), *Epilepsy: A handbook for the mental health professional* (pp. 158–188). New York: Brunner/Mazel.

Index